Vergil

Aeneid Book 3

VERGIL

Aeneid Book 3

Christine G. Perkell
Emory College

Focus Publishing
R. Pullins Company
Newburyport, MA
www.pullins.com

Vergil
Aeneid Book 3
© 2010 Christine Perkell

Focus Publishing/R. Pullins Company
PO Box 369
Newburyport, MA 01950
www.pullins.com

Interior illustration by Sam Kimball

ISBN 13: 978-1-58510-227-3

Printed in the United States of America

12 11 10 9 8 7 6 5 4 3

1112H

Table of Contents

Preface

This commentary is one of a projected series of commentaries on *Aeneid* 1-6, adapted from the T.E. Page commentaries of 1894, to be published by Focus Publishing. The purpose of the series is to make available to American college students the full help with translation that many of them, quite new to Latin, need, along with the addition of materials reflecting the breadth and interest of contemporary approaches to the *Aeneid*. Thus the Focus commentaries would be distinguished from available commentaries created for young British students, on the one hand, and graduates and professional scholars on the other. This *Aeneid* 3 commentary, then, aims to be sufficiently helpful in terms of grammar, syntax, and other translation issues to make the text easily accessible to students at the intermediate level of college Latin. At the same time it aims also to provide a rich range of material that will enhance appreciation of Book 3, especially with respect to its importance for the *Aeneid* as a whole.

Aeneid 3 is not often read on its own, Books 2, 4, and 6 being far more popular choices for single study. Yet it has great drama and interest. Dante clearly found this book haunting, for he brought together in *Inferno* 13 (the canto of those condemned for taking their own lives) two of its most striking images—the bleeding tree and the wailing Harpies. Dante's association of *Aeneid* 3 with the suicides may, in fact, be a key to Vergil's purposes in this book, which portrays some characters who, against the background of Trojan losses, have essentially given up on life. By contrast, Vergil shows Aeneas, having let go his own earlier thoughts of death (Aen.1.94-101, Aen. 2.348-54), seeking to live purposefully in response to a high calling.

Aeneid 3 illuminates the traits of character and values that made possible the Roman imperial achievement. Further, through the abundance of place names, allusions to techniques of sailing, navigation, city founding, prayer and sacrifice, this book evokes a whole world of the ancient Mediterranean and the movements of its various peoples. A rich text for class purposes, *Aeneid* 3 invites reading and discussion of such topics as Homer and Apollonius; Roman ethnicity, culture, and religion;

Augustus' religious renewals and foreign policy; ancient accounts of travel; literary criticism (internal vs. external narrators and readers, techniques of persuasive speech), to mention only some. In sum, students whose major desideratum is help with translation will find it here; those with time also for thematics, poetics, cultural context, etc. will find that the introductions to each subsection of the Book offer much of interest to think about.

Certain topics, useful to have in one place, are pulled together in the index (e.g., archaism, prayer language, characteristics of colonization narratives, etc.). When it falls to me to offer translation, I am as literal as possible, hoping not to obscure the imagination of Vergil's expression. The Latin text is Hirtzel's with few changes (362: *omnem* for *omnis*; 464: *ac secto* for *sectoque*; 533: *Euroo* for *euroo*; at 684-6 I follow Horsfall 2006). Grammar references are to Allen and Greenough, *New Latin Grammar* (1931). Throughout the text, terms defined in the glossary are marked by an asterisk. The vocabulary list is taken from Page's edition, with some revisions based on Lewis and Short, *A Latin Dictionary* (1962). Included also is a map of Aeneas' travels, with an appendix listing many place names mentioned in *Aeneid* 3.

My sincerest thanks go to Nicholas Horsfall who sent me proofs of his magisterial *Aeneid* 3 commentary, a great gift to Vergil studies, and who most generously offered to read my own manuscript, although I did not complete it in time to take advantage of the offer. Thanks, also, to my colleagues at Emory, Peter Bing, David Bright, and Niall Slater who read previous drafts; to Professor Sarah Spence, who kindly used an early draft of the manuscript in her seminar at the University of Georgia and shared her students' comments with me; and to the readers for Focus press. Finally and above all, I owe thanks to Randall Ganiban for his invitation to contribute this volume to the Focus *Aeneid* commentaries, and for his meticulous, thoughtful editing and saintly patience.

I dedicate this volume to Zeph Stewart, who set me on this Vergil path and always was a generous and exacting reader of whatever work I sent him. This is the first piece I will have sent out into the world that he did not read or know about or save from errors.

C.P.

Introduction to Vergil's *Aeneid*

[handwritten: 70 BCE]

Vergil's lifetime and poetry

Publius Vergilius Maro (i.e. Vergil)[1] was born on October 15, 70 BCE near the town of Mantua (modern Mantova) in what was then still Cisalpine Gaul.[2] Little else about his life can be stated with certainty, because our main source, the ancient biography by the grammarian Donatus (fourth century CE),[3] is of questionable value.[4] The historical and political background to Vergil's life, by contrast, is amply documented and provides a useful framework for understanding his career. Indeed, his poetic development displays an increasing engagement with the politics of contemporary Rome, an engagement that culminates in the *Aeneid*.

Vergil lived and wrote in a time of political strife and uncertainty. In his early twenties the Roman Republic was torn apart by the civil wars of 49-45 BCE, when Julius Caesar fought and defeated Pompey and his supporters. Caesar was declared *dictator perpetuo* ("Dictator for Life") early in 44 BCE but was assassinated on the Ides of March by a group of senators led by Brutus[5] and Cassius. They sought to restore the Republic, which, they

[handwritten: dictator perpetuo]

---

1   The spelling "Virgil" (*Virgilius*) is also used by convention. It developed early and has been explained by its similarity to two words: *virgo* ("maiden") and *virga* ("wand"). For discussion of the origins and potential meanings of these connections, see Jackson Knight (1944) 36-7 and Putnam (1993) 127-8 with notes.

2   Cisalpine Gaul, the northern part of what we now think of as Italy, was incorporated into Roman Italy in 42 BCE. Mantua is located ca. 520 kilometers north of Rome.

3   This biography drew heavily from the *De poetis* of Suetonius (born ca. 70 CE).

4   Horsfall (1995: 1-25; 2006: xxii-xxiv) argues that nearly every detail is unreliable.

5   Kingship was hateful to the Romans ever since Brutus' own ancestor, Lucius Junius Brutus, led the expulsion of Rome's last king, Tarquin the Proud, in ca. 509 BCE, an act that ended the regal period of Rome and initiated the Republic (cf. *Aeneid* 6.817-18). In killing Caesar, Brutus claimed that he was following the example of his great ancestor—an important concept for the Romans.

believed, was being destroyed by Caesar's domination and intimations of kingship.[6]

The assassination initiated a new round of turmoil that profoundly shaped the course of Roman history. In his will, Caesar adopted and named as his primary heir his great-nephew Octavian (63 BCE-14 CE), the man who would later be called "Augustus."[7] Though only eighteen years old, Octavian boldly accepted and used this inheritance. Through a combination of shrewd calculation and luck, he managed to attain the consulship in 43 BCE, though he was merely nineteen years of age.[8] He then joined forces with two of Caesar's lieutenants, Marc Antony (initially Octavian's rival) and Lepidus. Together they demanded recognition as a Board of Three (*triumviri* or "triumvirs") to reconstitute the state as they saw fit, and were granted extraordinary powers to do so by the Roman senate and people. In 42 BCE they avenged Caesar's murder by defeating his assassins commanded by Brutus and Cassius at the battle of Philippi in Macedonia, but their alliance gradually began to deteriorate as a result of further civil strife and interpersonal rivalries.   39 BCE

Vergil composed the *Eclogues*, his first major work, during this tumultuous period.[9] Published ca. 39 BCE,[10] the *Eclogues* comprise a sophisticated collection of ten pastoral poems that treat the experiences of shepherds.[11] The poems were modeled on the *Idylls* of Theocritus, a

---

6   For the reasons behind Caesar's assassination and the fall of the Republic, see the brief accounts in Scullard (1982) 126-53 and Shotter (2005) 4-19.

7   See below.

8   By the *lex Villia annalis* of 180 BCE, a consul had to be at least forty-two years of age.

9   Other works have been attributed to Vergil: *Aetna, Catalepton, Ciris, Copa, Culex, Dirae, Elegiae in Maecenatem, Moretum,* and *Priapea.* They are collected in what is called the *Appendix Vergiliana* and are generally believed to be spurious.

10   This traditional dating, however, has been called into question through re-evaluation of *Eclogue* 8, which may very well refer to events in 35 BCE. See Clausen (1994) 232-7.

11   Coleman (1977) and Clausen (1994) are excellent commentaries on the *Eclogues*. For a discussion of the pastoral genre at Rome, see Heyworth (2005). For general interpretation of the *Eclogues*, see Hardie (1998) 5-27 with extensive bibliography in the notes, and Volk (2008a).

Hellenistic Greek poet of the third century BCE (see below). But whereas
Theocritus' poetry created a world that was largely timeless, Vergil sets
his pastoral world against the backdrop of contemporary Rome and the
disruption caused by the civil wars. *Eclogues* 1 and 9, for example, deal with
the differing fortunes of shepherds during a time of land confiscations that
resonate with historical events in 41-40 BCE.[12] *Eclogue* 4 describes the birth
of a child during the consulship of Asinius Pollio (40 BCE) who will bring a
new golden age to Rome.[13] By interjecting the Roman world into his poetic
landscape,[14] Vergil allows readers to sense how political developments both
threaten and give promise to the very possibility of pastoral existence.

The *Eclogues* established Vergil as a new and important poetic voice,
and led him to the cultural circle of the great literary patron Maecenas,
an influential supporter and confidant of Octavian. Their association
grew throughout the 30s.[15] The political situation, however, remained
precarious. Lepidus was ousted from the triumvirate in 36 BCE because
of his treacherous behavior. Tensions between Octavian and Antony that
were simmering over Antony's collaboration and affair with the Egyptian
queen Cleopatra eventually exploded.[16] In 32 BCE, Octavian had Antony's

---

12   Octavian rewarded veterans with land that was already occupied.

13   This is sometimes called the "Messianic Eclogue" because later ages read it as
      foreseeing the birth of Christ, which occurred nearly four decades later. The identity
      of the child is debated, but the poem may celebrate the marriage between Marc
      Antony and Octavian's sister Octavia that resulted from the treaty of Brundisium
      in 40 BCE; this union helped stave off the immediate outbreak of war between the
      two triumvirs. For more on this poem, see Van Sickle (1992) and Petrini (1997)
      111-21, as well as the commentaries by Coleman (1977) and Clausen (1994).

14   In addition to the contemporary themes that Vergil treats, he also mentions
      or dedicates individual poems to a number of his contemporaries, including
      Asinius Pollio, Alfenus Varus, Cornelius Gallus, and probably Octavian,
      who is likely the *iuvenis* ("young man") mentioned at 1.42 and perhaps also
      the patron addressed at 8.6-13.

15   For the relationship between Augustus and the poets, see White (2005).
      White (1993) is a book-length study of this topic. For an overview of literature
      of the Augustan period from 40 BCE-14 CE, see Farrell (2005).

16   In addition to the political conflicts, there were also familial tensions: Antony
      conducted a decade-long affair with Cleopatra, even though he had married
      Octavia, Octavian's (Augustus') sister, as a result of the treaty of Brundisium
      in 40 BCE (see n. 13 above). Antony divorced Octavia in 32 BCE.

powers revoked, and war was declared against Cleopatra (and thus in effect against Antony as well). During a naval confrontation off Actium on the coast of western Greece in September of 31 BCE, Octavian's fleet decisively routed the forces of Marc Antony and Cleopatra, who both fled to Egypt and committed suicide in the following year to avoid capture.[17] This momentous victory solidified Octavian's claim of being the protector of traditional Roman values against the detrimental influence of Antony, Cleopatra, and the East.[18]

Vergil began his next work, the *Georgics*, sometime in the 30s, completed it ca. 29 BCE in the aftermath of Actium, and dedicated it to Maecenas. Like the *Eclogues*, the *Georgics* was heavily influenced by Greek models—particularly the work of Hesiod (eighth century BCE) and of Hellenistic poets[19] such as Callimachus, Aratus, and Nicander (third–second centuries BCE). On the surface, it purports to be a poetic farming guide.[20] Each of its four book examines a different aspect or sphere of agricultural life: crops and weather signs (book 1), trees and vines (book 2), livestock (book 3), and bees (book 4). Its actual scope, however, is much more ambitious. The poem explores the nature of humankind's struggle with the beauty and difficulties of the agricultural world, but it does so within the context of contemporary war-torn Italy. It bears witness to the strife following Caesar's assassination, and sets the chaos and disorder inherent in nature against the upheaval caused by civil war (1.461-514). Moreover, Octavian's success and victories are commemorated both in the introduction (1.24-42) and conclusion (4.559-62) of the poem, as well as in the beginning of

---

17   For the history of the triumviral period, see the brief accounts in Scullard (1982) 154-71 and Shotter (2005) 20-7; for more detailed treatments, see Syme (1939) 187-312, Pelling (1996). For discussion of the contemporary artistic representations of Actium, see Gurval (1995).

18   This ideological interpretation is suggested in Vergil's depiction of the battle on Aeneas' shield (8.671-713).

19   See discussion below.

20   Recent commentaries on the *Georgics* include Thomas (1988) and Mynors (1990). For interpretation, see the introduction to the *Georgics* in Hardie (1998) 28-52 with extensive bibliography in the notes, and Volk (2008b). Individual studies include Wilkinson (1969), Putnam (1979), Johnston (1980), Ross (1987), Perkell (1989), and Nappa (2005). For allusion in the *Georgics*, see Thomas (1986), Farrell (1991), and Gale (2000).

the third book (3.1-39). Thus once again, the political world is juxtaposed against Vergil's poetic landscape, but the relationship between the two is not fully addressed.[21]Octavian's victory represented a turning point for Rome's development. Over the next decade, he centralized political and military control in his hands. He claimed to have returned the state (*res publica*) to the senate and Roman people in 27 BCE.[22] His powers were redefined, and he was granted the name "Augustus' ("Revered One") by the senate. It is true that he maintained many traditional Republican institutions, but in reality he was transforming the state into a monarchy. So effective was his stabilization and control of Rome after decades of civil war that he reigned as *Princeps* ("First Citizen") from 27 BCE to 14 CE, creating a political framework (the Principate) that served the Roman state for centuries.[23]Vergil wrote his final poem, the *Aeneid*, largely in the 20s, during the first years of Augustus' reign, when the Roman people presumably hoped that the civil wars were behind them but feared that the Augustan peace would not last. The *Aeneid* tells the story of the Trojan hero Aeneas. He fought the Greeks at Troy and saw his city destroyed, but with the guidance of the gods and fate he led his surviving people across the Mediterranean to a new homeland in Italy.[24] As in the *Eclogues* and *Georgics*, Vergil interjects his contemporary world into

---

21   The overall meaning of the *Georgics* is contested. Interpretation of the *Georgics*, like that of the *Aeneid* (see below), has optimistic and pessimistic poles. Otis (1964) is an example of the former; Ross (1987) the latter. Other scholars, such as Perkell (1989), fall in between by discerning inherent ambivalence. For discussion of these interpretive trends, see Hardie (1998) 50-2.

22   Augustus, *Res Gestae* 34.

23   For general political and historical narratives of Augustus' reign, see the relatively brief account in Shotter (2005); longer, more detailed treatments can be found in A. H. M. Jones (1970), Crook (1996), and Southern (1998). A classic and influential book by Syme (1939) paints Augustus in extremely dark colors. For broader considerations of the Augustan age, see the short but interesting volume by Wallace-Hadrill (1993) and the more comprehensive treatments by Galinsky (1996, 2005). For the interaction of art and ideology in the Augustan Age, see Zanker (1988).

24   For general interpretation of the *Aeneid*, see the recent overviews provided by Hardie (1998) 53-101, Perkell (1999), Anderson (2005), Johnson (2005), Fratantuono (2007), and Ross (2007). For the literary and cultural backgrounds, see Martindale (1997), Farrell (2005), and Galinsky (2005).

his poetic world. In the *Aeneid*, however, the thematic connections between
these two realms are developed still more explicitly, with Aeneas' actions
shown to be necessary for and to lead ultimately to the reign of Augustus.
(See below for further discussion.)

Vergil was still finishing the *Aeneid* when he was stricken by a fatal
illness in 19 BCE. The ancient biographical tradition claims that he traveled
to Greece, intending to spend three years editing his epic there and in Asia,
but that early on he encountered Augustus, who was returning to Rome from
the East, and decided to accompany him. Vergil, however, fell ill during the
journey and died in Brundisium (in southern Italy) in September of 19 BCE.
The *Aeneid* was largely complete but had not yet received its final revision.
We are told that Vergil asked that it be burned, but that Augustus ultimately
had it published. While such details regarding Vergil's death are doubted,
the poem clearly needed final editing.[25] However, its present shape, including
its sudden ending, is generally accepted to be as Vergil had planned.

Vergil and his predecessors

By writing an epic about the Trojan war, Vergil was rivaling Homer, the
greatest of all the Greek poets. The *Aeneid* was therefore a bold undertaking,
but its success makes it arguably the quintessential Roman work because
it accomplishes what Latin poetry had always striven to do: to appropriate
the Greek tradition and transform it into something that was both equally
impressive and distinctly "Roman."

Homer's *Iliad* tells the story of the Trojan war by focusing on Achilles'
strife with the Greek leader Agamemnon and consequent rage in the tenth
and final year of the conflict, while the *Odyssey* treats the war's aftermath by
relating Odysseus' struggle to return home. These were the earliest and most
revered works of Greek literature,[26] and they exerted a defining influence on
both the overall framework of the *Aeneid* and the close details of its poetry.
In general terms, *Aeneid* 1-6, like the *Odyssey*, describes a hero's return (to
a new) home after the Trojan war, while *Aeneid* 7-12, like the *Iliad*, tells the
story of a war. But throughout the *Aeneid*, Vergil reworks ideas, language,

25   We can be sure that the poem had not received its final revision for a number
of reasons, including the presence of roughly fifty-eight incomplete or "half"
lines. See commentary note on 3.218.

26   These poems were culminations of a centuries-old oral tradition and were
written down probably in the eighth century BCE.

characters, and scenes from both poems. Some ancient critics faulted Vergil for his use of Homer, calling his appropriations "thefts." Vergil, however, is said to have responded that it is "easier to steal his club from Hercules than a line from Homer."[27] Indeed, Vergil does much more than simply quote material from Homer. His creative use and transformation of Homeric language and theme are central not only to his artistry but also to the meaning of the *Aeneid*.

Though Homer is the primary model, Vergil was also influenced significantly by the Hellenistic Greek tradition of poetry that originated in Alexandria, Egypt in the third century BCE. There scholar-poets such as Apollonius, Callimachus, and Theocritus reacted against the earlier literary tradition (particularly epic which by their time had become largely derivative). They developed a poetic aesthetic that valued small-scale poems, esoteric subjects, and highly polished style. Hellenistic poetry was introduced into the mainstream of Latin poetry a generation before Vergil by the so-called "neoterics" or "new poets," of whom Catullus (c. 84-c. 54 BCE) was the most influential for Vergil and for the later literary tradition.[28]

Vergil's earlier works, the *Eclogues* and *Georgics*, had been modeled to a significant extent on Hellenistic poems,[29] so it was perhaps a surprise that Vergil would then have turned to a large-scale epic concerning the Trojan war.[30] However, one of his great feats was the incorporation of the Hellenistic and neoteric sensibilities into the *Aeneid*. Two models were particularly important in this regard: the *Argonautica* by Apollonius of Rhodes, an epic retelling the hero Jason's quest for the Golden Fleece, and Catullus 64, a poem on the wedding of Peleus and Thetis.[31] Both works brought the great

---

27   *...facilius esse Herculi clavam quam Homeri versum subripere* (Donatus/ Suetonius, *Life of Vergil* 46).

28   Clausen (1987, 2002), George (1974), Briggs (1981), Thomas (1988, 1999), and Hunter (2006) display these influences, while O'Hara (1996) provides a thorough examination of wordplay (important to the Alexandrian poets) in Vergil.

29   The *Eclogues* were modeled on Theocritus' *Idylls*; the *Georgics* had numerous models, though the Hellenistic poets Callimachus, Nicander, and Aratus were particularly important influences. See above.

30   For example, at *Eclogue* 6.3-5, Vergil explains in highly programmatic language his decision to compose poetry in the refined Callimachean or Hellenistic manner rather than traditional epic. See Clausen (1994) 174-5.

31   On the influence of Apollonius on Vergil, see the important book by Nelis (2001).

and elevated heroes of the past down to the human level, thereby offering new insights into their strengths, passions and flaws, and both greatly influenced Vergil's presentation of Aeneas.

Of Vergil's other predecessors in Latin literature, the most important was Ennius (239-169 BCE), often called the father of Roman poetry.[32] His *Annales*, which survives only in fragments, was an historical epic about Rome that traced the city's origins back to Aeneas and Troy. It remained the most influential Latin poem until the *Aeneid* was composed, and provided a model not only for Vergil's poetic language and themes, but also for his integration of Homer and Roman history. In addition, the *De Rerum Natura* of Lucretius (ca. 94-55/51 BCE), a hexameter poem on Epicurean philosophy, profoundly influenced Vergil with its forceful language and philosophical ideas.[33]

Finally, Vergil drew much from Greek and Roman[34] tragedy. Many episodes in the *Aeneid* share tragedy's well-known dramatic patterns (such as reversal of fortune), and explore the suffering that befalls mortals often as

---

32   Ennius introduced the dactylic hexameter as the meter of Latin epic. Two earlier epic writers were Livius Andronicus who composed a translation of Homer's *Odyssey* into Latin, and Naevius who composed the *Bellum Punicum*, an epic on the First Punic War. Both Naevius and Livius wrote their epics in a meter called Saturnian that is not fully understood. For the influence of the early Latin poets on the *Aeneid*, see Wigodsky (1972).

33   See Hardie (1986) 157-240 and Adler (2003). The influence of the Epicurean Philodemus on Vergil (and the Augustans more generally) is explored in the collection edited by Armstrong, Fish, Johnston, and Skinner (2004). For Lucretius' influence on Vergil's *Georgics*, see especially Farrell (1991) and Gale (2000).

34   The earliest epic writers (Livius, Naevius and Ennius; see above) also wrote tragedy, and so it is not surprising that epic and tragedy would influence one another. Latin tragic writing continued into the first century through the work of, e.g., Pacuvius (220-ca. 130 BCE) and Accius (170-ca. 86 BCE). Their tragedies, which included Homeric and Trojan War themes, were important for Vergil. However, since only meager fragments of them have survived, their precise influence is difficult to gauge.

a result of the immense and incomprehensible power of the gods and fate.[35] As a recent critic has written, "The influence of tragedy on the *Aeneid* is pervasive, and arguably the single most important factor in Virgil's successful revitalization of the genre of epic."[36]The *Aeneid* is thus indebted to these and many other sources, the study of which can enrich our appreciation of Vergil's artistry and our interpretation of his epic.[37] However, no source study can fully account for the creative, aesthetic, and moral achievement of the *Aeneid*, which is a work unto itself.

The *Aeneid*, Rome, and Augustus

While Aeneas' story takes place in the distant, mythological past of the Trojan war era, it had a special relevance for Vergil's contemporaries. Not only did the Romans draw their descent from the Trojans, but the emperor

---

35 Cf., e.g., Heinze (1915, trans. 1993: 251-8). Wlosok (1999) offers a reading of the Dido episode as tragedy, and Pavlock (1985) examines Euripidean influence in the Nisus and Euryalus episode. Hardie (1991, 1997), Panoussi (2002), and Galinsky (2003) examine the influence of tragedy, particularly in light of French theories of Greek tragedy (e.g. Vernant and Vidal-Naquet (1988)), and draw important parallels between the political and cultural milieus of fifth-century Athens and Augustan Rome. On tragedy and conflicting viewpoints, see Conte (1999) and Galinsky (2003).

36 Hardie (1998) 62. See also Hardie (1997).

37 See Farrell (1997) for a full and insightful introduction to the interpretive possibilities that the study of intertextuality in Vergil can offer readers. For a general introduction to intertextuality, see Allen (2000). For the study of intertextuality in Latin literature, see Conte (1986), Farrell (1991) 1-25, Hardie (1993), Fowler (1997), Hinds (1998), and Edmunds (2001). For Vergil's use of Homer, see Knauer (1964b), Barchiesi (1984, in Italian), Gransden (1984), and Cairns (1989) 177-248. Knauer (1964a), written in German, is a standard work on this topic; those without German can still benefit from its detailed citations and lists of parallels. For Vergil's use of Homer and Apollonius, see Nelis (2001).

Augustus believed that Aeneas was his own ancestor.[38] Vergil makes these national and familial connections major thematic concerns of his epic.

As a result, the *Aeneid* is about more than the Trojan war and its aftermath. It is also about the foundation of Rome and its flourishing under Augustus. To incorporate these themes into his epic, Vergil connects mythological and historical time by associating three leaders and city foundations: the founding of Lavinium by Aeneas, the actual founding of Rome by Romulus, and the "re-founding" of Rome by Augustus. These events are prominent in the most important prophecies of the epic: Jupiter's speech to Venus (1.257-96) and Anchises' revelation to his son Aeneas (6.756-853). Together these passages provide what may be called an Augustan reading of Roman history, one that is shaped by the deeds of these three men and that views Augustus as the culmination of the processes of fate and history.[39]This is not to say that the associations among Aeneas, Romulus, and Augustus are always positive or unproblematic, particularly given the ways that Aeneas is portrayed and can be interpreted.[40] To some, Vergil's Aeneas represents an idealized Roman hero, who thus reflects positively on Augustus by association.[41] In general this type of reading sees a positive imperial ideology in the epic and is referred to as "optimistic" or "Augustan." Others are more troubled by Vergil's Aeneas, and advocate interpretations that challenge the moral and spiritual value of his actions, as well as of the role of the gods and

---

38   Augustus' clan, the Julian *gens*, claimed its descent from Iulus (another name for Aeneas' son Ascanius) and thus also from Aeneas and Venus. Julius Caesar in particular emphasized this ancestry; Augustus made these connections central to his political self-presentation as well. See, e.g., Zanker (1988) 193-210 and Galinsky (1996) 141-224.

39   See O'Hara (1990), however, for the deceptiveness of prophecies in the *Aeneid*.

40   For general interpretation of the *Aeneid*, see n. 24 (above).

41   This type of reading is represented especially by Heinze (1915, trans. 1993), Pöschl (1950, trans. 1962), and Otis (1964). More recent and complex Augustan interpretations can be found in Hardie (1986) and Cairns (1989).

fate. Such readings perceive a much darker poetic world[42] and have been called "pessimistic" or "ambivalent."[43] Vergil's portrayal of Aeneas is thus a major element in debates over the epic's meaning.[44]

Randall Ganiban, Series Editor

---

42   See, e.g., Putnam (1965), Johnson (1976), Lyne (1987), and Thomas (2001). Putnam's reading of the *Aeneid* has been particularly influential. Of the ending of the poem he writes: "By giving himself over with such suddenness to the private wrath which the sight of the belt of Pallas arouses, Aeneas becomes himself *impius Furor*, as rage wins the day over moderation, disintegration defeats order, and the achievements of history through heroism fall victim to the human frailty of one man" (1965: 193-4). For a different understanding of Aeneas' wrath, see Galinsky (1988).

43   For a general treatment of the optimism/pessimism debate, see Kennedy (1992). For a critique of the "pessimistic" view, see Martindale (1993); for critique of the "optimistic" stance and its rejection of "pessimism," see Thomas (2001). For the continuing debate over the politics of the *Aeneid* and over the Augustan age more generally, see the collections of Powell (1992) and Stahl (1998).

44   Indeed some readers also question whether it is even possible to resolve this interpretive debate because of Vergil's inherent ambiguity. See Johnson (1976), Perkell (1994), and O'Hara (2007) 77-103. Martindale (1993) offers a critique of ambiguous readings.

Introduction to Book 3:
Its Role in the *Aeneid*

Aeneid 3 is the second of the two books narrated by Aeneas to the Carthaginians. The first of these describes the desperate night of Troy's fall and the visions that call Aeneas to his city-founding mission for family and survivors. In this second book of his narrative, Aeneas tells of setting sail from Antandros, at the foot of Mt. Ida, and casting his fate to the winds. As he tells it, his wanderings are filled with false starts, terrifying sights, opaque prophecies, and much weariness; that is to say, his wanderings are quite lacking in conventional epic exploits. What does occur in this book, however, though not acknowledged as such by Aeneas, is of momentous significance for the poem; for in *Aeneid* 3 are revealed to Aeneas the true nature of his mission and the true identity of the Trojan people. While Hector's apparition in *Aeneid* 2 had spoken to Aeneas only of new walls for the survivors and the Penates (2.293-5), the voice of Apollo and vision of the Penates in *Aeneid* 3 tell of world empire (97-8, 158-60) and of Dardanus' Italian origin (94-6, 167-8), thus of a homecoming on a grand scale, a homecoming of a people.

With its explicit allusions to the *Odyssey*'s most famous episodes (e.g., the Cyclops, Scylla and Charybdis), *Aeneid* 3 is the most Odyssean book in this "Odyssean" half of the poem (*Aeneid* 1-6), as it has been termed. While Vergil alludes throughout the *Aeneid* to many other texts, Book 3 in particular invites readers to give attention to Odysseus, his adventures, and his homecoming, even as they read Aeneas' narrative of his voyaging from Troy to Carthage. Traditionally, readers have assumed that in thus alluding to the *Odyssey*, Vergil intended to rival Homer on Homer's terms—i.e., with the *same* purposes and values—and (sadly) failed. Yet this is surely to misapprehend Vergil's essential purposes in *Aeneid* 3. It is not through *imitation* of the *Odyssey* but instead precisely through *differences* from the *Odyssey* that Vergil constructs the character of Aeneas and the Roman achievement. Odysseus is famous for his cleverness—even brilliance—and

13

audacity in crisis. Who, after all, had not heard of Odysseus' tricky triumph over the Cyclops: the name of Nobody, the soporific wine, the blinding, the escape from the cave with his men lashed under the Cyclops' sheep? (e.g., Hom. *Od*.9.19-20). Yet, a word search of *Aeneid* 3, despite its pervasive allusions to *Odyssey* 9, shows the predominant motifs to be exhaustion, flight, uncertainty. It is these themes, so lacking in inherent drama, that Vergil juxtaposes to the *Odyssey*'s most exciting, most famous and extended episodes. Evidently Vergil is not out to show how Aeneas and Odysseus are heroic in the same ways, but, on the contrary, how different is the character of Aeneas from that of Odysseus and how different is the nature of the challenges he faces. The starkness of the differences is their very point. By implicitly contrasting Aeneas and Roman things to Odysseus and Greek things, Vergil adumbrates the singular identity of the Romans, their mission, and the characteristics that make their achievements possible.

Allusion functions in multiple ways. While it clearly functions to establish sameness with the model text (*imitatio*), it also invites attention to *differences* from the model text (*aemulatio*, "rivalry" or *oppositio in imitando*); and it is by way of these differences of content or context from his model that the alluding poet suggests his own purposes or new meanings. Indeed, as Wendell Clausen (1966) proposed: "*difference* is the *meaning* of the allusion" (editor's italics). Both "difference" and "meaning" are key terms for a responsive appreciation of allusion. We should, then, examine how *Aeneid* 3 differs from its Odyssean model and what these differences might suggest for interpretation. For example, to abbreviate Clausen's important discussion: the opening lines of Aeneas' first two speeches in the *Aeneid* (1.94-101, 198-207) explicitly imitate or allude to speeches of Odysseus in *Odyssey* 5.306-12 and 12.208-21, respectively; but as the speeches continue, crucial differences between the two speakers appear. Where Odysseus longs for glory, Aeneas longs for lost companions; where Odysseus trusts whole-heartedly in his own cleverness, Aeneas praises the endurance of his men, but in his own heart is despairing. Thus, both the heroic high confidence of Odysseus and also the initial despair of Aeneas are set into emphatic relief by the differences between Vergil's text and its model. Differences between Odysseus' narrative of his famous adventures in *Odyssey* 9-12 and Aeneas' narrative of his own difficult wanderings function to establish for readers Aeneas' non-traditional values in the *Aeneid*'s early books, as well as the new and Roman heroic paradigm that he comes to embody.

Some major differences between the Homeric model and Vergil's text that are significant for interpretation may be sketched as follows: "Resourceful" (his defining epithet) Odysseus narrates his wanderings to the peaceful Phaeacians (*Od.* 9-12); "pious" (his defining epithet) Aeneas narrates his to Rome's future enemy, the Carthaginians (*Aen.* 2-3). Odysseus, on an individual (because by this point his entire crew has perished) voyage of return to his established home, tells stories of his brilliant stratagems; and even his near failures elicit a certain awe. The Phaeacians, in response, endow him richly and arrange prompt transportation home to Ithaca, where, through his resourcefulness, Odysseus achieves his homecoming. Aeneas, by contrast, homeless, an exile "by fate," accepts the public mission of founding a new home for his surviving people. Defeated in the Trojan war, he must narrate to beautiful Dido not his triumphs, but, instead, the fall of his city and loss of his wife (*Aen.* 2), followed by abortive settlements in wrong places and, finally, the death of his father (*Aen.* 3). From his harrowing encounter with the ghost of Polydorus to the death of Anchises, Aeneas tells of failure, flight, exhaustion, and loss. Optimistic prophecies and omens show divine care for the Trojan mission; yet oracles and signs appear riddling (96), incomplete (147-71, 712), ambiguous (539-43), and thus liable to misinterpretation (103-17). For Aeneas, prophetic moments alternate with struggle towards the "always receding" (496) goal that disappoints, even as it beckons with promises of unanticipated good. Aeneas' initial desires are for rest and a stable home for his people (85-7), but he is met with prophecies of unprecedented power and more war (97-8, 539-40). Aeneas comes only in stages to grasp that Italy is the destined place and empire the destined outcome.

From this brief summary we see that the differences between the wanderings of *Odyssey* 9-12 (sometimes referred to by scholars as "temptations") and those of *Aeneid* 3 (never referred to as "temptations") point to the other-oriented character of Aeneas' journey; to his *pietas* that demands endurance and self-sacrifice; to his effortful struggle to let the past go and to commit himself, on behalf of others, to a new homeland and future in Italy. In reflecting on this portrait of Aeneas' labors, we see how Vergil illuminates the values of Homer's text for us, even as he constructs a new, Roman model of the heroic. Reading *Aeneid* 3 against the *Odyssey* will be a continuing focus of this commentary.

The journey of *Aeneid* 3 can be fruitfully read on several levels. On the personal level for Aeneas, it is a soldiering on in an unsought mission to an unmapped future. On the political level, it is a journey from the familiar to the new, as all attempts to replicate or preserve Troy as it was fail: the cities that Aeneas names after himself or Troy are stillborn; the imitation Troy of Helenus and Andromache does not invite tarrying. Taking emotional as well as physical leave of fallen Troy is thus a cost of making Rome. As Rome's new founder in contemporary history, Augustus himself, along with Vergil's other first readers, would have seen their present challenges reflected in those of Aeneas. Finally, on the poetic level, Vergil is undertaking the task of composing something new and greater than Homer, yet in the tradition of Homer. *Aeneid* 3 allows us to observe some of his strategies in this creative undertaking.

Traditional versions of Aeneas' travels, such as the *Alexandra* (a poem transmitted under the name Lycophron, possibly early second century BCE) and the *Roman Antiquities* of Dionysius of Halicarnassus (fl. 30 BCE), included a series of stopovers, with repeated founding of cities, temples, and ritual practices. That this tradition offered no high drama was perhaps a problem; that it offered almost nothing canonical was an opportunity. It will be seen that the most emotionally powerful, significant events of *Aeneid* 3 (i.e., Aeneas' encounters with Polydorus, Andromache, and Achaemenides) are Vergil's innovations.

The narrative of *Aeneid* 3, as Heinze (1993) 68-70 established, is modeled on Greek "foundation-legends" or "colonization narratives" (Horsfall (1989)) and therefore features certain commonplaces of this "ktistic" (i.e., related to city-founding) genre: riddling oracles of (especially) the god Apollo that propel the would-be colonists, inevitable misinterpretations, wrong settlements, corrective portents, and, finally, arrival at the destined location. The Trojans move unevenly westward to Italy, under Apollo's increasingly explicit guidance (a motif termed "progressive revelation"). The Trojans' stopovers from Troy to Sicily have been usefully divided by Lloyd (1957a) into three groups: those in the Aegean (13-191), Greece (209-505), and Italy/Sicily (521-715). In each of these sections there is both a prophetic incident and a novel encounter that adumbrate the book's major themes, as will be discussed *ad loc.*

Book 3 has seven unfinished lines, a remarkable range of tone (from the Euripidean pathos of the Polydorus episode to the learned Hellenistic character of the close), and some arguably ill-fitting choices of vocabulary by the narrating Aeneas. Horsfall (2006: xxviii-xxix) attributes such anomalies to the fact, as he argues, that Book 3 was the first book of the *Aeneid* to be composed and therefore reflects Vergil's not yet perfected epic technique. Other scholars' theories will be noted *ad loc.* Nevertheless, in considering these supposed anomalies, readers might take into account that the character Aeneas, who narrates *Aeneid* 2-3, reports the speech of as many as twenty other characters, whose utterances are demonstrably distinctive to varying degrees (Landis (2007)). Vergil's construction of character through speech and its relationship to tone and expression in *Aeneid* 3 are topics that merit further study. Finally, in assessing Aeneas' narrative, we may ponder to what extent, if at all, it has been shaped—as was Odysseus'— to move its primary audience, i.e., Dido.

In sum, while Vergil, had he lived to complete revisions, surely would have added to or otherwise altered some passages of *Aeneid* 3, we may nevertheless be confident that *Aeneid* 2 and 3 reflect his mature conception. Most fundamentally, Aeneas' narration of two books out of the twelve of the *Aeneid* corresponds to Odysseus' narration of four books out of the *Odyssey's* twenty-four. Further, rhetorically, both *Aeneid* 2 and 3 construct the same Aeneas, initially distrusting of his mission, yet driven by a conviction of duty and fatedness. The overall effect of Aeneas' narrative, despite any perceived anomalies, is of a pathos and elevation of purpose that powerfully engage the sympathy of listeners (Dido) and readers.

Bibliography

For important overall readings of *Aeneid* 3, see Allen (1951), Lloyd (1957a), DiCesare (1974) 61-93, Putnam (1980), Bright (1981), Horsfall (1986), Cova (1992), Quint (1993) 50-65, Stahl (1998) 37-84, and Hexter (1999). For construction of character through speech, see Highet (1972), Feeney (1991), Laird (1997), Johnson (1999), and Landis (2007). On "difference as the meaning of allusion," see Clausen (1966); for more recent, more complex discussions of allusion, see, e.g., Thomas (1986 and 2001:1-24 on "departures from" and "subversions of" the Homeric model), Farrell (1991: 5-14, 1997), Hinds (1998), and Nelis (2001). This last offers a comprehensive study of Vergil's allusions to the *Argonautica* of Apollonius of Rhodes (pp.1-66 for *Aeneid* 3), in particular the "two-tier" allusions, which draw simultaneously on the *Odyssey* and the *Argonautica* as "model texts." For an important reading of Vergil through his Homeric model text, see Barchiesi (1984).

The following modern commentaries on *Aeneid* 3 will be cited by the author's last name alone: Conington (1871), Pease (1935), R. D. Williams (1972), and Horsfall (2006), which has become the new standard edition. The fundamental debt of the volumes in this series to the commentary of Page (1894) has been described in the series Introduction. Frequent references will also be made to the commentary of the fourth century CE grammarian and commentator, Servius. This commentary exists in both a long and a short version. The long version (to be referred to throughout as "ServiusDan.") is believed to incorporate work of Aelius Donatus, also a grammarian of the fourth century CE. On the commentary of Servius, see Fowler (1997) and Thomas (2001: 93-121).

Translations of Homer's *Iliad* and *Odyssey* are by R. Lattimore (1951 and 1965).

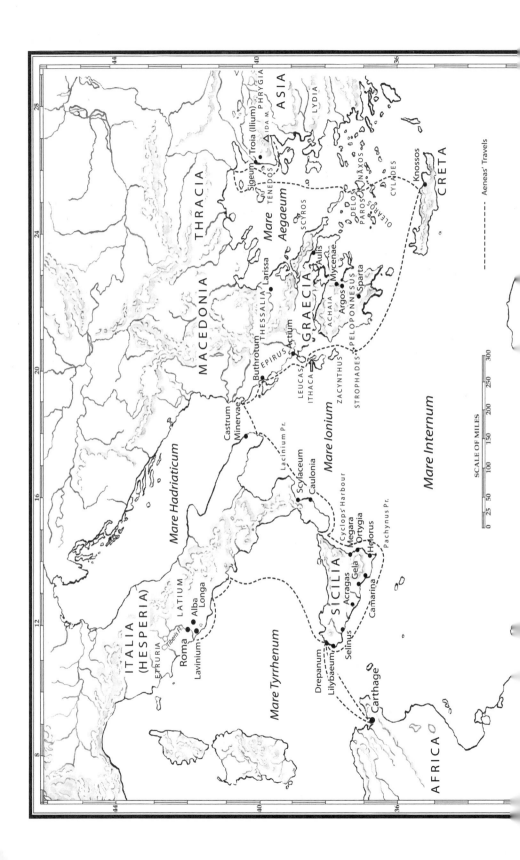

fumo, fumare, fumavi –
to smoke

cado, cadere, cecidi, casus
– fall

A   B   B   A
acc. gen gen acc.

Liber Tertius

the kingdom of Asia *to overthrow* *undeserving / nation*

"POSTQVAM res Asiae Priamique evertere gentem
(est) immeritam visum superis, ceciditque superbum
(nom) Ilium et omnis humo fumat Neptunia Troia, (nom)
diversa exsilia et desertas quaerere terras

to the gods.   and fell arrogant
Illium
Neptune-built Troy

impersonal visum est "It seemed" good to the gods to overthrow

distant places of exile   *from the ground / on it smokes*   *inf. of purpose*   *empty*

1–12. After the fall of Troy, Aeneas and his companions build ships for their journey to a new homeland.

Aeneas' narrative in Book 3 shows his uncertainty about the future, wherein he faces challenges of a different order (both moral and metaphysical) from those imposed by war in Book 2. Aeneas' deference towards his father reflects the traditional *pietas* accorded to the Roman *paterfamilias*. Throughout this book until shortly before his death, Anchises *Anchises* equals or even exceeds Aeneas in leadership of the Trojan mission. Although Aeneas predominates in matters of religion, his frequent use of verbs in the passive voice and in the first person plural (73 of these versus 53 first person singulars) characterize him initially as uncommanding. A theme of *Aeneid* 1–6 is Aeneas' growth into leadership independent of his father, whose judgment will, in fact, be shown to be fallible.

Lines 1–12 deploy rhetorical techniques (e.g., framing, interlocking* word order, alliteration*, varied rhythmical patterns, multiple place names evoking Troy) to achieve emphasis, solemnity, and pathos. See Lloyd (1957b) and Sanderlin (1975).

1. **POSTQVAM res…:** three long syllables lend solemnity to the opening of Aeneas' wanderings. (Contrast the openings of Books 1 and 2.) **res…gentem:** objects of *evertere*, the infinitive subject of the impersonal *visum* (*est*); "it seemed best," a common use of *visum*. Note chiastic* order of these nouns with their dependent genitives. As a noun, the infinitive is neuter. **res Asiae:** the kingdom of Asia. Priam is *regnatorem Asiae* (2.557).

2. **immeritam:** "undeserving," the enjambment* gives emphasis. Aeneas protests the gods' judgment also, importantly, in 2.402, 426-7. His distrust of the gods' justice, in tension with his sustained commitment to their will, is a pervasive motif of his narrative. The adjectives *immeritam…superbum* frame the line. Cf. Johnson (1999).

3. **Ilium…:** enjambed, thus emphatic, with *Troia* it frames the line. **humo:** "from the ground." **Neptunia:** "Neptune-built." Neptune and Apollo built the walls of Troy; when King Laomedon cheated them of their promised reward, they destroyed the city, cf. 2.610, 625.

4. **diversa exsilia:** "distant places of exile" rather than diverse places of exile (Williams *ad loc.*). The interlocking* order of adjectives (*diversa…desertas*) and nouns (*exsilia…terras*) and the alliteration* of *t* and *d* give rhetorical finish. **desertas:** "empty," either because the remaining Trojans are too few to conquer territory already occupied (Page) or by contrast with Troy and past experience (Horsfall). **quaerere…** infinitive of purpose after *agimur* (5). Infinitives of purpose are frequent throughout, replacing what in prose would be clauses of purpose or indirect command with the subjunctive. For discussion, see AG §457, 460-1, 563.

quaerere – to seek, ask
quaero, quaerere, quaesivi, quaesitus

Molior, moliri, molitus sum – struggle, build, found a city
mons, montis, m – mountain
fero, ferre, tuli, latus

auguriis agimur divum, classemque sub ipsa   5
Antandro et Phrygiae molimur montibus Idae,
incerti quo fata ferant, ubi sistere detur,
contrahimusque viros. vix prima inceperat aestas
et pater Anchises dare fatis vela iubebat,
litora cum patriae lacrimans portusque relinquo   10
et campos ubi Troia fuit. feror exsul in altum

(handwritten annotations: "2 indirect questions", "by omens we are driven", "gen. pl. of gods", "and the fleet", "strange", "uncertain where it is granted to stop", "we, gathering, the men scarcely, and begun summer was advising", "to give sails to the winds", "when I leave", "the port (m)", "also fields where Troy was", "I am carried", "as an exile", "fatum, fati (n.)", "contraho, contrahere, contraxi, contractus", "portus, portus", "exsul, exsulis (n.)")

5. **auguriis:** e.g., the omens of fire, thunder, shooting star (2.679-704). **agimur:** the passive voice suggests that Aeneas is driven literally by the winds and figuratively by destiny or divine will. On passives, see 1-12 n. **divum:** an archaic genitive plural. In epic poetry archaisms*, as they infuse a sense of a prior, distant time into the narrative, contribute to solemnity and rhetorical elevation.

6. **Antandro:** f., town at the base of Mt. Ida, near Troy. **Phrygiae:** *Phrygius* = "Trojan," not merely an ornamental epithet here. Three Trojan place names in the one line nostalgically evoke Troy. **molimur:** connotes great effort, cf. 1.33.

7. **incerti:** the Trojans grasp the meaning of prophecies only gradually (for the motif of progressive revelation, see Intro.), the significance of *Hesperia* and the *Tiber* (cf. Creusa at 2.781) being initially unclear to them. Typically the meaning of omens and prophecies becomes clear to mortals only in retrospect. Failure to undertand divine signs is a commonplace of colonization narratives (Horsfall (1989), Dougherty (1993)). **ferant... detur:** subjunctives in indirect question after *incerti*, in parallel clauses; note alliteration* of *f*'s. **sistere:** "stop," "settle," infinitive subject of *detur*, "it is granted" (i.e., by the gods).

8. **vix prima...et...cum (10):** "summer had scarcely begun *and* Anchises was advising...*when* I leave." Note inverted *cum* clause (*cum inversum*), wherein the formally subordinate clause in fact expresses the principal action of the sentence, in a temporal clause introduced by *cum* with the indicative (AG §546a.) Cf. Williams *ad* 8-10. Traditions vary on the season in which Troy fell.

9. **dare fatis vela:** this variation on the common phrase *dare ventis vela* "give sails to the winds," emphasizes that the Trojans are yielding themselves to whatever destiny brings.

10-11. Aeneas' grief (*lacrimans*) in leaving his *patria* encompasses *litora, portus, campos*, natural features. These he will not be able to replicate. As a city-founder, he will build walls (a motif throughout the book), temples, etc. Cf. *Aen.* 1.421-9 for the many constructions underway in Carthage. Nelis (2001) 25 observes that both Jason and Aeneas are crying at the start of their missions. Here, again, "difference is the meaning of the allusion": the situation of Jason, an untried, naïve youth, who has just taken farewell of his *mother* and is initially *rejected* as mission leader by his men (in favor of Heracles), illuminates by contrast the maturity of Aeneas, the magnitude of his mission, and the traumatic history that precedes it. See Beye (1982) on Apollonius' antiheroic portrait of Jason.

11. **ubi Troia fuit:** "was" (and now is no more), cf. 2.325. Pathos* inheres in the sad contrast between the past and the present. Such pathos, created in a variety of ways, characterizes Aeneas' narrative throughout. See 5 n. and Cic. *Inv.* 1.55-6.

no, nare, navi,
nascor, nesci, netus
natus, neti
sum

my son (Ascanius)
w/ companions + *perints* *+ the great gods*

cum sociis natoque penatibus et magnis dis.

At a little distance   *is cultivated*   *to the fields*

Terra procul vastis colitur Mavortia campis

(Thraces arant) acri quondam regnata Lycurgo   *dat. of agent*

plowing   *fierce*   *formerly*   *having been ruled*

the Thracians plow it

abl.

regno, regnor, regnavi, regnatus — to rule

12. **penatibus et magnis dis:** the spondaic line and monosyllabic ending are characteristic of Ennius (born 239 BCE), Rome's first great epic poet, as in: *dono ducite doque volentibu' cum magnis dis* (*Ann.* fr. 190 in Skutsch, 193 in Warmington). Thus Vergil makes Aeneas begin his narrative of the Trojans' journey with this (anticipatory) allusion to Rome's first great epic poet, closing the proem (the introduction to the book) with archaic, quintessentially Roman solemnity.

    penatibus: colonists customarily transport the sacred hearthfire of the mother city to the new colony. The Penates of the home protect the household, the Penates of the city, the city. These Penates, entrusted by Hector to Aeneas in 2.293-5, are the gods of the Trojan people, originally (in Vergil's version) brought from Italy by Dardanus and returned by Aeneas to their homeland, to become the household gods of the Roman state. Aeneas' rescue of the Penates from Troy (1.378, 2.717), with the promised continuity of their cult at Lavinium (12.192-4), is thematically and politically central to the poem. "The entire *Aeneid* is an *aition*, an explanation in mythological terms, for the presence at Lavinium of objects venerated and the Trojan Penates" (Horsfall (1989) 24). See Dougherty (1993) 15-30. The reference to *magnis dis* is (no doubt purposefully) imprecise.

13–18. The Trojans land in Thrace; Aeneas begins to found a town, naming it after himself.

The stop in Thrace is traditional in the Aeneas legend. Eponymous towns such as Aenus at the mouth of the Hebrus and Aeneia in Chalcidice suggest early Trojan settlement of the area, as founders of colonies typically name the colony either after themselves or after the mother city. However, the association of Polydorus' story with Aeneas is new with Vergil, as is the ghostly sequel to his murder related here.

13–16. These lines constitute a brief topographical ecphrasis*, signaled by the formula *Terra…colitur* (13) which introduces the description. The closing formula *feror huc* (16) re-establishes the connection with the narrative. See also 73, 163, 533, 692 and see Williams *ad loc.* for good notes.

13. **procul:** "at a little distance," "close by"; it is a short sail across the narrow Hellespont. (See map.) **colitur:** "is inhabited." **Mavortia:** archaic, hence poetic, adjectival form; cf. Hom. *Il.* 13.301 where Ares (Roman *Mars* or *Mavors*) comes from Thrace to do battle. Thracians are traditionally fierce. See 5 n. **campis:** ablative of quality or place where.

14. **Thraces arant:** parenthetical. Aeneas offers this explanation for the benefit of his listeners, of whom Dido is the most important. The final syllable of the Greek nominative plural *Thraces* is short. Understand *terram* as the object of *arant*. **acri…Lycurgo:** dative of agent with *regnata*; Lycurgus is termed fierce because he persecuted the Bacchants, female followers of Bacchus (Gr. Dionysus). For this impiety he was punished by Jupiter (Zeus). Thus impiety marks the Thracian episode from the start.

hospitium antiquum Troiae sociique penates   15
dum fortuna fuit, feror huc et litore curvo
moenia prima loco fatis ingressus iniquis
Aeneadasque meo nomen de nomine fingo.
Sacra Dionaeae matri divisque ferebam
auspicibus coeptorum operum, superoque nitentem   20

15. **hospitium…:** a land, "of long-standing (*antiquum*) a guest-host (*hospitium*) to Trojans and (whose) household gods (*penates*) (were: *fuerunt* omitted, as frequently) allied (*socii*) (i.e., with those of Troy)." They are allied because Polymestor is married to Iliona, Priam's daughter (Servius *ad loc.*). *Hospitium* may mean either (1) the relation of host to guest, hospitality, or, as here, (2) the place where such hospitality is shown; it is in apposition with *terra*, cf. 61.

16. **dum fortuna fuit:** note the pathos*, cf. 11 n. **feror:** again, note passive voice; Aeneas is carried by winds or fates. Note alliteration* of *f*'s that continues through 18.

17. **moenia prima:** building walls is an important commonplace of colonization narratives. The first action of Aeneas' wanderings is to build walls; by contrast, the first action of Odysseus' wanderings (also in Thrace) is the assault on the Ciconians (Hom. *Od.* 9.39-46). Cf. Horsfall *ad loc.* In this way, while the first action of Aeneas' wanderings is constructive, Odysseus' is destructive. In this way a moral contrast between the two heroes is established. See Intro. on allusion and difference. **fatis…iniquis:** lit. "fates being hostile," ablative absolute, portending an evil outcome. **ingressus** "beginning" or "entering upon" (the task).

18. **Aeneadas:** "men of Aeneas." Aeneas now calls his people after himself, in a typical founder's gesture, see 13-18 n. Vergil alludes here to the city of Aenus in Thrace. In Hom. *Il.* 4.520 a Thracian chieftain comes from Aenus (Gr. *Ainos*), which then became linked to the Aeneas legend. Servius (*ad* 3.17) says Aenus may have been named after a companion of Odysseus who died there; thus, as O'Hara (1996) 136 puts it, in making *Aeneas* the founder of Aenus, Vergil would be making a "polemical countersuggestion": Aeneas, not Odysseus, would be the key figure in the town's naming. Another town with a similar name, Aeneia (in Chalcidice) is traditionally said to have been founded by Aeneas (Dion. Hal. 1.49.4, Livy 40.4.9), but is likely too distant to be in Vergil's mind here (Williams *ad loc.*).

19–48. Aeneas rips myrtle and cornel shoots from a nearby mound to wreathe altars for sacrifice to his mother. To his astonishment, these drip blood. Aeneas repeats the gesture a second and third time. Polydorus' voice is then heard, imploring him to cease, for the blood is his own and each branch a spear thrust into his body. He urges flight.

The primary source for Polydorus' story is Euripides' *Hecuba,* wherein Polydorus' ghost, speaking the prologue, reveals that Priam had entrusted him, the youngest son, along with a quantity of gold, to his son-in law Polymestor, king of Thrace, in order to preserve his family line and wealth, should Troy fall. However, once Troy is lost, Polymestor murders Polydorus and throws his body into the sea. His mother Hecuba, though now a captive, contrives both to punish Polymestor for his violation of sacred trust and to bury Polydorus properly, as his ghost desired and foresaw (*Hec.* 10-15, 716-20,

caelicola - deity

corneus, cornea, corneum (adj)
cornel-tree (wood used to make weapons)

caelicolum regi mactabam in litore taurum.

forte fuit iuxta tumulus, quo cornea summo

virgulta et densis hastilibus horrida myrtus.

(by chance there was a mound nearby)
(dat) for the king I was sacrificing a bull on the shore
at the highest point
Myrtle bristling thick
neuter bristly thorns erant / thick spears w/ dense spearshafts / bristly and there were spearshafts

781-2). More generally the source is "Hellenistic mythological narrative…typically rich in horror, suffering nature, metamorphosis, and pathos" (Horsfall, 13-68 n.).

interlocking word order synchysis

This episode introduces two important motifs. The first is the failure of attempts to preserve, refound, or imitate Troy: in sending away his youngest son with much gold, Priam hoped to preserve his line (*Hec.* 80 "the last remaining anchor of my house"); equally, settlements that Aeneas names after himself (though such naming is a founder's or victor's prerogative) or Troy prove abortive; the imitation Troy of Andromache and Helenus is perceived by Aeneas as sterile. (See 294-505 n.) The enduring settlement will be named *Lavinium* after Aeneas' future, Latin wife (12.194, 823-42); Rome must be something new. Second is the motif of "inadvertent trespass" (editor's term), in which Aeneas stumbles into impiety or other violence, as will recur in the episode with the Harpies (209-77 n.).

Servius *ad* 3.46 cites the story of Romulus' throwing a spear onto the Palatine, which then took root and grew into a tree. Vergil's possible allusion here to this story would make of the Polydorus episode a "perverted foundation story" (Hardie (2007)). Thomas (1988) reads this episode as an instance of "tree violation," one type of inadvertent trespass. For a sustained reading of Aeneas' violence and moral infractions in Book 3, see Putnam (1980); for a fervent rejection of such a "moral reading" of this episode (and others), see Horsfall, 21 n. For another reading of Polydorus' significance, see 31 n. Nelis (2001) 27 compares the bleeding tree to Ap. Rhod. 2.476-85 (a wood nymph's tree violated) and 3.851-66 (Medea cuts the plant sprung from Prometheus' blood to make her magic ointment).

19. **Dionaeae matri:** Dione is mother of Venus.

20. **auspicibus:** in apposition with *matri* and *divis*: Aeneas was offering sacrifices to his mother and the gods as protectors of his task, i.e., to elicit the gods' goodwill in his new undertaking. Uncharacteristically, Aeneas' intended sacrifice occurs *after* work has begun (*coeptorum operum*); contrast, e.g., 119. Occasions for sacrifice were many, e.g., thank offerings or ritual obligations dictated by the sacred calendar. This one would be a "contractual sacrifice," associated with the making of vows. See Scheid (1998) 629-31. It is not to be assumed, however, that literary texts accurately represent normative Roman sacrifical practice. On the contrary, according to Feeney (2002), literary texts are more properly read as "explorations" of the "meaning and purpose of divinity and sacrifice" than as representations of actual practice. Indeed, Vergil's "departures" (Feeney (2002) 6) from Roman ritual conventions and assumptions are keys to his meaning. See also Feeney (1998). Dyson's (2001) reading of the *Aeneid* depends on numerous perceived ritual infractions on Aeneas' part. See Beard, North, Price (1998) 30-54 for an introductory overview of Roman gods and religious practice. **nitentem:** at verse end, with *taurum* (21), also postponed to verse end, an example of hyperbaton*.

21. **caelicolum:** the archaic-poetic form of *caelicolarum*; cf. 5 n. on archaisms; cf. 53 n. *Supero regi caelicolum* = Jupiter.

23. **virgulta et…myrtus**: supply *erant*. Myrtle was sacred to Venus, for whom Aeneas was preparing the sacrifice. **densis…:** "myrtle bristling (with branches that resemble) spear-shafts." Horrifically, the branches actually were spear-shafts.

[handwritten top margin: sanguis, sanguinis, (na.)]

[handwritten: so that I might cover leafy branches w/ leafy the altars]

> accessi viridemque ab humo convellere silvam
> conatus, ramis tegerem ut frondentibus aras,   25
> horrendum et dictu video mirabile monstrum.
> nam quae prima solo ruptis radicibus arbos
> vellitur, huic atro liquuntur sanguine guttae
> et terram tabo maculant. mihi frigidus horror
> membra quatit gelidusque coit formidine sanguis.   30
> rursus et alterius lentum convellere vimen
> insequor et causas penitus temptare latentis:
> ater et alterius sequitur de cortice sanguis.
> multa movens animo Nymphas venerabar agrestis

24. **viridem...silvam:** "the green thicket," *silva* denoting not forest, but bushy, low-lying plants. **convellere:** i.e., "rip," "tear," more violent than "pluck."

25. **conatus:** supply *sum*. **ramis...:** flowers and tree branches were common decorations for ritual occasions. **tegerem ut:** imperfect subjunctive in a purpose clause in secondary sequence. The postposition* of *ut* (i.e., succeeding instead of preceding the verb it governs) is only poetic. Postposition* (except in the case of certain prepositions, e.g., *tenus*) is poetic because it does not occur in prose or standard speech. See AG §435, §599d. For other instances, see index.

26. **dictu...mirabile:** i.e., amazing to tell; *dictu* is a supine in the ablative, typically in this traditional formulaic expression (cf. *horribile dictu*).

27–8. **ruptis radicibus:** ablative absolute, with alliteration*. **arbos:** archaic form of *arbor*. **huic:** dative of separation; it modifies *arbos*, which is attracted into the relative clause as a nominative: thus, "from the tree (*huic*) which (*quae prima...arbos*) was first torn (*vellitur*) from the ground (*solo*) dripped (*linquuntur*) drops of black blood (*sanguine guttae*)." **atro... sanguine:** ablative of description.

29. **tabo:** i.e., putrid, viscous fluid, more horrific even than blood (Horsfall *ad loc.*). **mihi:** dative of reference.

30. **gelidusque...:** Aeneas' blood did not freeze until *after* he saw the dripping blood, thus an instance of prolepsis*.

31–3. **rursus et alterius...ater et alterius:** "*again* I move to rip a pliant shoot from a second (tree)." Adler (2003) 281-5 reads Aeneas' tearing of the branches a second and third time as reflecting his (early) inclination to natural science, to know, as he says, the *causas penitus... latentis* "deeply hidden causes" (32) of this anomalous bleeding. Ultimately (on Adler's reading) Aeneas foregoes science to accept mission, religious revelation, and the divine will. See 19-48 n. on inadvertent trespass. **convellere:** characteristic Vergilian use of infinitive to express purpose; cf. 5 n. and 24, 31.

33. **ater...sanguis:** frame the line. Such framing is one of the pleasing patterns of epithet and noun interplay that characterize Vergil's verse. Wilkinson (1970) 217 calls this form of hexameter a "Bronze Line." Further on word patterns in the hexameter, see 108 n.

34. **movens:** "pondering," "my mind racing." **Nymphas...agrestis:** because Dryades and Hamadryades were the special guardians of woods and trees, respectively.

[handwritten bottom margin: horrendum et dictu video mirabile monstrum, / horrible to say I see a monster. — quiasmus (chiasmus) A B C / B C A]

Gradivumque patrem, Geticis qui praesidet arvis, 35
rite secundarent visus omenque levarent.
tertia sed postquam maiore hastilia nisu
adgredior genibusque adversae obluctor harenae
(eloquar an sileam?) gemitus lacrimabilis imo
auditur tumulo, et vox reddita fertur ad auris: 40
'quid miserum, Aenea, laceras? iam parce sepulto,
parce pias scelerare manus. non me tibi Troia
externum tulit aut cruor hic de stipite manat.

35. **Gradivum patrem:** i.e., Mars; this obscure epithet may mean "rejoicing" or "leaping in battle" (Servius, Horsfall *ad loc.*). The epithet serves to identify with precision the god being invoked in the prayer. **Geticis:** adjective; the Getae, here identified with Thracians, lived by the Danube. **praesidet:** referring to a tutelary deity's divine protection of a particular place, *praesidere* functions as a technical term. See Hickson (1993) 39 for other examples. **arvis:** dative after a compound verb.

36. **secundarent…levarent:** imperfect subjunctives in indirect command in secondary sequence after *venerabar*, lit. "I prayed them…that they might make favorable (*secundarent*) the vision and lighten (*levarent*) the omen," with omission of *ut*. (Note chiastic* order here of verbs and their objects.) Omens were understood to require fulfillment: hence, it was necessary, after an evil omen, to pray to the gods to fulfill it without harm. This is the first attested use of *secundare* ("to cause to be favorable") in a prayer (Hickson (1993) 79). Vergil tends, in fact, to avoid the technical language of prayer in his representations of prayer in epic, although cf. *praesidet* in 35 n. above. Cf. 20 n.

37. **sed**: postponed, thus poetic, emphasizing the word which now precedes; see 25 n. **hastilia:** plural, because each spear embedded in Polydorus' body had grown into a bristling shoot.

38. **genibusque…:** ablative of means, lit. "struggle with my knees against the opposing sand." **harenae:** dative after compound verb.

39–40. **eloquar an sileam?:** deliberative subjunctives. Aeneas shows concern that his narrative may be too disturbing for his listeners. **imo…tumulo:** from the very depth of the mound. **vox reddita:** "an answering voice"; Polydorus' ghost responds to Aeneas' action.

41-2. **miserum:** supply *me*. **Aenea:** Greek voc., cf. 475 *Anchisa*. **iam:** "at last," i.e., after lacerating my body twice. **sepulto:** supply *mihi*, dative after *parce*. **parce sepulto,/ parce… scelerare:** note the repetition and varied construction and meaning of *parce*: "spare a buried man, spare (i.e., cease) to defile." Polydorus sees Aeneas' otherwise pious (*pias* 42) hands now defiled.

42-3. **non…aut…:** *non* qualifies the whole sentence; therefore, translate *aut* as "nor." "Troy did not bear me foreign to you (*non me tibi externum…tulit*), nor does this blood drip from a tree (*cruor…de stipite manat*) (i.e., it drips from my body)." Dante Alighieri (1265-1321 CE), author of the *Divine Comedy*, takes up this image of bleeding trees to embody the condemned souls of suicides (*Inferno* 13). Dante's other allusions to *Aen.* 3 will be noted *ad loc*. **tibi:** dative of reference, dependent on *externus*.

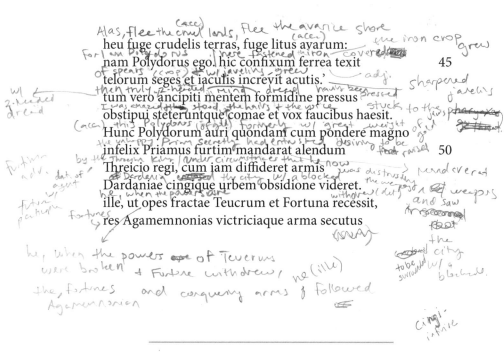

heu fuge crudelis terras, fuge litus avarum:
nam Polydorus ego. hic confixum ferrea texit   45
telorum seges et iaculis increvit acutis.'
tum vero ancipiti mentem formidine pressus
obstipui steteruntque comae et vox faucibus haesit.
Hunc Polydorum auri quondam cum pondere magno
infelix Priamus furtim mandarat alendum   50
Threicio regi, cum iam diffideret armis
Dardaniae cingique urbem obsidione videret.
ille, ut opes fractae Teucrum et Fortuna recessit,
res Agamemnonias victriciaque arma secutus

---

44. **crudelis…avarum**: transferred epithets* (i.e., transferred from Polymestor, to whom they really apply), in chiastic* order with *terras* and *litus*, direct objects of parallel clauses with anaphora* of *fuge*.

46. **iaculis…acutis**: ablative of quality or material with *seges*.

47. **ancipiti…**: the dread is *anceps* because it renders Aeneas doubtful of what to do. **mentem**: accusative of respect with *pressus*.

48. **steterunt**: perfect with short penult, archaic scansion, poetic.

49–72. Aeneas suspends the narrative of his own experiences to recount Polydorus' story to Dido, deploring, in an aside, the criminal greed for gold. He resumes his story with the Trojans' decision to flee after performing funeral rites for Polydorus.

49. **quondam**: elicits pathos* for what was but is no longer; cf. 11 n.

50. **mandarat**: syncopated form of *manda(ve)rat*. (See syncope*.) **alendum**: gerundive of purpose with dative of agent.

51. **Threicio regi**: the Thracian king is Polymestor, married to Priam's daughter, Iliona. **iam**: by now, i.e., towards the end of the war. **armis**: dative, as often, after a compound verb (*diffideret*).

51-2. **diffideret…videret**: subjunctives in *cum* circumstantial (or narrative) clause (AG §546 and nn. 1 and 2). Cf. 416, 626, 679, 712. **cingique urbem…**: accusative and infinitive construction after *videret*.

53. **fractae**: supply *sunt*. **Teucrum**: archaic-poetic genitive plural in -*um*; see 5 n. Teucer is an ancestor of the Trojans, who are often called Teucrians after him.

54. **res**: "fortunes" (of the Greeks). **victricia**: *victrix,* although a feminine adjective, is exceptionally used here with *arma*.

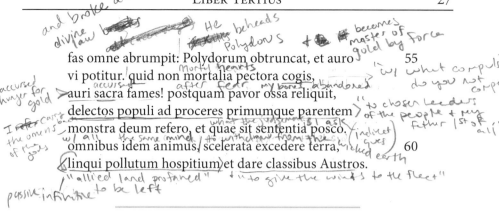

fas omne abrumpit: Polydorum obtruncat, et auro   55
vi potitur. quid non mortalia pectora cogis,
auri sacra fames! postquam pavor ossa reliquit,
delectos populi ad proceres primumque parentem
monstra deum refero, et quae sit sententia posco.
omnibus idem animus, scelerata excedere terra,   60
linqui pollutum hospitium et dare classibus Austros.

---

55. fas omne abrumpit: *fas omne* signifies all obligations imposed by the sacred laws of hospitality and of kinship; the line's two elisions* may suggest the breaking referred to. From Lycurgus to Polymestor to Aeneas, Thrace is a place of *pietas* violated. **obtruncat:** inconsistent with 45-6, but accords with Eur. *Hec.* 714-20, 782.

56. potitur: the short *i* makes *potitur* here third conjugation, not the usual fourth conjugation. Such variation in conjugation characterizes earlier stages of the development of Latin. *Potior* takes the ablative. **vi:** ablative of manner. **quid non….:** *quid* is cognate accusative*; *quid cogis* means "with what compulsion do you not compel?"

Aeneas' despairing exclamation about criminal desire for gold serves to relate his narrative to Dido's own story, as told to him by Venus, since Dido's brother Pygmalion killed her husband Sychaeus precisely for gold *auri caecus amore* (1.349). (Aeneas often takes note of his listeners in his narrative in Books 2-3; cf. 39-40 n.) Greed is never represented as a motive for Aeneas, however, who is defined by his other-directed virtues for the Roman mission. See, by contrast, e.g., Catullus 10, 28, 29, which point to Romans' desires to exploit the provinces for profit or, e.g., Propertius III.4, where greed for foreign gold is represented as the real motive for Roman conquests.

57. sacra: *sacer* may mean "holy" or "accursed," as common in the legal phrase *sacer esto,* "let him be accursed." Dante will exploit this ambiguity in *Purgatorio* 22.40-1. See 42-3 n. **postquam…:** Aeneas resumes his main narrative. **ossa:** understand *mea*.

58. delectos…: "to chosen leaders (*proceres*) of the people, and my father first of all (*primumque parentem*)."

59. refero: prodigies were regularly referred to the Roman Senate, *refero* being the technical term for laying a matter (*relatio*) before the Senate. Thus the *delecti proceres* prefigure the Roman Senate. Throughout the *Aeneid* Vergil retrojects the origins of defining Roman customs into Aeneas' epic past. **sit:** subjunctive in indirect question; note alliteration* of *p*'s, begun in 58.

60-1. excedere…linqui…dare: infinitives in apposition to *animus,* i.e., their decision is "to depart…"; note the tricolon*. However, the alternation of active (*excedere, dare*) and passive (*linqui*) infinitives has seemed suspiciously inelegant to some scholars; some late MSS have *linquere*. But *linqui* is read as more Vergilian by, e.g., Conington-Nettleship, Page, Horsfall, with Williams undecided. **linqui pollutum hospitium:**—the "hospitable" or "allied land profaned." Cf. 55 n. **dare classibus Austros:** "to give the winds to the fleet"; the fleet, thus succinctly personified, is impatient for a breeze. *Auster,* strictly the south wind, here means simply "wind," as frequently.

we renew   the funeral for Polydorus   and huge earth
ergo instauramus Polydoro funus: et ingens *gloomy*   *apposition*
is heaped on the mound   altars stand w/ heads   *gloomy altars*
aggeritur tumulo tellus; stant manibus arae,
blue   *gloomy*   *ribbons + black cypress tree*   *funeral*
caeruleis maestae vittis atraque cupresso,   *funeral*
dark-colored
it around the Ilian women, unbound   et circum Iliades crinem de more solutae;   *frothed bowls (acc)*   65
wet hair's custom according (nom.)   inferimus tepido spumantia cymbia lacte   *we brought w/ warm frothed bowls milk*
of sacred blood   cups   we secure his spirit in the tomb "
sanguinis et sacri pateras, animamque sepulcro   *w/ a great voice*
+ we call him for the last time
condimus et magna supremum voce ciemus.
Inde ubi prima fides pelago, placataque venti
transferred epithet   *thereupon when 1st there   (dat.)   the winds   is faith to the   having been calmed,   sea*   *confido, fides, +
w/ verbs of confiding   - confido, fidei, fides dat.*

62. **instauramus:** technical term for repeating a religious ceremony invalidated by some error or omission in the first performance (Livy 5.52). Vergil uses it for "renew," especially of something solemn or religious. Polydorus' body, covered only by the chance action of wind and wave, had not received formal burial; therefore this second, ritually correct, burial is an *instauratio funeris* (Page *ad loc.*, Bailey (1935) 247 n. 2). It is in the context of performing burial rites that the epithet *pius* is most often attributed to Aeneas (Camps (1969) 24-5). Note the detail of this description of the funeral; cf. the funeral for Misenus (6.175-235). At *Aen.* 2.646 Anchises, initially refusing to flee burning Troy, says (without conviction) *facilis iactura sepulcri.*

63. **aggeritur tumulo tellus:** earth is heaped upon the mound under which the body was lying (*tumulo*, dative). **stant manibus arae:** "altars stand" (i.e., "are raised") to the spirits of the dead, by Roman custom. Note alliteration* of *t* and assonance* of *a*.

64. **caeruleis:** "dark-colored," "somber." **atra:** "funeral"; cypress trees (f.), since they were associated with death, were called black.

65. **et circum…:** "and around (stand) the Ilian women, their hair unloosed according to custom (*de more*)." **crinem…solutae:** lit. "unbound as to their hair"; *crinem* is accusative of respect, a Greek construction, used, as often, of a body part. The purpose of untying the women's hair, a "fully Italian detail," is to avoid the interference of any knots with the "working of sacred influences" (Bailey (1935) 290); cf. 370.

66. **inferimus:** technical term, *inferiae* being offerings to the dead (cf. Cat. 101.2). **tepido… lacte:** it is warm because it has just been milked; bowls of new milk, wine, and blood are offered to Anchises' spirit at 5.77. Note chiastic arrangement of adjective-noun pairs, with *tepido…lacte* framing *spumantia cymbia* (thus abBA).

67. **sacri:** because sacrificed to the gods. **animam sepulcro | condimus:** "we bury" or "secure his spirit in the tomb." Postponed *et* is poetic.

68. **supremum…ciemus:** *supremum* is a cognate accusative* used adverbially, "we cry the last cry" or "we call to him for the last time." For this ritual last greeting to the dead, cf. 2.644, 11.97, 6. 506 n.; Cat. 101.10. First person plural verbs frame the verse, one of the framing patterns for which Wilkinson coined the term "Bronze Line" (Wilkinson (1970) 217). See 33 and 108 nn.

69. **pelago:** probably dative after *fides*, on analogy with the construction of *fido, fidere* (3) taking the dative; supply *est*. The sense is: "when the Trojans first had faith that the sea was again calm."

dant maria et lenis crepitans vocat Auster in altum, 70
deducunt socii navis et litora complent.
provehimur portu terraeque urbesque recedunt,
sacra mari colitur medio gratissima tellus
Nereidum matri et Neptuno Aegaeo,

---

70. **lenis crepitans:** "soft-rumbling" Southwind. Vergil frequently joins an adjective with a present participle when an adverb (e.g., *leniter*) would be normal, cf. 5.278 *arduus attollens*, 764 *creber adspirans*, 8.299 *arduus arma tenens*, 559 *inexpletus lacrimans* (Page).

71. **deducunt:** "launch." When sailors came ashore, they drew the ships up onto the beach (*subducta* 135); on departure they drew them down (*deducere*).

72. **portu:** ablative of separation. **terraeque urbesque:** the doubled –*que* is epic, recalling Homeric *te...te* ("both...and"), e.g., *Il.* 1.544

73–83. *The Trojans arrive at the island of Delos, where Apollo's city fills them with awe. Anius, king of Delos and Apollo's priest, welcomes the Trojans, Anchises especially, as an old friend.*

Aeneas' visit to Delos is traditional (e.g., Dion. Hal. 1.50). Delos is a "natural symbol" (Allen (1961) 122) of rest for the Trojans, since, as the story goes (see 75 n.), the island itself, once a restless wanderer like them, was, through Apollo's aid (of which the Trojans themselves are also beneficiaries), fixed in place and thus able to "disdain the winds." Delos, as Apollo's birthplace, was an important cult-center, rivaling Delphi, for worship of Apollo.

It was the Delphic oracle that frequently instigated colonizing missions. However, Vergil makes the Delian Apollo the divine patron of the Trojans' journey, a role he had not had previously (Heinze (1993)). Further, Vergil transfers symbols (laurel, mantic tripod) and powers of Apollo's cult site at Delphi to Delos (Paschalis (1986) 55). This elevation of the Delian Apollo over the Pythian (i.e., at Delphi) Apollo subtly serves Vergil's Roman purposes: he constructs a Delian-Trojan-Roman Apollo—morally grander than the Pythian (Delphic) Apollo of Greek epic and tragedy (Paschalis 50 n. 39)— whose oracles have the sole purpose of serving the Trojan-Roman mission (56). Augustus considered Apollo a divine patron of himself and built the famous temple of Apollo on the Palatine (dedicated in 28 BCE) (Suet. *Aug.* 29). See further 278-93 n. on Actium and Augustus.

73–8 form a topographical ekphrasis*, introduced by the formula *colitur...tellus*, closed by *huc feror*. See 13-16 n.

73. **sacra:** because it was the birthplace of Apollo. Note the elegant framing of the verse by *sacra...tellus* (see 33, 68, 108 nn.). **mari...medio:** "surrounded by sea," "in the sea-midst." **colitur:** is inhabited (cf. 13 *colitur*, 77 *coli*),

74. **Nereidum matri:** i.e., Doris, wife of Nereus, mother of the Nereids (sea-nymphs). The rhythm of this line, with hiatus* after both *matri* and *Neptuno*, and spondaic fourth and fifth feet, is highly unusual, calling attention to the Greek names with which it ends. Thus it suits the Greek site of Delos. **Neptuno Aegaeo:** for Neptune of the Aegaean Sea.

quam pius arquitenens oras et litora circum   75
errantem Mycono e celsa Gyaroque revinxit,
immotamque coli dedit et contemnere ventos.
huc feror: haec fessos tuto placidissima portu
accipit. egressi veneramur Apollinis urbem.
rex Anius, rex idem hominum Phoebique sacerdos,   80
vittis et sacra redimitus tempora lauro
occurrit; veterem Anchisen agnovit amicum.

75. **quam...revinxit** (76): extended hyperbaton*, encompassing two verses, encloses the wandering (*errantem*) island, suggesting both the island's wandering and its ultimate securing in place by the god. **pius:** in Vergil's version of this myth, Apollo shows *pietas* (the characteristic Roman virtue of Aeneas) to Delos, his birthplace. The goddess Latona, pregnant with Apollo and Diana, had vainly sought a land in which to give birth until she came to Delos, at that time a floating island, which received her. Apollo, in pious gratitude, bound the wandering island to the nearby islands of Myconos and Gyaros. Pre-Vergilian accounts, by contrast, omit mention of aid from Apollo (Paschalis (1986) 58 n. 78). Thus Vergil romanizes Apollo by terming him *pius,* and he makes the destiny of Delos prefigure the Trojans'. Through Apollo's aid, both achieve settlement after wandering (Paschalis (1986) 58 n. 79). The *pietas* associated with Apollo and Delos contrasts with the violations of *pietas* in Thrace. Cf. Williams *ad* 3.76. **arquitenens:** an epic, compound adjective. Since they are characteristic of Homeric Greek, compound adjectives contribute significantly to the epic tone of all Greek and Latin epic poetry thereafter. Note anastrophe* of *circum*.

76. **Mycono e celsa:** Myconos is a low-lying island; the epithet has puzzled commentors, one hypothesis being that any island seems, to approaching sailors, to rise from the sea.

77. **immotamque coli dedit...:** "and granted ([to] the island) to remain unmoved and to disdain the winds." Cf. 5 n. on infinitive of purpose, *coli*.

78. **huc...:** "to it (Delos) I am carried; it most peacefully welcomes (us) exhausted in its safe harbor." Note passive *feror* and adjective *fessos*, both motifs of Book 3: the Romanness of the Trojans' achievement is exemplified in endurance through exhaustion, loss, wandering. (See Intro.)

79. **veneramur:** "we reverence," "gaze with awe upon" (cf. 84). Both the island and the city are named Delos.

80. **idem:** early kings of Rome served also as priests. Note how *rex* and *sacerdos* frame the line (see 33, 68 nn.). Anius is a mythical figure, about whom there were various accounts; in one, his daughter Launa/ Lavinia, a priestess, marries Aeneas and accompanies him to Rome (Dion. Hal. 1.59.3, Horsfall *ad* 69-120). In the *Aeneid* Lavinia, the destined wife of Aeneas, is daughter of the Latin king Latinus.

81. **lauro:** sacred to Apollo, cf. 91. Vergil places Apollo's laurel and tripod (92) in Delos rather than Delphi (Paschalis (1986) 55), thus either creating or reviving an oracle of Apollo on Delos (see 73-83 n. and Paschalis (1986) 54-5).

iungimus hospitio dextras et tecta subimus.
Templa dei saxo venerabar structa vetusto:

[handwritten interlinear glosses: we join ... hospit... right hand ... (recedes) houses ... we ascend; the temples of the god w/ ... regarding / I was reverently ... ancient stone ... having been built]

---

83. **hospitio:** ablative of manner. Contrasts with violated *hospitium* of Polymestor (15).

84–120. Aeneas prays that Apollo may preserve the Trojans and grant them their own city. From the temple's inner sanctum, a divine voice instructs the Trojans ("sons of Dardanus") to seek their "ancient mother" and promises universal rule. Anchises interprets the "ancient mother" as Crete, native land of their ancestor Teucrus. He commands the Trojans to sacrifice and set sail.

In understanding the Trojans' "ancient mother" to be Crete, Anchises misses the clue inherent in the address "sons of Dardanus." The Penates' subsequent appearance to Aeneas is necessary to set the Trojans again on the right path. (On the characteristic ambiguity of oracles in colonization narratives, see Dougherty (1993) 157-63.) The Penates' revelation of the *Italian* origin of Dardanus and hence of his descendants Aeneas and the other Trojans is a key passage in the *Aeneid*, since it makes of the Trojans' arrival in Italy a *return* to their true home.

In the *Aeneid*, as is revealed piecemeal (see also 3.94-9, 147-91; 7.205-11, 8.134-42), Dardanus, ancestor of Aeneas, is a son of Jupiter and Electra, born in a town or region in Etruria called Corythus or Corythum. He immigrates first to Samothrace and then to the Troad, where he founds Troy, marries Bateia, daughter of Teucer (or Teucrus), fathers the Trojan race, and ultimately is apotheosed. (Elaborated versions of this story are found in later commentators, such as Servius *ad* 3.104, 167.) That Dardanus comes from Etruria is a significant innovation on Vergil's part (Horsfall (1973), R.Wilhelm (1992)), with important thematic and political implications.

Other versions of Aeneas' heritage were current in Vergil's time. The Greek historian Dionysius of Halicarnassus, essentially contemporary with Vergil, relying apparently on Varro (Servius), represented Dardanus, the Trojans' ancestor, as ethnically Greek, from Arcadia, thereby implicitly claiming that Rome was a Greek city. On the other hand, if Dardanus, whom Aeneas (*Aineios*) claims as his ancestor already in Homer, *Iliad* 20.215-43, is Italian (as Vergil tells it), then Aeneas' voyage is a return, a homecoming, a *nostos*; and his settlement in Italy has unarguable legitimacy. As Syed argues (2005) esp. 194-227, the idea of an Italian Aeneas is crucial to the Romans' sense of their distinctive selfhood—neither Greek nor wholly Eastern (like the Phrygian Trojans). An Italian Dardanus and/or Aeneas as founder embodies an assimilation of Italian and Roman identity, thereby making a community of Romans with a shared past. See further the notes on 168, 180.

On Dardanus and the Romans' ethnicity see Horsfall (1973, 1987), Jocelyn (1991), and Wilhelm (1992).

84. **Templa...venerabar:** "regard reverently," cf. 79 n. **saxo...vetusto:** the temple, built from stone ancient even to Aeneas, would pre-exist (and therefore have primacy over) Apollo's temple in Delphi (Paschalis (1986) 60).

'da propriam, Thymbraee, domum; da moenia fessis   85
et genus et mansuram urbem; serva altera Troiae
Pergama, reliquias Danaum atque immitis Achilli.
quem sequimur? quove ire iubes? ubi ponere sedes?
da, pater, augurium atque animis inlabere nostris.'

---

85. **da...da:** an elegant prayer. Its special sound effects (note the repetition, anaphora* (*da...
da...da*), alliteration* (of *d*), consonance (of *m*)) are characteristic of ancient prayers, which
were spoken aloud, and serve to attract the attention of the god that is being invoked. After
the brief invocation with epithet (*Thymbraee*), two tricola* *abundantia* (*moenia...et genus...
urbem* (85-6) and *quem...quo...ubi* (88) follow; the last verse (89) is framed by imperatives
da and *inlabere*, one active, one deponent, from different conjugations. In sum, an elegant
composition. **propriam:** to be "our own," i.e., lasting, permanent. **Thymbraee:** epithet of
Apollo. *Thymbra* is a city near Troy, sacred to Apollo. **moenia:** building of walls is defining
of city-founders, along with *domum* 85, *genus, urbem* 86; on *fessis*, see 78 n. Aeneas prays
only for walls, homes, etc., but receives prophecies of power and rule.

    Hom. *Il.* 1.36-42 offers a "complete set of constitutive elements of ancient prayer,"
i.e., "invocation," "argument," and "prayer proper." The invocation may include the god's
cult names, patronymics* (denoting descent from the father or other ancestor), residences,
and functions; the argument encompasses reasons the god may wish to grant the prayer;
finally, the prayer proper expresses the petitioner's wish (Versnel (1998) 570). A familiar
example may be Catullus 34, the hymn to Diana, which preserves traditional material: an
invocation with abbreviated ancestry (*Latonia*), spheres of concern (*montium, silvarum,
saltuum, amnium*), alliteration*, anaphora*, archaic liturgical language (*sospites*), and
formulae; see Fordyce (1973). Nevertheless, literary prayers largely fail to coincide with
actual prayers attested in inscriptions, historical accounts, etc. In Aeneas' prayer here,
for example, only *serva* (86) occurs as a technical term of prayer (Hickson (1993) 79-80).
"The most striking characteristic of prayers in the *Aeneid* is the total absence of technical
formulae...Vergil's dominant concern was to employ a literary language...which would
recall the Greek epics he sought to rival" (Hickson (1993) 141, 144). (See Hickson (1993)
161-6 for listing of all petitionary prayers in the *Aeneid*.) See also Feeney (1998, 2004).

86. **altera Troiae | Pergama:** Aeneas speaks of himself and his followers as Troy's "other
(one of two) citadel." In fact, Rome will not be (merely) another Troy. See on Buthrotum
episode, 294-505 nn.

87. **reliquias...Achilli:** repeated from 1.30, in apposition to *altera Troiae Pergama*. The first
syllable of *reliquias* is artificially lengthened in thesis* (i.e., the stressed syllable of the foot,
AG §611, 642), a frequent practice in Homer; the word is sometimes spelled *relliquias*.

88. **quem sequimur?:** "whom do we (are we to) follow?" In short questions the indicative,
often used instead of the deliberative subjunctive, lends directness and urgency, cf. 367
quae prima pericula vito? The questions form a *tricolon* abundans* (*quem...quo...ubi...*).

89. **animis...nostris:** dative after compound verb. **inlabere:** deponent imperative. Aeneas
prays that the god may "slip into" and inspire their spirits.

Vix ea fatus eram: tremere omnia visa repente, 90
liminaque laurusque dei, totusque moveri
mons circum et mugire adytis cortina reclusis.
summissi petimus terram et vox fertur ad auris:
'Dardanidae duri, quae vos a stirpe parentum
prima tulit tellus, eadem vos ubere laeto 95
accipiet reduces. antiquam exquirite matrem.
hic domus Aeneae cunctis dominabitur oris
et nati natorum et qui nascentur ab illis.'

90. **Vix...fatus eram...visa:** sc. *sunt*, "scarcely had I spoken: all things seemed…"; note parataxis* that emphasizes the suddenness of the response. Cf. 2.172. **tremere:** in response to the god's presence.

91. **liminaque laurusque:** the first -*que* is artificially lengthened in thesis* (see 87 n.), the stressed syllable of the foot. This is characteristic of Homeric metrical practice, as is the double –*que*; see 87 n. Note pleasant alliteration* of *l*'s.

92. **mons:** Mt. Cynthus. **mugire:** the roar that precedes the divine voice. **reclusis:** the temple doors "fly open" (Conington).

93. **summissi petimus terram:** "humbled we fall to the ground," whether by kneeling or by prostrating themselves is unclear (Horsfall); cf. Lucr. 1.92 *muta metu terram genibus submissa petebat.*

94–5. **Dardanidae duri:** by addressing the Trojans as "sons of Dardanus" the oracle hints that their ancient mother is Italy, (in the *Aeneid*) the original home of Dardanus; *duri* refers both to the Trojans' character and to their hardships. **quae vos…:** lit: "which land (*quae… tellus* 95) first (*prima*) bore (*tulit*) you (*vos*)…this same one (*eadem*) will welcome you…." The relative clause precedes the main clause, with *tellus* attracted into the relative clause; *quae* and *tellus* then elegantly frame the relative clause. This reversed order of clauses and the emphatic hyperbaton* of *quae…tellus* dramatize the land and the revelation concerning it. Both *ubere* and *laeto* have meanings appropriate to both *terra* and *mater*: *uber* means (1) a mother's breast, (2) fertility of soil; *laetus* means (1) joyful, i.e., giving a joyful welcome, (2) fertile, fruitful.

96. **reduces:** the Trojans' arrival in Italy is a return; similarly in 101 *reverti.* See 84-120 n.

97. **hic:** "here," i.e., in this land just mentioned; English idiom would say "there," cf. 111 *hinc.* **cunctis dominabitur oris:** ablative of place or dative after *dominor.* This and the following line allude to Hom. *Il.* 20. 307-8, Poseidon speaking:
"but now the might of Aineias shall be lord over the Trojans,
    and his sons' sons, and those who are born of his seed hereafter."
Poseidon's narrower prophecy of Aeneas' rule over (an Asian) Troy is transformed here, presumably to Aeneas' surprise, into a promise of universal empire. As Horsfall (*ad loc.*) well observes, this foretelling of universal empire should alarm the Carthaginians.

98. **et nati…:** "and his children's children and their children after them."

haec Phoebus; mixtoque ingens exorta tumultu
laetitia, et cuncti quae sint ea moenia quaerunt,   100
quo Phoebus vocet errantis iubeatque reverti.
tum genitor veterum volvens monimenta virorum
'audite, o proceres,' ait 'et spes discite vestras.
Creta Iovis magni medio iacet insula ponto,
mons Idaeus ubi et gentis cunabula nostrae.   105
centum urbes habitant magnas, uberrima regna,
maximus unde pater, si rite audita recordor,

---

99. **haec Phoebus:** "these things Phoebus (spoke)," i.e., thus spoke Phoebus. **exorta:** sc. *est.*

100–1. **sint…vocet…iubeat:** subjunctives in indirect questions after *quaerunt.* As oracles were characteristically ambiguous, they required decoding. Hence the Trojans seek to understand the meaning of this one. **ea moenia:** "those (i.e., the promised) walls," implicit in Apollo's prophecy; see 17 and 85 nn. **errantis:** sc. *nos.*

102. **veterum…virorum:** pondering traditions of "earlier generations"; alliteration* here is appropriately archaizing.

103. **spes…vestras:** i.e., "the object of your hopes."

104. **Iovis magni…insula:** Crete is the birthplace of Jove. Saturn, Jove's father, consumed his children at birth to prevent their overthrowing him. This deeply displeased their mother, the goddess Rhea, who saved the newborn Jupiter by concealing him on Mt. Aegaeum in Crete, giving Saturn a stone wrapped in swaddling clothes in his place (Hes. *Theog.* 459-91). The Corybantes (111), by clashing their cymbals, prevented the baby's cries from being heard. **medio…ponto:** "in the midst of the sea."

105. **mons Idaeus ubi:** note the omission of *est*; the poetic postposition of *ubi* emphasizes the preceding word(s). The existence of a Mt. Ida in Crete as well as in the Troad makes possible Anchises' inference that Crete was the birthplace of the Trojan race as well as of many Trojan religious practices.

106. **habitant:** understand the Cretans as subject. **uberrima regna:** the fertile land supports many kingdoms, cf. Hom. *Il.* 2.649.

107. **maximus…pater:** "our great ancestor," i.e., Teucrus (also *Teucer*), who left Crete during a time of famine and settled in the Troad. As father of Bateia, who became the wife of Dardanus, he is also an ancestor (on the maternal side) of the Trojans, who are therefore often referred to as Teucrians (e.g., 1.555, 6.562, 6.648, 8.470, 8.513). (On Teucer, see Servius *ad* 3.108.) **audita:** "things heard," the story.

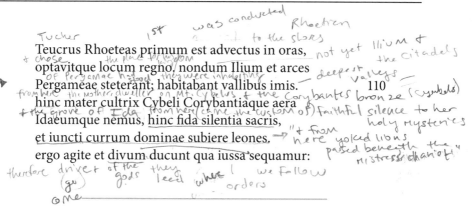

Teucrus Rhoeteas primum est advectus in oras,
optavitque locum regno, nondum Ilium et arces
Pergameae steterant; habitabant vallibus imis.   110
hinc mater cultrix Cybeli Corybantiaque aera
Idaeumque nemus, hinc fida silentia sacris,
et iuncti currum dominae subiere leones.
ergo agite et divum ducunt qua iussa sequamur:

108. **Rhoeteas**: adjective from *Rhoeteum*, a promontory on the Hellespont. The agreement of the adjective before the caesura* with the noun at the end of the verse (as here) is one of the recurrent, elegant patterns in Vergil's verse. Framing*, chiastic* and interlocking* order of verbal elements, agreement of adjectives either before or after the main caesura with the noun at the end of the line are esthetically pleasing aurally and visually. Further, these patterned arrangements may often be seen to enrich meaning in various ways. See Wilkinson (1970) 213-20 on the esthetic and intellectual pleasure readers derive from the patterned interplay between nouns and their epithets.

109. **locum**: i.e., the Rhoetean coast. **regno**: dative of purpose.

110. **steterant**: i.e., had been built. **habitabant**: as subject, understand "they" (the inhabitants), cf. 106.

111. **hinc|...hinc (112)**: "from here," i.e., from Crete, (came) the Mother, dweller (*cultrix*) on Mt. Cybelus (*Cybeli*),...and the Corybantes' bronze (*Corybantiaque aera*)," i.e. "cymbals," see 104 n. Note the alliteration* of *c*'s and anaphora* of *hinc,* giving emphasis.

 Anchises identifies the goddess Rhea with the Phrygian goddess Cybele (the name derived from Mt. Cybelus in Phrygia), also known as the *Magna Mater* (cf. *domina,* "mistress" in 113). The *Corybantes,* her attendants, like the *Curetes* of Crete, clash cymbals and dance ecstatically in their worship of the goddess. Cybele is represented riding in a chariot drawn by lions or other wild animals, symbolizing her power over wild nature. Lucretius (2.600-43) captures the spectacular impact of Cybele's processions; Catullus 63, by contrast, paints a terrifying picture of the orgiastic rites that accompanied her mysteries. References to Cybele recur in the *Aen.*: the transfigured Creusa tells Aeneas that she is in Cybele's care (2.788); Cybele prays that her Trojan ships may be rescued (9.82-122); Cybele is invoked by Aeneas (7.139, 10.252-5).

112. **Idaeumque nemus**: the Idaean grove was sacred to Cybele; note that the second syllable of *nemus* is artificially lengthened in thesis*; see 87 and 91 nn. **hinc fida silentia sacris**: "from here (*hinc*) (came) (the custom of) faithful (*fida*) silence (*silentia*) to her holy mysteries (*sacris*)," i.e., initiates into the mysteries were prohibited from revealing their contents.

113. **et iuncti**: "and (from here) yoked lions (*iuncti...leones*) passed beneath (*subiere*) the mistress's (*dominae*) chariot (*currum*)." Note the suggestive framing of the verse with *iuncti...leones*.

114. **divum**: archaic genitive plural, see 5 n. **qua**: in postposition, a poetic practice; see 25 n. Note alliteration* of *d*'s.

placemus ventos et Gnosia regna petamus. 115
nec longo distant cursu: modo Iuppiter adsit,
tertia lux classem Cretaeis sistet in oris.
sic fatus meritos aris mactavit honores,
taurum Neptuno, taurum tibi, pulcher Apollo,
nigram Hiemi pecudem, Zephyris felicibus albam. 120
Fama volat pulsum regnis cessisse paternis
Idomenea ducem, desertaque litora Cretae,

115. **Gnosia regna:** Cnossos, the chief town of Minoan Crete. Note the chiastic* order of verbs (framing the line) and their accusatives, as well as alliteration* of *p*.

116. **longo…cursu:** ablative of degree of difference. **modo Iuppiter adsit:** subjunctive in a proviso clause "(provided) only that Jove be favorable" (cf. AG §528). Anchises refers either literally to the god Jove or to the weather, which Jove personifies.

117. **lux:** sc. *diei*. **Cretaeis…in oris**: here as elsewhere (e.g., 321, 326) the adjective (*Cretaeis*) is more poetic and elevated than would be the genitive (*Cretae*) (Horsfall *ad loc.*), as is also the case in English.

118. **meritos:** "deserved," "due." **honores** "sacrifices," "offerings."

119. **Neptuno…:** they sacrifice to Neptune in prayer for their future sailing, to Apollo (note apostrophe* to Apollo) in thanks for the past oracle (Servius *ad loc.*).

120. **nigram…:** first a black victim to the storm god to ward off harm, then a white victim to the beneficent West Wind to secure good (Servius *ad loc.*). Note the verse is framed by the two colors.

121–46. The Trojans hear that Idomeneus has been driven from Crete, leaving the island open for settlement by them. Aeneas begins to build a city, calling it Pergamum; but plague strikes. Anchises urges a return to Delos for consultation of the oracle; but the Penates' revelations to the sleeping Aeneas render the trip unnecessary.

Anchises, once informed of Aeneas' vision of the Penates, accepts its validity, remembering, if late, indications that Italy, not Crete, is the destined land. A visit to Crete does not figure in the Aeneas tradition, although there was a Pergamum in Crete in historical times (see 190 n.).

121. **Fama volat:** introduces the accusative and infinitive of indirect speech. Each of the infinitives (*cessisse, deserta* (*esse*), *vacare, astare*) has its own subject accusative.

122. **Idomenea:** = Greek accusative of Idomeneus, who led the Cretan ships to Troy. Caught by storms on his return, he vowed to the sea gods, should he arrive safely, to sacrifice whatever he might first see on reaching Crete. In the event, this was his own son, whom he did duly sacrifice. As punishment the gods sent plague on his people, who expelled him, whereupon he emigrated to Italy (Servius *ad* 121). Idomeneus' story is one of several *nostoi* alluded to in Book 3, Odysseus' being the most important. The *nostoi*, i.e., tales about (difficult) returns or homecomings of Greek heroes after the fall of Troy, reflected actual Greek colonization around the Mediterranean (Horsfall (1989) 8). The motif* of the "victorious" Greeks' many bad homecomings functions to diminish the value of their victory at Troy by suggesting how ephemeral it was. (See 328, 332 nn. on Neoptolemus.) **desertaque…:** Crete was "deserted," not by all its inhabitants, but by Idomeneus and his people.

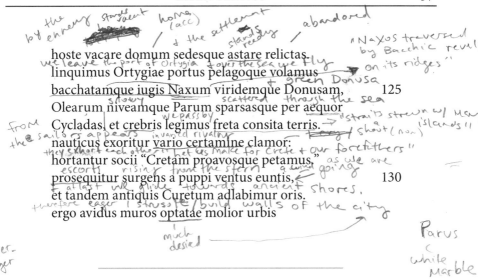

hoste vacare domum sedesque astare relictas.
linquimus Ortygiae portus pelagoque volamus
bacchatamque iugis Naxum viridemque Donusam,   125
Olearum niveamque Parum sparsasque per aequor
Cycladas, et crebris legimus freta consita terris.
nauticus exoritur vario certamine clamor:
hortantur socii "Cretam proavosque petamus,"
prosequitur surgens a puppi ventus euntis,   130
et tandem antiquis Curetum adlabimur oris.
ergo avidus muros optatae molior urbis

---

123. **astare:** "stand ready (at hand)" (Conington), i.e., "available for our project."

124. **Ortygiae:** genitive, the ancient name of Delos, from Gr. quail, thus "Quail Island."
pelago: "on" or "over" the sea, ablative of "space over which," "extent" (AG §429.4a).

125–6. **bacchatamque iugis Naxum:** *bacchatam* from *bacchor*, "to honor or traverse in Bacchic dance," used passively; lit. "Naxos traversed by bacchic revels on its ridges"; cf. 460, 475. **Naxum…Donusam, Olearum…Parum:** Aegean islands; *Paros* was famed for its white marble. The piling up of place-names is evocative.

127. **crebris…freta consita terris:** from *consero* ("scatter" or "strew"), thus "straits strewn with many islands," with etymological play on the name of the *Sporades* (Gr. "scattered about"), islands north and west of the Cyclades. Although *sparsas* strictly modifies *Cycladas*, it also serves as a gloss for the *Sporades*, "scattered" off the coast of Asia Minor (O'Hara (1996) 137). (See 401 n. on the poetic purposes of wordplay.) Page and Williams (*ad loc.*) read *concita*, "made rough by," because the narrow straits between the islands cause strong currents and rough water. **legimus:** governs the preceding accusatives (*Naxum, Donusam…Cycladas*) in the sense of "pass by"; with *freta* it has the meaning of "pick one's way through," "cross." The original meaning of *lego*, "pick," "gather," "cull," expands to encompass "pass lightly by" or "over" and is used especially of ships skirting a coast (cf. 292 *litoraque Epiri legimus*) or skimming the surface of the sea. When used of passing the eye over writing it means "read" (Page *ad loc.*).

128. **nauticus…clamor:** a loud cheer from the men. The phrase emphatically frames the line; note chiasmus* (abBA) with *vario certamine*. **vario certamine:** "in varied rivalry," i.e., they are racing each other.

129. **hortantur socii…:** they exhort each other: "Let us make for Crete and our forefathers!" **petamus:** hortatory subjunctive in direct speech. The verbs frame the verse.

130. **prosequitur…:** "escorts," a technical term. **euntis:** sc. *nos*.

131. **antiquis…oris:** adjective before the main caesura* with noun at verse end, an elegant, characteristic pattern, see 108 n.

132. **muros:** a motif, cf. 17, 85, 100. **optatae:** "much desired." **optatae…urbis:** adjective *after* main caesura* with noun at verse end, a variation from the pattern just above. See 108 n.

Pergameamque voco, et laetam cognomine gentem
hortor amare focos arcemque attollere tectis.
    Iamque fere sicco subductae litore puppes;   135
conubiis arvisque novis operata iuventus;
iura domosque dabam: subito cum tabida membris
corrupto caeli tractu miserandaque venit
arboribusque satisque lues et letifer annus.
linquebant dulcis animas aut aegra trahebant   140
corpora; tum sterilis exurere Sirius agros,

133. **Pergameamque voco:** sc. *urbem*, and "I call it the Pergamene city." See 13-18 n. **laetam cognomine:** "rejoicing in the name." A *cognomen*, strictly, is a co-name, i.e., a name that goes with another name. Vergil, however, frequently uses *cognomen* to connote a new entity (here the new city) named after an established or old one (here, *Pergama* or "Troy"); cf. 334, 350, 702 (Williams *ad loc.*).

134. **hortor amare focos…:** On the poetic use of the infinitive to express indirect command, see 4 n. **focos:** for worship of the Penates, gods of the hearth. **tectis:** probably dative of reference, for (i.e., to protect) their homes. Lines 134-7 list characteristic actions of city founders, e.g., building homes and citadel, distributing land, sanctifying marriages, establishing laws (Horsfall 1989). Cf. *Aen.* 1.421-9 listing the Carthaginians' construction projects in their establishment of a new city.

135. **Iamque fere:** "about now." With words indicating time, *fere* indicates that the specified time is only approximate. **subductae:** sc. *erant.*

136. **conubiis:** scanned as if *conubjis*, three long syllables. **conubiis arvisque:** ablatives of means or dative. **operata:** supply *erat*, "was busied with." There may be zeugma* here, as *operata* seems not equally appropriate to both marriages and fields.

137. **iura domosque dabam:** cf. 1.507 *iura dabat legesque viris* of Dido, still establishing her new city (cf. 134 n.). **subito cum…:** (very literally)
    "when suddenly, wasting, on our limbs,
    from an infected expanse of sky, piteous, came
    both to trees and crops a plague and death-bringing season."

    On *cum inversum*, see 8 n. The jagged word order here, with the verb in the middle and subjects at the end, with the extreme hyperbaton* of subject and modifiers, suggests Aeneas' distress in making sense of the experience. Note how a rendering of the sentence into standard English would eliminate the achieved incoherence of the Latin. See Perkell (1989) 152-66 for discussion of portents and plague in Lucr. 6.1138-1286 and Verg. *Geo.* 3.478 ff.

138. **corrupto caeli tractu:** ablative absolute or ablative of source.

140-1. **linquebant…animas:** conventionally, life is said to leave the dead; here pathos* accrues, as the dead leave their "sweet" lives. **trahebant | corpora:** subjects are "the dying." **sterilis:** proleptic*, see 30 n. **exurere:** historic infinitive. **Sirius,** the Dog-Star (that appears with late, hot summer "dog" days) burned the life from the fields.

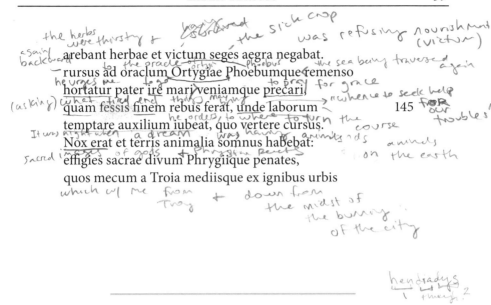

Troy → Thrace → Delos → Crete →

measure/ trace

the herbs were thirsty +   the sick crop was refusing nourishment (victum)

...arebant herbae et victum seges aegra negabat.

back to the oracle Ortygia Phoebus   the sea being traversed again

rursus ad oraclum Ortygiae Phoebumque remenso

he urges me to go   to pray for grace

hortatur pater ire mari veniamque precari,

(asking) what tired end things may   "where to seek help

quam fessis finem rebus ferat, unde laborum   145   FOR our troubles"

he orders, to where to turn the course

temptare auxilium iubeat, quo vertere cursus.

It was night when   a dream   was having animals

Nox erat et terris animalia somnus habebat: animals on the earth

sacred   images of gods + Phrygian penates

effigies sacrae divum Phrygiique penates,

quos mecum a Troia mediisque ex ignibus urbis

which w/ me from Troy + down from the midst of the burning of the city

hendiadys

142–5. **oraclum:** syncopated form. **remenso…mari:** ablative absolute. Past participles of many deponent verbs may have a passive sense, as here "the sea being traversed again," cf. 125 *bacchatam*. **hortatur…ire…precari, | quam…:** "He urges me to go…to pray for grace, (asking) what end…"; for the construction, see 134 n. *Precari* occurs consistently with *venia* in petitions for pardon, often with implicit acknowlegment of a prior offense that would render the deity disinclined to grant the request (Hickson (1993) 51).

145–6. **fessis:** a motif, emphatic through alliteration* with *finem* and *ferat*; see 78 n. **ferat… iubeat:** subjunctives in the indirect question implicit in *veniam precari*. Note the tricolon*: *quam…, unde…, quo…*, with last element the shortest. This divergence from the usual pattern of *tricolon* abundans* may suggest Anchises' distress. **unde…:** "whence (i.e., from what quarter) to seek help for our troubles."

147–91. *As Aeneas sleeps, the Penates appear to him in a dream, promising empire and glory for his descendants. They identify the homeland of Dardanus, the ancient mother of Apollo's oracle, as the land called Hesperia by the Greeks, but Italy by its inhabitants. Anchises, recalling other signs that confirm Aeneas' vision, orders the Trojans again to set sail.*

    The descent of the Trojans from Italian Dardanus and the consequent placing of their true homeland in Italy is thematically central to the *Aeneid*. At the behest of Apollo, consistently the Trojans' divine ally, the Penates appear to Aeneas to reveal the Trojans' true homeland. The awesome effect of the Penates' utterances is achieved by alliteration* (an archaic, incantatory, solemn feature), omission of verbal elements (for "oracular brevity" see Williams *ad loc.*), repetition of *nos* (affirming emphatically the gods' presence), juxtaposition of *nos* and *te* (affirming the felt unity of the Penates with Aeneas and the Trojans, both in their present difficult journey and in their shared grand future).

147. **nox erat:** an atmospheric start to temporal ecphrasis; "it was night when…" Cf. 2.250, Ap. Rhod. 3.744, and Horsfall *ad loc.*

148. **effigies…penates:** hendiadys*, as the images are not distinct from the Penates. **divum:** see 5 n. This is "the most explicit identification of the Penates of Troy with those of Rome" (Bailey (1935) 93).

extuleram, visi ante oculos astare iacentis   150
in somnis multo manifesti lumine, qua se
plena per insertas fundebat luna fenestras;
tum sic adfari et curas his demere dictis:
'quod tibi delato Ortygiam dicturus Apollo est,
hic canit et tua nos en ultro ad limina mittit.   155
nos te Dardania incensa tuaque arma secuti,
nos tumidum sub te permensi classibus aequor,

150-3. **visi…:** the infinitives *astare*, *adfari*, and *demere* are complementary of *visi sunt*. "They
seemed to stand (*astare*)…and to address (*adfari* 153)…and to take away (*demere* 153)…."
Cf. Aeneas' visions of Hector at 2.271 and Creusa at 2.773.

150-1. **extuleram:** emphatic enjambment*. **visi…somnis:** lit. "seemed to stand before the
eyes of me, lying in sleep…" (with *iacentis*: sc. *mei*). **manifesti:** "clear," "manifest" agrees
with *penates* (148), the nearer of its two subjects (cf. also *effigies* in 148). *Manifesti* is a
forceful word, indicating something not only visible but seeming touchable, as by hand.
Aeneas distinguishes between a true dream, seen in light sleep (*in somnis* 151) and an unreal
or false dream seen in deep sleep (*sopor* 173, where see n.). Cf. 4.358 *manifesto in lumine
vidi* (of Mercury). **qua:** adv. "where," as often.

152. **insertas…fenestras:** a much debated line, fortunately of no thematic importance. For
Aeneas to describe the windows as "inserted" into the walls seems overly obvious. The sense
must, therefore, be that bright moonlight comes through open (not "inserted") windows,
illuminating the Penates. Therefore, *insertas* must mean the windows are "unshuttered,"
"open" (Williams) or, alternatively, the epithet *insertas* "inserted" is transferred from *luna*
(Horsfall), with the moonlight being "inserted" through the windows. (See transferred
epithet*.) This is a Golden Line* (abVAB), as *plena…luna* and *insertas…fenestras* are in
interlocking* order encircling *fundebat*. See 108 n. on word patterns.

153. **adfari…demere:** see 150-3 n; alternatively, these infinitives may be taken as historical.

154. **tibi delato Ortygiam…:** lit. "to you (*tibi*) having been conveyed (*delato*) to Ortygia…,"
meaning, "once you will have arrived…" *Ortygiam* is accusative of motion towards a place.

155. **canit:** oracles were almost always uttered in hexameter verse; *canere* therefore often has
the sense of "utter an oracle," "prophesy." **en:** "lo!," "behold!" **ultro:** "voluntarily," "of his
own accord."

156-7. **nos…nos:** emphatic anaphora*; note also the repeated conjunction of *nos* with *te, tu,
tibi*. **nos…secuti, | nos…permensi** (*sumus*). Gods sometimes desert a defeated city; the
Penates are steadfastly loyal. Contrast *Aen.* 2.351-2: *excessere omnes adytis arisque relictis/ di
quibus imperium hoc steterat*. Cf. also *Aen.* 2.402. **Dardania incensa:** ablative absolute. **sub
te:** "under you" (as leader).

idem venturos tollemus in astra nepotes
imperiumque urbi dabimus. tu moenia magnis
magna para longumque fugae ne linque laborem.　160
mutandae sedes. non haec tibi litora suasit
Delius aut Cretae iussit considere Apollo.
est locus, Hesperiam Grai cognomine dicunt,
terra antiqua, potens armis atque ubere glaebae;
Oenotri coluere viri; nunc fama minores　165

158-9. In these verses, the Penates prophesy fame reaching the stars for Aeneas' descendants, *imperium*, and great walls for great (things). This is the grandest, most precise prophecy of power that Aeneas has heard thus far, a stage of "progressive revelation."

158. **idem…:** long *i*, thus plural, "(we) shall likewise exalt to the stars…" **tollere in astra:** likely refers to the fame of Aeneas' descendants generally, not uniquely to the deification of Julius and Augustus Caesar.

159. **imperium…urbi:** "empire to the (your) city," for Roman readers a stirring juxtaposition; *urbi* is to be understood in the sense of "*the* city," i.e., Rome. **moenia:** see, e.g., 85 n. **magnis:** possible meanings of *magnis* are "mighty gods," "mighty descendants," or (as dative of *magna*) "a mighty destiny."

160. **fugae…laborem:** i.e., in this instance, flight is not shameful, since it is divinely willed, cf. *Aen.* 1.2 *fato profugus*: in important contrast to, e.g., Odysseus, Aeneas is an exile by fate, not a mere wanderer (Bliss (1964)). *Labor*, a motif. Note how suffering and endurance characterize Aeneas' wanderings, as opposed to Odysseus' seeming adventurism and many exciting encounters (Circe, Sirens, Calypso, Nausicaa). **ne linque:** *ne* with the imperative is archaic, thus poetic. (Analogously in English: "leave not" is archaic and therefore may sound poetic to contemporary speakers, versus "don't leave," as occurs in ordinary speech.) Similarly archaic are the simplex verb (*linque*, not compounded), as well as the alliteration* (of *longum…linque laborem*), which lend solemnity and rhetorical elevation to the Penates' utterance (Horsfall).

161. **mutandae:** sc. (*sunt*), gerundive expressing necessity.

162. **Cretae:** locative.

163–6. **est locus:** introduces an ecphrasis*, see 13-16 n; the verses are repeated from 1.530-3. This ecphrasis focuses on name-change (metonomasia), reflecting Hellenistic interest in such aetiologies* (see O'Hara (1996) 73). **Hesperiam:** the "Western Land," so called formerly by the Greeks, named as the future homeland by Creusa at 2.781, is now identified by the Penates as the former *Oinotria* (165), currently called *Italia* (166) by its inhabitants. (In 171 the Penates refer to Italy as *Ausonia*.) **Grai:** scanned as two longs. Note the asyndeton* and parataxis*, further archaic features (cf. 160 n. and Horsfall) throughout this ecphrasis.

164. **armis…ubere:** ablatives of respect.

165. **Oenotri:** according to Servius (*ad* 1.532), Oenotria refers to the best wine, which is Italian, or to an ancient king of the Sabines, Oenotrus. See further O'Hara (1996) 127. **coluere:** = *coluerunt*. **fama:** sc. *est*, "the rumor is," "they say," introducing indirect statement.

Italiam dixisse ducis de nomine gentem;
hae nobis propriae sedes, hinc Dardanus ortus
Iasiusque pater, genus a quo principe nostrum.
surge age et haec laetus longaevo dicta parenti
haud dubitanda refer: Corythum terrasque requirat   170
Ausonias: Dictaea negat tibi Iuppiter arva.'
talibus attonitus visis et voce deorum
(nec sopor illud erat, sed coram agnoscere vultus
velatasque comas praesentiaque ora videbar;
tum gelidus toto manabat corpore sudor)   175

---

166. **ducis:** referring to Italus, king of the Oenotrians, after whom Italy is now (*nunc*) named.

167. **propriae:** cf. 85 n. *hae sedes (sunt); Dardanus ortus (est).* The three clauses from *hae nobis* (167) through *principe nostrum* (168) without a main verb contribute to the effect of "oracular brevity" (Williams).

168. **Iasiusque pater, genus a quo principe nostrum:** supply *ortum est.* **Iasius…:** Iasius and Dardanus are half-brothers, sons of Electra (8.134-41, Servius *ad* 3.104, 167), Corythus being the father of Iasius, Zeus the father of Dardanus. Iasius settles in Samothrace; Dardanus travels on from there to found Troy and becomes apotheosed (7.205-11 Latinus speaking). See Horsfall (1973) and (2000) 165-9.

170. **refer:** "report" or "deliver"; *re-* in composition may have the sense of "duly" rather than of "again" or "back;" thus *referre* is not only "carry back" but "carry to the proper recipient." **Corythum:** in the *Aeneid*, a town or region in Etruria, presumably named after a legendary early king, Corythus. Vergil makes this (probably fictive) location the birthplace of Dardanus and hence of the Trojan people (see Jocelyn (1991)). **requirat:** sc. *Anchises,* jussive subjunctive, "Let him seek," "make for."

171. **Ausonias:** i.e., Italian. **tibi:** i.e., Aeneas.

173. **nec sopor illud erat:** "nor was that (a false vision arising from) heavy sleep," as contrasted with *in somnis* at 151. There is an allusion here to Hom. *Od.* 19.547, where Odysseus, still in beggar disguise, tells Penelope that her dream of his return and vengeance on the suitors was not an *onar* ("a (mere) dream"), but a *hupar esthlon* (an "authentic waking-vision"). The words from *nec sopor* to *sudor* (175) form a parenthesis, and *attonitus* (172) goes grammatically with *corripio* (176) "astounded by such a vision…(for it was no dream…) I tear myself from bed." **sudor:** probably because his heart is racing.

174. **velatas:** "crowned" or "garlanded," i.e., with *vittae,* fillets. Cf. 405 where Helenus will instruct Aeneas in (what will become) a defining Roman custom of veiling the head. Vergil locates origins of important Roman customs in Aeneas' experiences; cf. 59 and n.

175. **tum…:** the cold sweat which came upon him after (cf. *tum*) the vision. Note chiasmus* of *gelidus toto…corpore sudor.*

corripio e stratis corpus tendoque supinas
ad caelum cum voce manus et munera libo
intemerata focis. perfecto laetus honore
Anchisen facio certum remque ordine pando.
agnovit prolem ambiguam geminosque parentis, 180
seque novo veterum deceptum errore locorum.
tum memorat: 'nate, Iliacis exercite fatis,
sola mihi talis casus Cassandra canebat.
nunc repeto haec generi portendere debita nostro
et saepe Hesperiam, saepe Itala regna vocare. 185
sed quis ad Hesperiae venturos litora Teucros
crederet? aut quem tum vates Cassandra moveret?

176-7. **supinas…manus:** cf. 1.93 *duplicis tendens ad sidera palmas,* i.e., with palms up. Note the hyperbaton* of adjective and noun, that frames the elements *ad caelum* and *cum voce,* dissolving all into a single gesture: "I stretch to heaven my hands with my voice." Aeneas offers prayer or sacrifice after a vision also at 5.743 and 8.70. **munera…:** "pour undefiled (i.e., pure, unmixed) offerings"—in this case, wine—"on the hearth."

178. **honore:** a "ritual act," a "sacrifice," as often.

179. **Anchisen facio certum:** i.e., "I inform Anchises."

180. **adgnovit…:** the Trojans are *prolem ambiguam,* doubtful offspring, because they might be considered descendants either, on the paternal side, of (Italian) Dardanus by his marriage to Bateia or, on the maternal side, of (Cretan) Teucer, father of Bateia (Dardanus and Teucer thus being the *gemini parentes*). (On Teucer, see Servius *ad* 3.108.) Anchises now understands that Apollo's oracle, citing Dardanus, pointed to Italy.

181. **seque novo veterum…:** the meaning of the antithesis between *novo* and *veterum* seems to be that the lands and stories were old, but Anchises' mistake is new or recent. Cassandra's fate was to speak truths, but never be believed. (See 186-7 n. on Cassandra). **veterum…locorum:** "extended" use of the objective genitive (Williams *ad loc.*). Perhaps the unusual syntax reflects Anchises' embarrassment. Note interlocking* of *novo…errore* and *veterum…locorum.* **deceptum:** sc. *esse.*

182. **nate, exercite:** vocatives. **Iliacis exercite fatis:** "tested by the (hard) fates of Ilium."

184. **portendere:** "that she (Cassandra) used to foretell this (i.e., a settlement in Italy) as due our race." Understand *Cassandram* as accusative subject of *portendere* and *vocare* (185).

185-6. **Hesperiam…Hesperiae:** polyptoton*; emphatic.

186-7. **quis…crederet…moveret :** past potential subjunctives, "who would have believed?" (cf. AG §446-7). **tum:** emphatic. Apollo had punished Cassandra for betraying him by ordaining that her prophecies would be true, but never believed.

cedamus Phoebo et moniti meliora sequamur.'
sic ait, et cuncti dicto paremus ovantes.
hanc quoque deserimus sedem paucisque relictis   190
vela damus vastumque cava trabe currimus aequor.
Postquam altum tenuere rates nec iam amplius ullae
apparent terrae, caelum undique et undique pontus,
tum mihi caeruleus supra caput astitit imber
noctem hiememque ferens, et inhorruit unda tenebris.   195
continuo venti volvunt mare magnaque surgunt
aequora, dispersi iactamur gurgite vasto;
involvere diem nimbi et nox umida caelum
abstulit, ingeminant abruptis nubibus ignes.
excutimur cursu et caecis erramus in undis.   200

---

188. **cedamus…sequamur:** hortatory subjunctives framing the line, with alliteration* of *m*.
Phoebo: because it was he who sent the Penates. **meliora:** "better counsels" or "plans."

189. **dicto:** dative after *pareo*.

190. **paucis…relictis:** this detail accounts for the origin of the town of Pergamum (see 121-46 n.), still in existence in Vergil's day; alternatively, it may to refer to those who died there.

191. **vela damus:** sc. *ventis*. **trabe:** metonymy* for *nave*. *currimus aequor*: "run (over) the sea," accusative of extent of space.

192 **tenuere:** = *tenuerunt*.

193. **caelum undique…:** "(but) sky and sea on *every* side…" Note the repeated *undique*, emphatically framed by *caelum* and *pontus*; *apparet* is to be supplied from *apparent*, forming a contrasted clause, but without any adversative to mark the contrast. The effect is of abruptness.

194. **caeruleus:** deepest blue or smoke black, like a thunder-cloud.

195. **inhorruit unda tenebris:** "the wave roughened with (or in) the darkness." Dactylic fourth and fifth feet, with coincidence of ictus* and accent* in last three feet may express sea swells.

196. **venti volvunt mare magnaque…:** alliteration*, with *aequora* emphatically enjambed into the following verse.

198. **involvere:** = *involverunt*.

199. **abstulit:** emphatic enjambment.

ipse diem noctemque negat discernere caelo
nec meminisse viae media Palinurus in unda.
tris adeo incertos caeca caligine soles
erramus pelago, totidem sine sidere noctes.
quarto terra die primum se attollere tandem   205
visa, aperire procul montis ac volvere fumum.
vela cadunt, remis insurgimus; haud mora, nautae
adnixi torquent spumas et caerula verrunt.

201-2. **negat discernere…nec meminisse:** supply *se* (the personal pronoun may be omitted in
indirect statement when there is no ambiguity, cf. 603 *fateor petiisse*), "says that he neither
distinguishes…nor remembers." The Trojans are deprived both of landmarks (the normal
basis of navigation in antiquity) and of stars (the rarer method in heroic times) (Horsfall,
and see his further notes on navigation *ad loc.*). See Adler (2003) 288-91 for discussion of
Palinurus as exemplifying scientific knowledge or method in the *Aeneid*. The juxtaposition
of *diem noctemque* exemplifies Palinurus' difficulty in distinguishing between them. **viae:**
genitive after *meminisse*.

203. **tris adeo…:** "three whole nights"; *adeo* gives emphasis to the preceding word.
incertos…soles: accusative of duration of time; the use of *soles* as "days" is common;
"uncertain suns" means "clouded," "dark days." See 108 n. for *incertos…soles*, and note
chiastic* arrangement with *caeca caligine*.

204. **erramus pelago:** again the motif of wandering (used of Trojans, islands, returning
Greeks), recurrent in this book; ablative of "space over which," see 124 n.

205-6. **terra visa:** sc. *est*. **volvere fumum:** "swirl up smoke," a sign of an inhabited country.

207. **vela cadunt:** "sails fall," brisker than "we lower the sails." **remis insurgimus:** "we
rise onto our oars"; *remis* is dative after a compound verb. The sequence of asyndetic*,
paratactic* cola (*vela cadunt, remis insurgimus; haud mora nautae…spumas*) expresses
speed. "Rowers raise themselves from the benches in order that the weight of their bodies
returning to their places may be added to the force with which they pull the oar" (Page *ad
loc.*).

208. **caerul(e)a:** neuter of the adjective used as a noun; sc. *aequora*.

209–77. The Trojans find themselves on the Strophades islands, where herds of cattle roam without (apparent) guard. They kill some to eat and to sacrifice. Suddenly the Harpies swoop down and defile their food. Withdrawing to a different spot, the Trojans again attempt to eat, with the same result. Aeneas orders his men to arm for battle, but the Harpies prove invulnerable. Celaeno (Gr. "the dark one"), the eldest of the Harpies, rebukes the Trojans, prophesying that famine will drive them to eat their tables before they have a city. The men exhort Aeneas to seek peace with the Harpies, and Anchises prays to the gods to avert the threatened famine. The Trojans sail to Mount Leucates and the temple of Apollo, where they come ashore.

The prophecy (attributed variously to the oracle of Jupiter at Dodona, the Erythraean sibyl, or Venus) that the Trojans will eat their tables is part of the traditional Aeneas legend, as found in, e.g., Lycoph. 1250-8, Dion. Hal. 1.55.3, Varro cited by Servius *ad* 3.256 f. However, other features of this account—the landing on the Strophades, the encounter with the Harpies, their invulnerability to human weapons—are unique to Vergil.

In Homer, the Harpies, whose name means the Snatchers (Gr. *harpazein*), are personified storm-winds, later evolving into goddesses of famine, who snatch others' food, but are always hungry. They are represented as birds with faces of women or as women with wings. To Vergil's readers the most familiar account would have been that of Apollonius of Rhodes (*Arg.* 2.178-300), where Phineus, the Thracian king, for having revealed divine secrets, is punished by visitations of the Harpies, who befoul his food. He promises the Argonauts to prophesy their future (to the degree allowable) in return for deliverance from the Harpies. The sons of Boreas (the North wind), Calais and Zetes, who can, of course, fly, pursue the Harpies, turning back at the Strophades (hence called islands of turning (Gr. *strephesthai*), where the goddess Iris promises that the Harpies' torture of Phineus will cease. (Apollonius has the Harpies settle in Crete, not in the Strophades. There are variant versions also of the original offense.)

The eating of the cattle recalls the other significant model text of this episode, i.e., *Od.* 11.104-17, where Tiresias, the underworld seer, reveals to Odysseus that he will have his homecoming if he and his companions can "contain their desire" and refrain from eating the cattle of Helios (the sun god). If they do not, they and their ship will be destroyed. In *Od.* 12.278-390, despite Odysseus' explicit prohibition, the companions fail to "contain their desire" and do eat the cattle. Thereafter they and their ship are destroyed by Zeus, with Odysseus alone surviving.

Differences from the epic models of this passage suggest interpretations (see Introduction). In contrast to the companions of Odysseus, the Trojans, in eating the Harpies' cattle, have *not violated an explicit taboo*. Nevertheless, their actions may be seen as morally questionable. The smoke that Aeneas sees rising from the island (206) suggests civilization (cf. the smoke rising from Circe's island in *Od.* 10.149, 197). Therefore, although the cattle may be without apparent guard (221), Aeneas might have suspected that these are domestic animals.

Aeneas' order to his men to arm for attack proves ill-conceived, since the Harpies are invulnerable (as they are *not* in Apollonius). In his recourse to arms against immortal

servatum ex undis Strophadum me litora primum
excipiunt. Strophades Graio stant nomine dictae 210
insulae Ionio in magno, quas dira Celaeno
Harpyiaeque colunt aliae, Phineia postquam

creatures, Aeneas inadvertently recalls the over-confident Odysseus who proposes to take up arms against Scylla, despite Circe's prior instruction. She rebukes his *hubris*:
"Hardy man, your mind is full forever of fighting
and battlework. Will you not give way even to the immortals?
She is no mortal thing but a mischief immortal, dangerous,
difficult and bloodthirsty, and there is no fighting against her."

Od. 12.116-19

(Cf. Ap. Rhod. 2. 288-9 where Iris announces to the sons of Boreas that it is not "permitted" (Gr. *themis*) to strike the Harpies ("dogs of great Zeus") with swords). That the Harpies are repellent, Aeneas surely establishes. However, Celaeno's charges against the Trojans are not without justice and stand unrebutted; her retaliatory prophecy has Apollo's authority (251).

In sum: Vergil connects the traditional table-eating prophecy with an unacknowledged (by Aeneas) moral infraction (the violation of the divinely owned cattle and then the attack on the Harpies), if not with the flagrant impiety of Odysseus' companions. The Trojans leave the Strophades islands filled with apprehension, to some degree morally compromised, and with no divine reassurance. Unlike the Argonauts, who, in rescuing Phineus from the Harpies, perform a good deed and are rewarded with a prophecy, the Trojans, having eaten the Harpies' cattle, an impious deed, are rewarded with a curse. (Putnam (1980) 14 observes that, unlike Odysseus, Aeneas seems no more aware of any impiety than his men.) Vergil has, thus, through allusion to *Odyssey* 12, injected into the prophecy of famine a connection with the symbolic world of monsters (the Harpies and, still to come, Scylla and Charybdis, Etna, and Polyphemus), a morally dangerous world of "inadvertent trespass" and unfamiliar hazards. (See Horsfall *ad* 209-69 for useful bibliography and for objections to such "modern moral criticism" as is suggested here.) See esp. Harrison (1985) 147-58 for the literary history of the Harpies; see Nelis (2001) 32-8 on the Harpies and Phineus' prophecy: Vergil's Harpy episode has more of "death, mystery, and corruption" (33) than its Apollonian model. The Harpies, along with the bleeding tree image from *Aen.* 3, occur in Dante, *Inferno* 13, where the suicides are punished. See 57 n.

209. **servatum:** emphatic in hyperbaton* with *me.*

210. **excipiunt:** emphatic enjambment. **Strophades...Graio nomine dictae:** for the Greek etymology of Strophades, see 209-77 n. Most derive the word from the "turning back" of the Harpies' pursuers at this point. **stant:** = *sunt*, with further connotation of endurance or stability. **dictae:** "called."

211. **insulae* Ionio:** in imitation of Homeric metrical practice, Vergil sometimes shortens a final long vowel or diphthong in hiatus. Cf. 5.261 *Ilio* alto*; 6.507 *te*, amice.* [Here the * marks hiatus.]

212. **Harpyiae:** the word scans as three longs, the middle syllable being the Greek diphthong *ui*. **Phineia:** a quadrisyllabic adjective, with the *e* long and both *i* and *a* short. The adjective in place of a genitive is elevated, poetic, see 117 n. **postquam:** note its postposition*, unusual as a line ending.

clausa domus mensasque metu liquere priores.
tristius haud illis monstrum, nec saevior ulla
pestis et ira deum Stygiis sese extulit undis.   215
virginei volucrum vultus, foedissima ventris
proluvies uncaeque manus et pallida semper
ora fame.
huc ubi delati portus intravimus, ecce
laeta boum passim campis armenta videmus   220
caprigenumque pecus nullo custode per herbas.
inruimus ferro et divos ipsumque vocamus
in partem praedamque Iovem; tum litore curvo

---

213. **clausa:** supply *est*; **mensas...priores:** accusative object of *liquere* = *liquerunt*. **metu:** ablative of cause.

214. **illis...:** ablative after the comparative *tristius*. **monstrum:** sc. *se extulit*; the word is used also of Polyphemus (658).

215. **pestis et ira deum:** i.e., divine anger, resulting in *pestis*, a compound subject or an instance of hendiadys*. For *deum*, see 5 n.

216–17. **virginei...vultus:** supply *erant*. Note alliteration* of *v*'s. The Harpies are birds with the faces of maidens. **foedissima...proluvies:** foul discharge from their belly. Donatus (the late fourth century CE commentator), cited by Williams on 3.216-18, infers from *proluvies* that the Furies suffer constantly from hunger because of a digestive ailment, their discharge being intestinal excreta. **uncae...manus:** "taloned hands" (Conington); **pallida:** "pale with hunger," a detail that verges perhaps on the pitiable.

218. **fame:** ablative of cause. This line is unfinished, as are 316, 340, 470, 527, 640, 661 in this book. See Introduction for discussion.

219. **delati:** *defero* is often used of bringing a ship into harbor, cf. 71 n. The passive may imply lack of volition on Aeneas' part.

220. **laeta:** "fat."

221. **caprigenum... pecus:** "goat-born flock"; *caprigenum* is a compound adjective of the archaic/epic type. **nullo custode:** ablative absolute. Aeneas means "no *apparent* guard."

222-3. **ferro:** ablative of means. **divos ipsumque...Iovem:** "the (other) gods and above all Jupiter." **in partem praedamque:** = *in partem praedae*, "to share the spoil," hendiadys*. The Trojans misguidedly call on Jupiter to accept a share of the ill-gotten spoils (see Harrison (1985)). **litore curvo:** along the shore, see 124 n.

exstruimusque toros dapibusque epulamur opimis,
at subitae horrifico lapsu de montibus adsunt   225
Harpyiae et magnis quatiunt clangoribus alas,
diripiuntque dapes contactuque omnia foedant
immundo; tum vox taetrum dira inter odorem.
rursum in secessu longo sub rupe cavata
[arboribus clausam circum atque horrentibus umbris]   230
instruimus mensas arisque reponimus ignem;
rursum ex diverso caeli caecisque latebris
turba sonans praedam pedibus circumvolat uncis,

---

224. **exstruimusque…:** "and pile up the couches (*toros*) and feast on the rich banquet." *exstruere* occurs of "piling up" the couches on which the Romans reclined at meals: in contrast to the formality of language (*epulamur, dapibus*), the couches on this occasion would be made of turf. **dapibus:** ablative after *epulamur*. Here the noun after the main caesura is modified by the adjective at the end of the line, a less frequent pattern than adjective *before* the caesura with the noun at the end of the line. See 108, 132 nn. (Note, too, that ordinarily the adjective comes before its noun, thereby keeping essential elements of meaning in suspension until the end of the verse.)

225. **lapsu:** "swoop."

226. **Harpyiae:** a dramatic revelation of the subject of *adsunt* (225), emphatic through enjambment*. **clangoribus:** describing not voice (*vox* 228), but beating wings.

227. **diripiunt…foedant:** note chiasmus of verbs and their objects, as well as framing of the line by the verbs.

228. **immundo:** enjambed, thus emphatic. **tum vox…:** "then (came) (sc. *est* or *fit*) a dread voice amid the foul smell."

229. **rursum…rursum (232):** the archaic form of *rursus*. Note the parallelism: the renewed attempt to feast is matched by a renewed attack of the Harpies. Similarly, Aeneas makes two attempts to pull the bleeding branches of Polydorus' tree before, on the third attempt, he elicits the rebuke of impiety (41-2). See 247-57 for Celaeno's rebuke.

230. This line is omitted by Servius, but included by Donatus (for whom, see 216-7 n.). Presumably it is copied from 1.311 and wrongly inserted here, where it does not fit the syntax of adjoining verses. It is bracketed by Horsfall (see his discussion *ad loc.*) and other editors (Hirtzel, Mynors, Williams).

231. **arisque reponimus ignem:** i.e., in order to perform the sacrifice (see 223 n.) which had been interrupted. Note parallel order of verbs and direct objects.

232. **ex diverso caeli:** "from a different quarter of the sky"; *diverso* is the neuter of the adjective used as a substantive.

233. **turba:** i.e., of Harpies. **pedibus:** ablative of means.

polluit ore dapes. sociis tunc arma capessant
edico, et dira bellum cum gente gerendum.   235
haud secus ac iussi faciunt tectosque per herbam
disponunt ensis et scuta latentia condunt.
ergo ubi delapsae sonitum per curva dedere
litora, dat signum specula Misenus ab alta
aere cavo. invadunt socii et nova proelia temptant,   240
obscenas pelagi ferro foedare volucris,
sed neque vim plumis ullam nec vulnera tergo
accipiunt, celerique fuga sub sidera lapsae
semesam praedam et vestigia foeda relinquunt.
una in praecelsa consedit rupe Celaeno,   245

234–5. **ore:** commentators dispute what might be the nature of this *oral* pollution. **sociis… gerendum (235):** note the double construction after *edico*, which has the sense "I order" with *capessant* (paratactic* subjunctive in indirect command, with *ut* omitted) and "I say" introducing accusative/ infinitive of indirect statement, *bellum gerendum (esse)*. "Then I order my comrades to seize (i.e., that they should seize) their arms and (I say) that war must be waged…." **gerendum:** gerundive expressing necessity.

235. **edico:** Aeneas gives the command for the armed attack on the Harpies; Anchises interprets omens and offers the public prayers.

236. **haud secus ac iussi faciunt:** "not otherwise than as ordered they do," i.e., they do as they are bidden. *Ac* or *atque* may be translated "than"; with *iussi* supply *sunt*. **tectosque…:** "and place their hidden-in-grass swords"; *tectos* and *latentia* (*scuta*) are used proleptically, see 30 n., 141 n. (See prolepsis*.)

238. **dedere:** = *dederunt*, the subject is the Harpies (*delapsae*).

239. Misenus sounds his trumpet to mark the Harpies' approach. (The story of his death is told in *Aen.* 6.162-74.)

240. **aere cavo:** "with the hollow brass," i.e., the trumpet; note synecdoche*. **nova proelia:** "strange battles," i.e., against the other-worldly Harpies. The infinitive *foedare* in apposition to *proelia* clarifies the nature of the strange combat, i.e., "to defile with a sword…"

241. **pelagi…volucris:** Harpies are, variously, daughters of the Sea and Earth or of Neptune (Servius *ad loc.*), or of Electra, daughter of Ocean (Hes. *Th.* 265). Note framing of line with *obscenas* and *volucris*.

242. In Ap. Rhod. 2.284 the Harpies are not invulnerable, a significant change made by Vergil, and are saved from slaughter by the intervention of Iris.

243. **sub sidera:** "towards the stars," "upwards."

244. Note chiastic* arrangement of adjectives and nouns.

245. **praecelsa:** to strengthen an adjective Vergil often prefixes *prae* instead of the more usual *per*; cf. *praedives, praedulcis, praepinguis, praevalidus* (Page).

infelix vates, rumpitque hanc pectore vocem:
'bellum etiam pro caede boum stratisque iuvencis,
Laomedontiadae, bellumne inferre paratis
et patrio Harpyias insontis pellere regno?
accipite ergo animis atque haec mea figite dicta, 250
quae Phoebo pater omnipotens, mihi Phoebus Apollo
praedixit, vobis Furiarum ego maxima pando.
Italiam cursu petitis ventisque vocatis:
ibitis Italiam portusque intrare licebit.
sed non ante datam cingetis moenibus urbem 255
quam vos dira fames nostraeque iniuria caedis

246. **infelix vates:** a prophet of ill. **rumpitque...vocem:** because emotion is *breaking through* her previously restrained silence (Servius *ad loc.*), thus, "speaks with unrestrained anger." Literally, "broke forth this word from her chest." **pectore:** supply *ex*.

247–8. **bellum etiam...bellumne...:** "war indeed...is it war that you prepare to wage?" Note the emphatic outrage in the repeated *bellum*, which recalls Aeneas' repeated *rursum... rursum* (229, 232). **Laomedontiadae:** "descendants of Laomedon": Celaeno knows (without asking) who the Trojans are and where they are going, thereby revealing that she is somehow superhuman, divine or demonic. She implies that, like their impious ancestor Laomedon, these Trojans too are treacherous (cf. 4.542, Dido speaking). **bellum inferre:** sc. *nobis*.

249. **patrio:** Celaeno claims the Strophades are the "ancestral domain" of the Harpies; cf. 241, they are offspring of the sea. **patrio...regno:** i.e., *(e) patrio regno (nostro)*. The line is framed by *patrio...regno*; the adjective/noun pattern here (aBbA) may be seen as a variation on chiastic*.

250. **animis:** supply *in* and construe with *accipite*, but not *figite*.

251. **quae Phoebo pater omnipotens:** sc. *praedixit*. The *pater omnipotens,* cited as the highest authority, is Jupiter, through whose will come Apollo's revelations; cf. Apollo's other prophetic interventions at 73-120, 162, 360 on Delos, and 371 in Buthrotum. Celaeno invokes awesome authorities as guarantors of her truthfulness.

252. **Furiarum...maxima:** "greatest" or "eldest *(maxima natu)* of the Furies." Harpies are identified with Furies elsewhere (Hom. *Od.* 20.78, Aesch. *Eum.* 50-1) and cf. *ira deum* (215). Cf. 12.845-52 for Furies as gods' agents in punishing human wickedness.

253–4. **Italiam...petitis...ibitis Italiam:** the repetition of *Italiam* is highly rhetorical, as with *bellum* in 247-8. Celaeno achieves oracular portentousness through alliteration*, emphatic repetition, brevity, and (above all) riddling revelation. **Italiam:** the accusative of motion towards a place, without a preposition, common in poetry (cf. 293, 441, 507, 601).

255–7. **ante...quam:** "sooner than." **datam:** here "promised." **nostraeque iniuria caedis:** "the wrong of our murder," i.e., the "wrong of attempting to murder us," an appositional or defining genitive (AG §343d). **subigat :** subjunctive of anticipated action after *ante... quam*, AG §551c.

ambesas subigat malis absumere mensas.'
dixit, et in silvam pennis ablata refugit.
at sociis subita gelidus formidine sanguis
deriguit: cecidere animi, nec iam amplius armis,   260
sed votis precibusque iubent exposcere pacem,
sive deae seu sint dirae obscenaeque volucres.
et pater Anchises passis de litore palmis
numina magna vocat meritosque indicit honores:
'di, prohibete minas; di, talem avertite casum   265

257. **ambesas...absumere mensas:** "to consume your gnawed-around (*ambesas*) with-your- jaws (*malis*) tables." *absumere* is a complementary infinitive after verbs of inducing or permitting, a Vergilian usage (Horsfall *ad loc.*); cf. 4-5 n. and AG §457, 563a. Note framing of verse, and cf. *semesam* (244). The prophecy is fulfilled without harm at 7.109-17 when the Trojans use thin cakes as plates or "tables" for their meat; cf. Lycoph. 1250-4; Dion. Hal. 1.55.3 for other versions of the table-eating story. Note that at 7.124-7 Aeneas attributes this prophecy to Anchises.

259. **sociis:** dative of reference. **gelidus:** predicative.

260–1. **cecidere:** = *ceciderunt*. **nec iam...exposcere pacem:** *pacem votis exposcere* is a religious formula (cf. Livy 1.16.3 *pacem precibus exposcunt*, 3.7 *supplicatum ire, pacemque exposcere deum;* Ov. *Met.* 9.545 *opemque tuam timidis exposcere votis*), appropriate since the men suspect the Harpies are divine. The goal is to restore the *pax deorum*, the right relationship with the gods. **iubent:** sc. *me*. Note the zeugma*: the men order Aeneas to "seek peace" not "with arms" (*armis*), but with "vows and prayers" (*votis precibusque*). Williams (*ad loc.*) translates: "They urged me not *to trust*...in weapons, but *to seek peace* by vows..."

262. **sive deae seu...dirae...volucres:** The usual formula of address to unknown deities is *si divus si diva* ("whether you be god or goddess"). Vergil uses a variant of that formula to fit this problematical circumstance (Hickson (1993) 41-3). **sint:** subjunctive in a subordinate clause in indirect statement. **obscenae:** "filthy," "ominous," applied especially to things ill-omened. The men suspect the Harpies are goddesses because of their invulnerability; but even if they are (mere) birds, they are nevertheless bad omens and should be appeased (Servius *ad loc.*).

263. **passis...palmis:** cf. 1.93.

264. **meritosque indicit honores:** "proclaims appropriate offerings" (i.e., due sacrifices are to be made).

265. **di...di:** anaphora*, characteristic of prayer, serves to draw the gods' attention. **avertite:** technical term in formal prayers requesting that the gods "turn aside" some ill, often disease (Servius Dan. *ad loc.*, Hickson (1993) 85); cf. 620. See 85 n. for features of a more elaborate prayer. Anchises now steps in to utter the prayer.

et placidi servate pios.' tum litore funem
deripere excussosque iubet laxare rudentis.
tendunt vela Noti: fugimus spumantibus undis
qua cursum ventusque gubernatorque vocabat.
iam medio apparet fluctu nemorosa Zacynthos   270
Dulichiumque Sameque et Neritos ardua saxis.
effugimus scopulos Ithacae, Laertia regna,
et terram altricem saevi exsecramur Vlixi.
mox et Leucatae nimbosa cacumina montis
et formidatus nautis aperitur Apollo.   275
hunc petimus fessi et parvae succedimus urbi;

---

266. **placidi:** (having now been) placated, i.e., "propitious"; an early, if not the first, use in this sense (Hickson (1993) 58), alluding to the *pax deorum* (260-1). **servate:** "preserve," a term recurrent in "petitions seeking preservation" (Hickson 79); cf. 86. **pios:** the Trojans' defining attribute (understand *nos*). **funem:** the mooring rope.

267. **excussos...laxare rudentis:** "to free the shaken-out sheets"; *rudentis* are ropes (nautical term "sheets") fastened to the bottom corners of the sail to adjust it to the wind. Here they "shake the sail out full" (*excutere*) for speed; cf. 682-3 *rudentis excutere*.

268. **spumantibus undis:** ablative of extension, cf. 124 *pelagoque volamus* with note.

269. Doubled *–que* imitates Homeric usage, gives epic character; see 71 n.

270. **nemorosă Zacynthos:** note the shortened vowel *a* in arsis* (an unstressed syllable, see AG §642, 611), before the following double consonant z of Zacynthos. Artificial shortening of a vowel in arsis is characteristic of Homeric practice. In *Aen.* 3.270-3 Vergil alludes simultaneously to Hom. *Od.* 9.21-8 and Ap. Rhod. 4.573-6 (an instance of two-tier allusion), thus combining the tradition of Homeric formulas with Apollonius' "highly varied, geographically detailed, aetiologically learned" style (Nelis (2001) 60). Five place names in two and half lines offer learning and poetic color.

271. **Neritos ardua saxis:** "Neritus steep with crags," in Homer a mountain in Ithaca; here, as context and gender (f.) show, an island; *saxis* is ablative of cause. This line has three cola, the last the longest (tricolon abundans*).

272. **effugimus:** a motif* in this book. **scopulos Ithacae, Laertia regna:** the epithet "rocky" is used of Ithaca in the *Odyssey*. Laertes is Odysseus' father.

273. **terram altricem:** "nurturing land," i.e., that nursed Ulysses. *Vlixi* is the genitive of *Vlixes*, Ulysses. **saevi...Vlixi:** contrasts with *infelix* used of Ulysses at 613, 691; see nn.

275. **formidatus nautis:** "dreaded by sailors," because built on a dangerous site; *nautis* is dative of agent or reference. **aperitur:** "comes into view." **Apollo:** i.e., his temple, a common metonymy*.

276. **hunc:** sc. *Apollinem*, as in 275. **fessi:** a motif in this book.

ancora de prora iacitur, stant litore puppes.
Ergo insperata tandem tellure potiti
lustramurque Iovi votisque incendimus aras,
Actiaque Iliacis celebramus litora ludis.   280

277. **stant litore puppes:** "the sterns stand along the shore"; *litore* is ablative of extension, cf. 124 *pelagoque volamus.*

278–93. *At Actium, the Trojans make expiatory offerings to Jupiter and celebrate games. Before departing, Aeneas dedicates the shield of Abas in the temple of Apollo. The Trojans then sail along the coast of Epirus, putting in at Buthrotum.*

In traditional accounts, the Trojans build a temple at Actium (Dion. Hal. 1.50.4). Vergil, however, locates games there and a shield dedication, which other sources place elsewhere (Zacynthos for the games in Dion. Hal. 1.50.3, Samothrace for the shield in Servius Dan. on 3.287). Here the Trojans perform sacrifices, celebrate games, and dedicate spoils of war, alluding in this way to Augustus' future victory over Antony and Cleopatra at Actium in 31 BCE and to his restoration of the ancient temple to Apollo there. (The significance of Actium is developed further in *Aeneid* 8.)

The Trojans' religious observances are both expiatory (for the inauspicious sacrifice to Jupiter in the Strophades) and thank offerings for safe passage through Greek territory. The dedication of the Shield of Abas signifies differently. Conventionally, dedications are made on behalf of the *victors*; here, irony* inheres in Aeneas' dedication of a shield on behalf of the *vanquished* Trojans. More specifically, the shield in question was a famous talisman of the power of Argive Hera, because it protected the city even after the death of the family of Abas (an early Argive king), its original owners (Servius Dan. on 286). Abas' grandfather, Danaus, presumably first carried the shield, then his father Lynceus, then Abas, who re-dedicated it in Hera's temple.

To explain Aeneas' possession of the shield, ancient even from his perspective, readers must infer that an Argive member of the Trojan expedition had carried the shield to Troy and lost it in combat with Aeneas. In then dedicating this shield to Apollo, defender both of the Trojans and of the future Augustus, Aeneas transforms a symbol of Hera's power — or of Greek victory generally— into a symbol of Trojan and Roman victory under Apollo. In sum, this is a complex, subtle, polemical allusion. For full discussion and references, see Miller (1993, 2009) and Lloyd (1957b).

278. **insperata...tellure:** ablative after *potior*; *insperata* means "unhoped for," because of the dangers mentioned in 282-3.

279. **lustramurque Iovi:** "we purify ourselves in honor of Jupiter," *lustramur* functioning as a middle voice; purification is preliminary to sacrifice and celebration of sacred games in the next line. **votis:** i.e., sacrifices offered in fulfilment of a vow; ablative of means, not dative of purpose. **incendimus aras:** "we set ablaze the altars," i.e., for sacrifices.

280. **Actiaque...:** these games constitute an ancient precedent for the quinquennial games that Octavian instituted at Actium to memorialize his victory there in 31 BCE, cf. notes on 59, 174. In the adjective *Actia*, there is another instance of etymological wordplay: while *Actia* in Latin means "relating to Actium," in *Greek*, esp. as an epithet of gods, it means "of the shore." (Thus *Pan Aktios* = Pan of the Shore.) The "play" is that *actia* both *means* (in Greek) and *modifies* (in Latin) shore (O'Hara (1996) 141). On etymological play, see 401, 693 nn. **Iliacis...ludis:** ablative of means; note the adjective (before the main caesura*) and noun (at line end) placement.

exercent patrias oleo labente palaestras
nudati socii: iuvat evasisse tot urbes
Argolicas mediosque fugam tenuisse per hostis.
interea magnum sol circumvolvitur annum
et glacialis hiems Aquilonibus asperat undas: 285
aere cavo clipeum, magni gestamen Abantis,
postibus adversis figo et rem carmine signo:
AENEAS HAEC DE DANAIS VICTORIBVS ARMA.
linquere tum portus iubeo et considere transtris.
certatim socii feriunt mare et aequora verrunt.   290
protinus aërias Phaeacum abscondimus arces
litoraque Epiri legimus portuque subimus
Chaonio et celsam Buthroti accedimus urbem.

---

281. **patrias:** "traditional," "Trojan." **oleo labente:** the oil makes the wrestlers' bodies slippery. **palaestras:** "wrestling-bouts." Note the same adjective and noun placement as in 280.

282. **iuvat evasisse…:** sc. *eos* or *nos.*

283. **Argolicas:** emphatic through enjambment*. At this point the Greeks constitute the greatest danger; later, various monsters will have that role. **fugam tenuisse:** "to have held (our course of) flight."

284. **interea magnum…:** "meantime the sun rolls through the year"; the sun is thought to make a circuit in a year. *Annum* is the object of *circum* in *circumvolvitur*, and expresses duration of time. **magnum:** an ornamental epithet*.

286. **aere cavo:** ablative of quality. The round shield (*clipeus*) is made by beating out a brass plate until it becomes hollow. **magni gestamen Abantis:** "gear of great Abas," see 278-93 n.

287. **postibus adversis:** "on the doors facing" as one enters. **carmine:** an inscription, often on dedicatory objects and usually in verse.

288. **AENEAS…:** verbs are commonly omitted in such inscriptions; understand *dedicat* or *dat, dicat, dedicat* (abbreviated as D.D.D.). **DE:** supply *erepta,* "won from."

289. Alludes to Hom. *Od.* 9.103-4:
    and the men quickly went aboard and sat to the oarlocks,
    and sitting well in order dashed the oars on the gray sea.

290. Note chiasmus* of verbs and objects.

291. **abscondimus arces:** the sense is "we lose the citadels (from our view)," cf. Hom. *Od.* 5.279. After the Phaeacians returned Odysseus to Ithaca in their magic ship, Poseidon threatened to cover their city with a mountain in vengeance (13.146-52); nevertheless, in antiquity Phaeacia was identified with Corcyra (Ap. Rhod. 4.990-2).

292. **legimus:** "skirt," cf. 127 n.; **portu:** dative after a compound.

293. **Buthroti:** an appositional genitive; i.e., a "limiting" or "defining" genitive, used in apposition to a noun (AG §343d).

here

Hīc incredibilis rerum fama occupat auris,
Priamiden Helenum Graias regnare per urbis   295

---

*294–355. Aeneas hears that Helenus, a son of Priam, rules over the kingdom of Pyrrhus (=
Neoptolemus), the son of Achilles, and is now married to Andromache, widow of the great
Trojan hero Hector. Aeneas comes upon Andromache making offerings in Hector's memory
at his (empty) tomb. She recounts how she became Pyrrhus' slave, bore him a child, and was
subsequently given over by him to Helenus, also a captive, who, at Pyrrhus' death, succeeded to
his kingdom. Helenus enters with a retinue.*

In the traditional accounts, Aeneas does meet Helenus, who had settled at Buthrotum
(Dion. Hal. 1.51), although not Andromache, whose marriage with Helenus is prophesied
in Euripides' *Andromache*, but is not integrated by any earlier author into Aeneas' story.
(For other sources and variants, see Nelis (2001) 39.)

In Buthrotum Aeneas comes upon a city that is not merely a namesake of the great
Troy of the past, but a wholesale imitation, so that Troy's monuments are somehow
instantly recognizable, if on a small scale (*parvam Troiam* 349). Aeneas himself has tried
twice to build a new Troy; yet he responds negatively to this replica, which he sees as arid
(*arentem* 350), false (*falsi* 302, *simulata* 349), a mere image (*effigiem* 497). The structure of
the episode reinforces Aeneas' negative judgment of this imitation Troy, as it begins with
Andromache's offerings at Hector's empty tomb and concludes with her gifts to Ascanius,
who, she says, resembles Astyanax, her dead son. (On Andromache, see 297 n.) Between
these intensely emotional scenes comes Helenus' unengaging prophecy.

Nugent (1999) has observed that limitless, self-destructive grief characterizes female
figures throughout the *Aeneid*, and nowhere is this truer than in the case of Andromache.
Andromache has lost a son and a spouse, but does have a city; Aeneas has lost a city and a
spouse, but has a son. Andromache longs for persons; Aeneas longs for a city, but not this
one. In their bitter, asymmetrical losses, they fail to comfort each other.

The diminished quality of this "Little Troy" is exemplified in Helenus, Hector's
brother, a lesser son of Priam, now Andromache's husband. (On Helenus see notes on 295
and 344-55.) Commentators and Helenus himself draw attention to his overall loquacity
(a significant contrast to Aeneas' characteristic proto-Roman terseness); Aeneas later draws
attention to his omissions (712-3; cf. also 374-462 n.) (See O'Hara (1990) for the motif*
of prophetic omissions in the *Aeneid*.) Helenus has the gift to see into the future, but not
to enter it. This lack on Helenus' part points up by contrast the special courage of Aeneas.
Thus, just as there is asymmetry between the sorrows of Andromache and Aeneas, so
there is asymmetry between the virtues of Helenus and Aeneas, to whom, as we see, the
Roman mission is appropriately given. Aeneas observes the derivative physical appearance
(*falsi* 302, *simulata* 349, *parvam* 349, *effigiem* 497) and emotional sterility of Helenus' and
Andromache's Troy, wherein the couple exchange no words and whose marriage is without
offspring. Aeneas' experience of this Troy constitutes a lesson for him on the unfruitful
seduction of nostalgia and the inadequacy of mere imitation. (See Introduction.) With
respect to his own composition of the *Aeneid*, Vergil acknowledges implicitly, through this
representation of the inadequacy of mere imitation, that no poet can rival or transcend
Homer merely by imitating him.

For further discussion: Grimm (1967), Anderson (1969, 1989), Putnam (1980) 56-9,

Achilles' father Aeacus *son of Achilles* *Helenus son of Priam* *Andro-Mache*

marriage *& the scepters* *having acquired*

coniugio Aeacidae Pyrrhi sceptrisque potitum,
et patrio Andromachen iterum cessisse marito. *again yielded*
obstipui miroque incensum pectus amore
compellare virum et casus cognoscere tantos.
progredior portu classis et litora linquens, 300
sollemnis cum forte dapes et tristia dona *by chance*

Bright (1981), G.S. West (1983), Feeney (1983), O'Hara (1990) 26-31, Cova (1992, 1994), Quint (1993) 53-65, Bettini (1997), Hexter (1999), Nugent (1999), Nelis (2001) 38-44.

294. **auris:** sc. *nostras.*

295. **Priamiden…:** the patronymic lends epic character, cf. *Aeacidae* 296. Helenus and Andromache were both given as prizes to Pyrrhus (Neoptolemus), the son of Achilles, at the fall of Troy. Helenus, a seer, forewarned Pyrrhus of the sea storms that would destroy many Greeks on their return home. In consequence, Pyrrhus took the land route without incident. At his death (he is murdered by Orestes, see 328 n.), in gratitude, he left Helenus a share in his kingdom and Andromache for wife. Pyrrhus is regularly described as king of Epirus and was regarded as the ancestor of the historical kings of Epirus who bore his name. **regnare:** infinitive of indirect statement dependent on the verb of saying implicit in *fama.*

296. **coniugio:** for *coniuge*, i.e., Andromache; ablative, along with *sceptris* (i.e., *regnis*) after *potior*; both nouns are synecdochic*. **Aeacidae:** "descendant of Aeacus," a patronymic*, in the genitive; the order of descent is Aeacus, Peleus, Achilles, Pyrrhus.

297. **patrio marito:** a husband of her own race, i.e., Trojan. Although Andromache is from Thebes, she is described as Trojan because of her marriage to Hector. **cessisse:** "passed into the possession of," cf. 333. This legal use of *cedo* with the dative is found also in prose (e.g., Livy 31.46 *captiva corpora Romanis cessere*). It is also used of booty passing to a new owner (Horsfall *ad loc.*), a meaning compatible with Andromache's sorrowful narrative.

Andromache figures in the *Iliad*'s most heart-wrenching scenes (6.369-529, 22.437-515, 24.723-450), where she is defined by her passionate love for Hector and their son, Astyanax, both of whom are slain at Troy. In Euripides' *Trojan Women* she argues in vain for Astyanax' life; in Euripides' *Andromache*, as the intended victim of Hermione's murderous jealousy, she is again the defender of her child (with Pyrrhus), Molossus. Her marriage with Helenus is prophesied at the end of the play.

298-9. **amore:** ablative of means, with *compellare* ("longing to address"); the infinitive dependent on *amor* is poetic. **incensum:** supply *est.* **pectus** sc. *meum.*

300. **portu:** ablative of separation.

301–2. **sollemnis cum forte…:** "when (*cum*), by chance (*forte*), before the city (*ante urbem*) in a grove (*in luco*)…by the water of a false Simois (*falsi Simoentis ad undam*) was offering (*libabat*) to ashes (*cineri*) ritual feasts (*solemnis…dapes*) and mourning gifts (*tristia dona*) Andromache…." Information builds up in pieces as Aeneas comes to understand what he is seeing. On *cum inversum*, see 8 n. *Libo* is a technical term for any offering that can be "poured" upon the altar. These could include wine, milk, oil, honey, eggs, beans, even corn or fruit. Andromache calls Hector's *manes* to the tomb to partake of the offerings. **solemnis:** "ritual," perhaps referring to the *parentalia,* the private celebration of rites for the family dead. Note parallel adjective and noun sequence (aAbB) in 301.

ante urbem in luco falsi Simoentis ad undam
libabat cineri Andromache manisque vocabat
Hectoreum ad tumulum, viridi quem caespite inanem
et geminas, causam lacrimis, sacraverat aras.   305
ut me conspexit venientem et Troia circum
arma amens vidit, magnis exterrita monstris
deriguit visu in medio, calor ossa reliquit;
labitur et longo vix tandem tempore fatur:
'verane te facies, verus mihi nuntius adfers,   310
nate dea? vivisne? aut, si lux alma recessit,
Hector ubi est?' dixit, lacrimasque effudit et omnem
implevit clamore locum. vix pauca furenti
subicio et raris turbatus vocibus hisco:

302. **falsi:** "counterfeit," "pretended," i.e., the river is named *Simois* after the real Simois in Troy.

303. **cineri:** of Hector, as will be revealed. Andromache as subject is also postponed.

304. **tumulum...inanem:** a cenotaph (empty tomb), because Hector's ashes were buried in Troy where he was killed (Hom. *Il*. 24.795-804). The verse is framed by *Hectoreum* and *inanem*, emphasizing Hector's absence. For the elevated tone of such adjectival forms as *Hectoreum*, see 117 n. **caespite:** ablative of material.

305. **geminas...aras:** probably to Dis and Proserpina. The dead like even numbers (Servius *ad loc.*). **causam lacrimis:** "a focus for tears," as she had built the two altars in order to lament.

306-7. **ut:** with indicative means "as," "when." **Troia circum arma:** "Trojan arms about me" (Horsfall) or "Trojan warriors with me" (Williams). Trojan arms are identifiable to Andromache, as they are later to Achaemenides, whom the Trojans in their turn recognize as Greek, despite his deteriorated state. *Troia* scans as a dactyl. **amens:** "out of her mind," "hysterical." **magnis exterrita monstris:** "terrified by the portentous apparitions." Andromache, engaged in invoking Hector's spirit, mistakes Aeneas for a shade; cf. 313 *furenti*.

308. **deriguit visu in medio:** "she stiffened at the sight," lit. "in the midst of the sight."

309. **longo tempore:** "in time," "after some time."

310. **vera...facies, verus...nuntius:** "as a true form...a true messenger," in apposition to an implied *tu*, the subject of *adfers*. Note anaphora* in parallel clauses.

311. **si lux alma recessit:** "if life-sustaining light has departed," i.e., "if you are dead."

312. **Hector ubi est?:** i.e., "if you are a shade, why is Hector not with you?" Cf. Dante, *Inf*. 10.59-60.

313-14. **vix pauca furenti...:** lit. "with difficulty (*vix*) some few (words) (*pauca*) I offer (*subicio*, throw under) to her hysterical (*furenti*)...and I stammer (*hisco*)..." **raris...vocibus:** ablative of manner, "with halting words." Aeneas is represented as deeply disconcerted (*turbatus*) by Andromache's extreme emotional state.

'vivo equidem vitamque extrema per omnia duco;   315
ne dubita, nam vera vides.
heu! quis te casus deiectam coniuge tanto
excipit, aut quae digna satis fortuna revisit,
Hectoris Andromache? Pyrrhin conubia servas?'
deiecit vultum et demissa voce locuta est: 320
'o felix una ante alias Priameia virgo,
hostilem ad tumulum Troiae sub moenibus altis

[handwritten marginalia: "from such a husband", "what misfortune saved you", "(gen.)", "do you keep marrying of Pyrrhus?", "she lowered her eyes and with downcast voice she spoke"]

---

315. **extrema:** "things beyond which one cannot go," "utmost dangers" or "difficulties." Aeneas responds to Andromache by speaking of his own difficulties and thus fails to offer sympathy or consolation. Indeed, his subsequent questioning (see 319 n.) strikes some commentators as remarkably unsympathetic. Feeney (1990) offers a sustained discussion of Aeneas' represented avoidance of authentic emotional exchange, a feature of Vergil's characterization of Aeneas.

316. **ne dubita:** *ne* + imperative is archaic, thus poetic; see 160 n. This is an incomplete verse (cf. 218 n.).

317. **deiectam coniuge tanto:** "fallen" or "cast down from such a (noble) husband." *Casus, deiectam,* and *excipit* connote an actual fall; commentators take the referenced fall to be a loss of rank, although a fuller emotional response is called for.

318. **digna satis:** "sufficiently worthy," i.e., of you.

319. **Hectoris Andromache…:** "Andromache wife of Hector." **Pyrrhin conubia servas?:** "Are you still keeping marriage with Pyrrhus?" (The *n* in *Pyrrhin* is the interrogative enclitic *-ne*.) Heinze makes no comment on these verses (82, 222, 273 n. 11); yet some readers find Aeneas' question tactless (West (1983) 260), "an unfeeling reproach" (Conington *ad loc.*). Cova (1994) *ad loc.* understands Aeneas to be distinguishing between Andromache's felt moral state (marriage to Hector) and her subsequent marriages (unwilled). Donatus (cf. 216-17 n.; cited by, e.g., West (1983) 260 n. 7) reads Aeneas as implicitly charging Andromache with sexual immorality, which her own speech is designed to refute (a suggestion that likely reveals more about Donatus' cultural context than about Vergil's text). See also Highet (1972) 6 and 6 n. In any case, Aeneas' address to Andromache as "Hector's wife" accords with Andromache's own perception of herself as *univira*, married to only one man (West (1983) 261), an admired (if not widely exemplified) status among Roman women. Andromache speaks of Pyrrhus with loathing and of Helenus not at all.

321. **felix una ante alias:** "O happy alone above others," a strong superlative. Polyxena is the *Priameia* (see 117 n.) *virgo*, virgin daughter of Priam, sacrificed by Pyrrhus on the tomb of Achilles at Troy. Euripides' *Hecuba* treats this event, but places it in Thrace, not Troy. Aeneas, in his first utterance in the poem (1.94-6), expresses the same thought (better to have died at Troy) in the same kind of construction. His last speech in the poem (12.947-52) has a very different character, while Andromache's last speech is consistent in its pathos* (486-91) with her first.

[handwritten note at bottom: "Polyxena > young daughter of Priam. Neoptolemus - Pyrrhus] sacrifices Polyxena at Troy"]

iussa mori, quae sortitus non pertulit ullos
nec victoris heri tetigit captiva cubile!
nos patria incensa diversa per aequora vectae   325
stirpis Achilleae fastūs iuvenemque superbum
servitio enixae tulimus; qui deinde secutus
Ledaeam Hermionen Lacedaemoniosque hymenaeos

323. **mori:** poetic use of the infinitive for indirect command (4 n.). **sortitus...ullos:** Andromache, as wife of the Trojan commander, was not assigned by lot, but instead was chosen by Pyrrhus (Eur. *Tro.* 274). In using the plural (*sortitus*), she speaks of the enslaved captive Trojan women generally.

324. **nec victoris heri...:** note the emphasis of each word: "conqueror," "master," whose bed she is compelled as a "captive" to "touch." Vergil thus makes Andromache describe her forced sexual service to Pyrrhus as a fate worse than death. This is a fine touch on Vergil's part, for Hector in the *Iliad*, when speaking of Andromache's future life as a slave after his death (Hom. *Il.* 6.455-8), omits from his explicit imaginings precisely the sexual slavery that Vergil's Andromache experiences as the greatest torment.

325. **nos:** strongly antithetical. Note the chiastic* order of the adjective and noun pairs *patria incensa, diversa...aequora.*

326-7. **stirpis Achilleae:** Andromache speaks of the arrogance of Achilles' race, as exemplified in his arrogant son Pyrrhus (*iuvenem...superbum*), who became her master (see 321 n. on *Priameia*). She had to endure (*tulimus*) both his arrogance (*fastus*) and the enforced bearing of his children (*servitio enixae*), a zeugma*. **servitio:** "in slavery," ablative both of time and cause. **enixae:** "having born (children)," the participle being used absolutely. The child to whom she refers is Molossus (cf. 327-8 n.), who became the eponymous ancestor of the Molossian kings of Epirus.

327-8. **qui:** connective relative pronoun, "and he." **deinde:** "thereafter," i.e., "when he was tired of me." **Ledaeam Hermionen:** Hermione is the daughter of Helen who is the daughter of Leda (thus the matronymic), and Menelaus, king of Sparta (Lacedaemon). In Euripides' *Andromache* the jealous Hermione conspires (unsuccessfully) to murder Molossus and Andromache, since her own marriage to Pyrrhus is barren. **Lacedaemonios hymenaeos...:** these polysyllabic Greek words at line end give a Greek feel to the verse. Note adjective/ noun order parallel with the preceding *Ledaeam Hermionen* (aAbB), the elevated adjectives, and the resulting ponderousness of the whole. The effect of these features together may function to express Andromache's scorn.

Before the Trojan war, Hermione was promised to Orestes. Subsequently, nevertheless, Menelaus gave her to Pyrrhus instead. Orestes, both for love of Hermione and also maddened by Furies as punishment for killing his mother Clytemnestra, murders Pyrrhus—in Vergil's version—at his father's altars (*patrias...ad aras* 332). In other accounts the murder transpires in Apollo's temple at Delphi (e.g., Pind. *Nem.* 7.34-43, Eur. *And.* 1073-5, 1117-60), because Apollo is avenging the murder of Priam by Pyrrhus at Priam's own altar (Pind. *Paean.* 6.110-20). Because involvement in such primitive retribution would compromise the morally elevated figure of the god that he has constructed, Vergil omits Apollo from the murder story (Paschalis (1986) 52). See notes on 73-83 and 85.

me famulo famulamque Heleno transmisit habendam.
ast illum ereptae magno flammatus amore 330
coniugis et scelerum furiis agitatus Orestes
excipit incautum patriasque obtruncat ad aras.
morte Neoptolemi regnorum reddita cessit
pars Heleno, qui Chaonios cognomine campos
Chaoniamque omnem Troiano a Chaone dixit, 335
Pergamaque Iliacamque iugis hanc addidit arcem.
sed tibi qui cursum venti, quae fata dedere?
aut quisnam ignarum nostris deus appulit oris?
quid puer Ascanius? superatne et vescitur aura?

---

329. **me famulo famulamque Heleno:** the *-que*, grammatically unnecessary, is therefore emphatic— both *to a slave* and *to be* a slave. **habendam:** gerundive expressing purpose, the term being devoid of any feeling. Andromache does not acknowledge explicitly her marriage to Helenus.

331. **scelerum Furiis agitatus:** "maddened by the Furies of his crimes," i.e., the Furies who avenge blood killings. Orestes murdered Clytemnestra to avenge her murder of Agamemnon (his father and her husband), whose sacrifice of their daughter Iphigenia caused Clytemnestra to murder him. This story of serial vengeance and its ultimate judicial resolution is told in Aeschylus' *Oresteia*.

332. **excipit incautum:** "catches unawares." **patriasque obtruncat ad aras:** see 327-8 n. Pyrrhus' slaughter of Priam and his son Polites at the altar is vividly described in *Aen.* 2.506-8. The resemblance between the two passages implies that retributive justice is at work also in the murder of Pyrrhus, but not through Apollo's agency. (Cf. *obtruncat* 55.) The tragic fates of the Greeks alluded to by Andromache, as with the episode of the shield of Abas (278-93 n.), demonstrate the fleeting nature of the Greeks' triumph at Troy.

333. **morte:** ablative of time. **reddita:** "duly given." Pyrrhus (Neoptolemus) gives over this share of his kingdom (*regnorum…pars*) and Andromache for wife in gratitude for Helenus' prophecy to him.

334. **Chaonios:** traditionally, the Chaonians existed before the Trojan War; as inhabitants of a tribal state in North Epirus in the sixth century, their royal house claimed descent from Helenus. The figure of Chaon is not attested elsewhere; the etymology may, therefore, have been created by Vergil (Williams *ad loc.*). **cognomine:** a "like" or "related name," cf. 133 and 350 n.

337. **sed tibi:** note the emphatic position: I have told you *my* history, "but now about *yourself,* what winds, what fate …?" **dedere** (= *dederunt*): its subjects are both *venti* and *fata*.

338. **ignarum:** sc. *te*. **oris:** dative after the compound *appulit*.

339. **quid puer Ascanius:** "what (of) the boy Ascanius?" **superatne:** "does he survive?" Cf. 2.643. **aura:** ablative after *vescor*.

quem tibi iam Troia— 340
ecqua tamen puero est amissae cura parentis?
ecquid in antiquam virtutem animosque virilis
et pater Aeneas et avunculus excitat Hector?'
talia fundebat lacrimans longosque ciebat
incassum fletus, cum sese a moenibus heros 345
Priamides multis Helenus comitantibus adfert,
agnoscitque suos laetusque ad limina ducit,
et multum lacrimas verba inter singula fundit.
procedo et parvam Troiam simulataque magnis

---

340. **quem tibi iam Troia**—: see 218 n. for other half-lines. While half-lines would seem to indicate incompleteness, some commentators, in this particular case, suggest that the broken off verse may be purposeful, expressing Andromache's literally unspeakable grief. Other scholars, however, say that such an irregularity would be unacceptable in epic.

341. **tamen** refers to *amissae* "still, in spite of her loss." **amissae...parentis:** the "lost parent" is Creusa, whose disappearance is described in *Aen.* 2.736-95.

342-3. **ecquid…:** lit. "Does the (image of) his father Aeneas and his uncle Hector excite (him) at all (*ecquid*) to ancestral courage (*virtutem*) and manly (*virilis*) spirit(s)?" An instance of "geneological protreptic," (Horsfall *ad* 3.340 and cf. *Aen.* 12.439). *Ecquid* is cognate accusative* used adverbially after *excitat*, cf. 56 n. **avunculus:** Hector was Ascanius' uncle because Creusa was Hector's sister. This pairing of Aeneas and Hector elevates Aeneas, who, in the *Iliad*, is not the equal of Hector (other instances: *Aen.* 6.170, 11.291, 12.440). In 343 *Aeneas* is before the caesura, with *Hector* at the end of the verse, a variation on a recurrent verbal pattern (see 108 n.) that serves implicitly to associate the two, as if they were an adjective and noun in agreement.

344. **talia fundebat lacrimans:** Andromache's tears prevent her waiting for an answer. For unresponded-to speeches in the *Aeneid* (a suggestive motif), see Highet (1972), Johnson (1976), Feeney (1983).

345-6. **cum…heros:** on *cum inversum*, see 8 n. **heros** "hero," refers to Helenus (346), further elevated by the epic patronymic *Priamides*. In Hom. *Il.* 6.76 Helenus is "best of the augurs." He tells Hector to instruct the Trojan women to offer sacrifice to Athena (6.86-98), but the goddess is unmoved (6.311). He urges Hector to single-combat, foreseeing correctly that his death is not nigh (7.44). Elsewhere he is mentioned as a warrior (12.94, 13.576 -8, 759-73) and a still surviving son of Priam (24.248).

347-8. **suos:** his fellow Trojans. **laetus…lacrimas:** Helenus' tears, by contrast to Andromache's, are of joy. **multum:** adverb. Helenus has a large escort (*multis comitantibus*) and great wealth (cf. 353-5), despite the diminutives that predominate in Aeneas' description of the city.

349. **parvam Troiam…:** Aeneas "recognizes a tiny Troy and a (tiny) Pergamum mimicking its great namesake." **magnis:** understand *Pergamis*, dative after *simulata*.

Pergama et arentem Xanthi cognomine rivum   350
agnosco, Scaeaeque amplector limina portae.
nec non et Teucri socia simul urbe fruuntur.
illos porticibus rex accipiebat in amplis;
aulai medio libabant pocula Bacchi
impositis auro dapibus, paterasque tenebant.   355
Iamque dies alterque dies processit, et aurae
vela vocant tumidoque inflatur carbasus austro:
his vatem adgredior dictis ac talia quaeso:
'Troiugena, interpres divum, qui numina Phoebi,

---

350. **arentem Xanthi…rivum:** a contrast to its famous original "the whirling Xanthus" (Hom. *Il.* 5.479). **cognomine:** ablative of description.

351. **limina:** Aeneas expresses emotion openly in embracing the threshold.

352. **nec non:** "likewise." **socia…urbe:** ablative after *fruor*.

353. **porticibus…in amplis:** in Greek houses the "porticoes" surrounded an open-air courtyard in front of the house. In the center of this (*aulai medio*) stood the altar on which libations were poured (*libabant pocula Bacchi*). **rex:** like Anius, Helenus is both king and priest.

354. **aulai:** archaic-poetic first declension genitive singular, scans as three longs; cf. 6.747 *aurai*, 7.464 *aquai*, 9.26 *pictai*. **Bacchi:** Bacchus, the wine god, by metonymy* for wine.

355. **impositis…dapibus:** ablative absolute. **auro:** dative after compound; synecdochic* for golden plates. Cf. Willliams' (*ad loc.*) full note on Vergil's "fondness" for parataxis: in hypotaxis* one would find *paterasque tenentes* instead of *paterasque tenebant.*

356–73. *Aeneas asks Helenus to confirm Italy as the destined homeland and to instruct him on future challenges. Helenus leads Aeneas to Apollo's temple where he prepares to receive the god's message.*

358. **his vatem adgredior dictis:** "I thus address (lit. approach with words) the seer."

359. **Troiugena:** vocative "Trojan-born," archaic, epic-type compound. **interpres:** "an intermediary" between two parties, here between the gods and men, either as the gods' mouthpiece or as interpreter of the gods' communications. Helenus fulfills both functions. **divum:** archaic genitive. **numina:** "will."

359–61. Note the *tricolon* abundans* with anaphora* of *qui* (359-60). Aeneas' elaborate address to Helenus, detailing his attributes, is not unlike an invocation to a god: note the epithets (*Troiugena, interpres divum*); the powers that justify the request (he can interpret the god's will, his cult objects, birds' song and flight paths); the prayer itself (*fare age* 632). See 85 n. for conventional features of prayers.

qui tripodas, Clarii lauros, qui sidera sentis   360
et volucrum linguas et praepetis omina pennae,
fare age (namque omnem cursum mihi prospera dixit
religio, et cuncti suaserunt numine divi
Italiam petere et terras temptare repostas;
sola novum dictuque nefas Harpyia Celaeno   365
prodigium canit et tristis denuntiat iras
obscenamque famem) quae prima pericula vito?
quidve sequens tantos possim superare labores?'
hic Helenus caesis primum de more iuvencis

360. **qui...sentis:** "you who sense"; implies access to a higher order of things. In a kind of zeugma*, *sentis* applies to a range of things: tripods ("you have knowledge about"), cult objects, to stars ("you interpret the movements of"), bird omens. **Clarius:** epithet of Apollo from his oracle at Claros, near Colophon. **lauros:** laurels were sacred to Apollo. **sidera:** cf. 4.519 *conscia fati sidera*. Astrology was popular at Rome in Vergil's day; cf. Hor. *Carm.* 1.11.

361. **volucrum...:** note short *u* before the stop/liquid combination c/r. The poet's choice determines the scansion of a stop + liquid after a short vowel. Birds could manifest the divine either through their cries (an *augurium*) or through their flight patterns (an *auspicium*); in the former case the birds were called *oscines*, in the latter, *praepetes*.

362–3. **fare:** imperative of *for, fari. fare age:* almost colloquial, means "come (on) now, say!" **omnem cursum mihi prospera dixit | religio:** "positive oracles (*prospera...religio*) have affirmed (lit. "told of") all my voyage"; *religio* denotes all the oracles Aeneas has received. Note the hypallage* (transferring) of both epithets, the sense of the whole being *omnis religio* (all the oracles) *dixit* (have foretold) *prosperum cursum* (a prosperous voyage) (Servius *ad loc.*).

364. **petere...temptare:** infinitives complementary to *suaserunt* (363), poetic indirect command (cf. 134, 144, 465, 609). **terras...repostas:** "remote lands"; syncopated form of *repositas*. (See syncope*.)

365–6. **novum dictuque nefas...prodigium:** *dictu*, ablative of the supine in *u*, frequently occurs after the indeclinable substantives *fas* and *nefas*. Here, however, *nefas* functions either as an adjective (*nefandum*) with *prodigium*—the prodigy is "startling and unlawful to tell"—or as a noun essentially in apposition to *prodigium*. Like *monstrum, prodigium* describes anything that is contrary to ordinary experience and therefore attributable to divine intervention.

367. **quae prima pericula vito:** "what dangers do I first avoid?" The indicative for the subjunctive is more vivid in this indirect question, cf. 88 n.

368. **possim:** potential subjunctive or subjunctive in the apodosis* of a future less vivid condition (the implied protasis* being: *si sequar*, "if I were to follow").

369. **hic:** temporal. **caesis...iuvencis:** ablative absolute; for the adjective-noun pattern, see 108 n. **de more:** "according to custom."

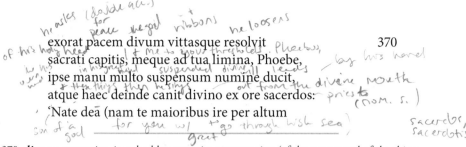

exorat pacem divum vittasque resolvit   370
sacrati capitis, meque ad tua limina, Phoebe,
ipse manu multo suspensum numine ducit,
atque haec deinde canit divino ex ore sacerdos:
'Nate dea (nam te maioribus ire per altum

370. **divum:** accusative, in a double accusative construction (of the person and of the thing requested, *pacem*) after *exorat*. **vittasque resolvit:** the hair is unbound to free the seer for possession by the god. Similarly, the Sibyl's possession by Apollo in 6.46-51 includes her hair coming undone. For the "hampering influence of knots in religion and magic," see Horsfall *ad loc* and *ad* 7.394. Cf. 65 n.

371. **limina:** i.e., threshold of the *adytum*, the inner sanctum of the temple, where the oracle is delivered; sacrifice is offered outside.

372. **ipse manu:** with his own hand, implying personal attention, cf. 4.344 n. **suspensum:** sc. *me*.

374–462. The prophecy of Helenus. Helenus affirms that divine will sustains Aeneas' mission. The sign of a white sow surrounded by thirty piglets will mark the destined site. Prescriptions and prohibitions follow. In particular, at Castrum Minervae, the first stop in Italy, Aeneas is to institute the practice of sacrifice with head veiled. At Cumae the Sibyl will offer further revelation.

Helenus' prophecy consists, essentially, of two prohibitions, each followed by a prescription: avoid Greeks along the eastern coast of Italy (396-402) and institute the practice of sacrifice with head veiled (403-9); avoid the monsters Scylla and Charybdis (413-32) and establish rites for Juno (433-40). The stop at Cumae to see the Sibyl (441-60) breaks this pattern, perhaps because there Aeneas will receive a prophecy of a different kind from that of Helenus.

In its focus on of-this-world prescriptions that will make possible the greater revelation in the Underworld, Helenus' prophecy resembles that of Circe (Hom. *Od.* 10.488-540, 12.37-141), whose prescriptions enable Odysseus to speak with Tiresias, the blind seer in the Underworld, who reveals the secret of homecoming ("contain your desire," "do not eat the cattle of the sun" (*Od.* 11.90-137)). Cf. also Phineus' prophecy to the Argonauts (Ap. Rhod. 2.311-407) and Nelis (2001) 38-44.

Helenus' prophecy is admonitory, didactic, emphatic, alliterative (375-6, 424-8, 455-9), and repetitive (383, 412, 433), all of which are characteristic features of oracular speech. In its length, however, the prophecy deviates from characteristic oracular style. (Contrast Creusa at 2.776-89, Apollo at 3.94-8, Penates at 3.154-71, Celaeno at 3.247-57, Anchises at 5.724-39, Sibyl at 6.83-7.) Helenus himself calls attention to his loquacity, as do commentators ("ponderous solemnity and long-winded repetitiousness," G. Williams (1983) 265; "definite verbosity," "vexatious repetition," Horsfall *ad* 374-462). The purpose of this characterization of Helenus may be to draw a contrast between him and Aeneas, both Trojan princes and both, in that sense, potential founders of a new Troy. The superiority of Aeneas as Roman founder is exemplified in several ways, one of which is his proto-Roman terseness (see Feeney (1983)).

Despite its length, Helenus' prophecy contains significant omissions: the storm that drives the Trojans to Carthage, the death of Palinurus, the death of Anchises, and

auspiciis manifesta fides, sic fata deum rex   375
sortitur volvitque vices, is vertitur ordo),
pauca tibi e multis, quo tutior hospita lustres
aequora et Ausonio possis considere portu,
expediam dictis: prohibent nam cetera Parcae
scire Helenum farique vetat Saturnia Iuno.   380
principio Italiam, quam tu iam rere propinquam
vicinosque, ignare, paras invadere portus,

---

the visit to the Underworld. At the conclusion of this book, Aeneas laments explicitly
that the prophecy omitted the death of Anchises (712-13). Nor does Helenus reveal the
ineffectiveness of his insistently prescribed sacrifices to Juno, who remains hostile to the
Romans for centuries after the conclusion of the *Aeneid* (Feeney (1984)). O'Hara (1990)
has shown, more generally, that prophecies in the *Aeneid* characteristically omit death and
other difficulties. Phineus (Ap. Rhod. 2.311 ff.) concedes that, even as a prophet, he cannot
reveal what the gods wish to keep secret. On Helenus, see O'Hara (1990) 25-31, 54-60,
123-7; Nelis 37-45.

374–5. te...ire: accusative and infinitive construction with *manifesta fides (est)*. maioribus...
auspiciis: "with the gods' will." Originally *auspicium* denotes omens manifest in birds'
flight or other specific celestial signs. In Vergil (only nine occurrences) it signifies more
generally (as here) "exceptional occurrences," thus "the gods' will" (Cova *ad loc.*). See 361
n. manifesta fides: "there is manifest proof." sic fata...: "thus does the king of heaven allot
the fates and turn the changes: this is the cycle (of events) that is turning (unfolding)." This
imprecise but suggestive turning imagery implies a wheel of changes, turned by Jupiter,
but also turning on its own. deum: archaic genitive plural. rex: monosyllabic ending lends
archaic, Ennian solemnity, appropriate for oracular speech.

376. Alliteration* (of *v*'s) suits oracular style.

377. quo: connective relative equivalent to *ut eo*; introduces a relative clause of purpose in
primary sequence. tutior: Helenus' prescriptions are resolutely practical. hospita: neuter
plural adjective, meaning either "stranger" or "host," or, in this case, possibly both.

379. prohibent nam cetera...: the future is partly unknown to Helenus, partly
incommunicable because of the gods' prohibition against human omniscience. Cf. Phineus'
admission to the Argonauts that he is not allowed to reveal their whole future (Ap. Rhod.
2.311-16). The accusative *cetera* is governed by both *scire* and *fari* (380). Note postposition
of *nam*; see 25 n.

380. Helenum: Helenus' use of his own name may suggest self-importance, although other
readings are possible. Iuno: enemy of the Trojans since the judgment of Paris, cf. *Aen*. 1.27
n. Her hostility parallels to some degree Poseidon's wrath against Odysseus in the *Odyssey*
(e.g., Hom. *Od*. 1.68-79).

381. Italiam: not "Italy" as a whole, but the destined western coast, as opposed to the eastern,
nearer coast (*hanc oram* 396). iam: "now," i.e., now that you have arrived on the shore
opposite Epirus. rere: alternative form for *reris* from *reor*.

longa procul longis via dividit invia terris.
ante et Trinacria lentandus remus in unda
et salis Ausonii lustrandum navibus aequor   385
infernique lacus Aeaeaeque insula Circae,
quam tuta possis urbem componere terra.
signa tibi dicam, tu condita mente teneto:
cum tibi sollicito secreti ad fluminis undam
litoreis ingens inventa sub ilicibus sus   390

---

382. **ignare:** cf. 8.730.

383. **longa procul…:** various features of this line evoke oracular style—the jingling effect (*via invia*, "pathless path"), repetition of *longa*/*longis*, rhyme of a word before the caesura* with a word at line end (*longis…terris*), coincidence of ictus* and accent* and also of word and foot in the second half of verse. **dividit:** governs *Italiam* (381), and signifies "separates" or "divides (from you)"; note the ablative *longis terris* after *dividit*: "divides by a long stretch of country."

384. **ante et…quam** (387)**…possis:** the subjunctive after *ante quam* expresses an anticipated action; the indicative, a completed one. AG §551b-c. **Trinacria:** Sicily, so called because of its triangular shape. **lentandus:** a gerundive, expressing necessity (with *est* to be understood); a rare word, referring to the bending of the oar as the rower drags it through the water.

385. **salis Ausonii:** the sea to the southwest of Italy, commonly called the Tyrrhenian Sea. *Ausonia* is identified as Aeneas' promised land (378). **salis:** metonymy* for sea. **lustrandum:** gerundive "must be traversed" (understand *est*); see 384 n. on *lentandus*.

386. **inferni…lacus:** the Lucrine and Avernian lakes, near Cumae, the latter associated with the Underworld. **Aeaeae…insula Circae:** In the *Odyssey*, Circe's island, Aeaea, is in the east; it is she, both frightening and nurturing, who (temporarily) turns Odysseus' men into pigs. In the *Argonautica* Circe is the daughter of the sun, aunt of Medea, and strongly associated with magic. Vergil, in accordance with later tradition, places Circe's island between Cumae and the mouth of the Tiber. The Trojans simply pass by Circe's island after leaving Cumae and Caieta (7.10-24).

388. **teneto:** future imperative, archaic in tone, hence formal, elevated; cf. 408. Note alliteration* of *t*'s and the polyptoton* of *tu* and *tibi*.

389. **tibi sollicito:** dative of agent with *inventa*. Aeneas will be anxious (*sollicito*) because of Turnus' marshalling of forces against him. **secreti ad fluminis undam:** i.e., at some point where the stream (the Tiber) is secluded.

390. **litoreis:** occurs only rarely, as here, of a riverbank. **ilicibus sus:** the monosyllabic ending is archaic, thus appropriate to this traditional oracle. Other versions of the sow prodigy, traditional in the Aeneas legend, are found in Lycophron (1255-60) and Dionysius of Halicarnassus (1.56). Helenus says the sow will mark the site of the future city (i.e., Lavinium); Tiberinus (at 8.43-8) repeats the prophecy (fulfilled at 8.81-3), adding that it signifies the foundation of Alba Longa from Lavinium in 30 years—as many years as the sow has offspring. See Dougherty (1993) 20 with n. 31 on animal guides in colonization narratives.

triginta capitum fetus enixa iacebit,
alba, solo recubans, albi circum ubera nati,
is locus urbis erit, requies ea certa laborum,
nec tu mensarum morsus horresce futuros:
fata viam invenient aderitque vocatus Apollo.   395
has autem terras Italique hanc litoris oram,
proxima quae nostri perfunditur aequoris aestu,
effuge; cuncta malis habitantur moenia Grais.
hic et Narycii posuerunt moenia Locri,
et Sallentinos obsedit milite campos   400

391. **triginta…:** "shall lie having given birth (*enixa*) to a litter of thirty young," the huge number of offspring being prodigious in itself (Horsfall). **capitum:** descriptive genitive after *fetus*; *caput* is used in counting men or animals, cf. *per capita*. **enixa:** object is *fetus*.

392. **solo:** ablative of place where, without preposition. **albi…nati:** sc. *iacebunt*. The anaphora* of *alba/ albi* suggests an etymological link with Alba Longa (see Horsfall *ad loc.* for references).

393. **requies…certa laborum:** Aeneas will never achieve *requies*, according to Jupiter's prophecy in *Aeneid* 1.263-6. Nevertheless, at, e.g., 1.241 (Venus) and 495 (Aeneas), rest is an explicit goal.

394. **nec…horresce:** *ne* with imperative is archaic (see 160 n.), thus poetic. Cf. *Geo.* 2.96 and R. Thomas (1988b) *ad loc.* for another instance of *nec* linking a prohibition to a preceding positive statement.

395. **fata viam:** see 257 n., uttered also by Jupiter (10.113). **aderit:** *adsis* or *ades* was commonly used in invoking the presence of a god. **vocatus…:** "when invoked."

396-7. **has…hanc:** demonstrative, "this nearer border of the Italian shore," that is, the one "which, nearest, is steeped in the tide of our (i.e., the Ionian) sea."

398. **effuge:** emphatic through enjambment*. Flight (particularly but not only of the Trojans) is a recurrent motif. **malis…Grais:** dative of agent. *Graiis* scans as two longs. The mention of Greeks is anachronistic, since Greek colonization of what came to be called *Magna Graecia* did not occur until centuries after the Trojan war.

399. **hic:** adverb, as scansion shows. **Narycii…Locri:** Naryca was a town of the Locrians, where Ajax son of Oileus was born. Returning from Troy, the impious Ajax was shipwrecked by Pallas Athena (*Aen.* 1.39-45); some surviving companions made their way to Southern Italy, where they founded another Locri. This passage alludes to leaders of the Trojan expedition (Ajax, Idomeneus, Philoctetes), with their geographical epithets. Movement of peoples around the Mediterranean and establishment of new colonies are reflected in these *nostoi*, stories of the returns of Greek heroes from the Trojan war; see 401-2 n. **moenia:** defining of city founders; see 85 n.

400. **Sallentinos…campos:** in the southeastern extremity of the Apulia region, in the heel of Italy. **milite:** ablative of means; a collective noun.

[handwritten top margin: Idomeneus of Lyctos (from Crete)]
[handwritten top margin right: Velare - passive imperative]

Lyctius Idomeneus; hic illa ducis Meliboei
parva Philoctetae subnixa Petelia muro.
quin ubi transmissae steterint trans aequora classes
et positis aris iam vota in litore solves,
purpureo velare comas adopertus amictu, 405

[handwritten annotations interspersed: "the first well known city of the Meliboean leader"; "relying on the wall of Philoctetes"; "(do not settle on the Adriatic coast)"; "when your ships having crossed the sea will have stopped"; "the altars having been placed at last you will perform your vows on the shore"; "cover hair covered w/ a red"; "middle (for yourself) having perp..."; "but take advantage of the stop to sacrifice & initiate the practice of veiling the head during sacrifice"]

401. Lyctius: adjective; Idomeneus was from the city of Lyctos in Crete, whence he was expelled, see 122 n. He founds, among other cities, Castrum Minervae, Aeneas' first stop in Italy. **hic illa…:** *illa* implies "well known": "there is that (well known city) of the Meliboean leader (*ducis Meliboei*), small Petelia (*parva…Petelia*), relying on the wall of Philoctetes." Philoctetes, king of Meliboea, also exiled from Crete, founded Petelia in Bruttium. *Petelia* is likely connected with the Old Latin word *petilus*, thin or small. In this case *parva…Petelia* would be an etymological wordplay (Williams *ad loc.*). For other possible derivations of the root *pet-,* either from an augury from bird *flight* (Gr. *petomai,* "fly") related to the founding of the town or because Philoctetes sought (*petivit*) a place for the town, see Servius *ad loc.* On Petelia, see also O'Hara (1996) 143-4. See 692-711 n. for further instances of etymological play. Such learned etymological wordplay functions to create a particular tone, affirming Vergil's adherence to the tradition of Alexandrian poetry, as exemplified by Callimachus and Apollonius of Rhodes. For an important discussion of the poetic importance of such etymological wordplay for Vergil, see O'Hara (1996) 102-11.

403–4. quin: "but no, indeed." It both corrects and exhorts: thus 1) (but no) "do not settle on the Adriatic coast," but 2) (indeed) "take advantage of the stop to sacrifice and initiate the practice of veiling the head during sacrifice." **steterint:** used often of ships, "are anchored," future perfect (for a future action that takes place before another future action) from *sto,* used intransitively. Translate: "when your ships, having crossed [been sent over] (*transmissae…classes*) the sea (*trans aequora*) stand (i.e., at anchor, *steterint,* lit. "will have stood") and, the altars having been placed (*positis aris*), at last (*iam*) you will perform your vows (*vota…solves*) on the shore (*in litore*), then cover…" **iam:** "at last."

405. purpureo…amictu: frame the line, as if to exemplify the covering. The *amictus* (from *amicio:* "throw on" or "about"), a garment mentioned ten times in the *Aeneid,* is a draped mantle, worn by both male and female figures (Amata 12.602, Juturna 12.885). Bender suggests that it has "sacerdotal significance" as a kind of proto-toga, when Aeneas, following Helenus' instructions, dons an *amictus* to make his first sacrifice on arrival in Italy (3.545). **velare:** "veil your hair," passive imperative with middle sense. Romans covered their heads during prayer and sacrifice, while Greeks did not. In the *Origo Gentis Romanae* 12.2 (an anonymous compilation of earlier sources, made probably c. 360 CE), this custom is attributed to a moment when, just as Aeneas was sacrificing on shore, Odysseus/ Ulysses and his fleet chanced to arrive. To avoid recognition by Ulysses and consequent sacrilege, should he interrupt the ritual, Aeneas covered his head. See Harrison (1985). A sense of Roman identity results from marking or establishing differences from other peoples (e.g., Syed (2005) esp. 194-233). In this case, Roman sacrificial ritual marks Romans' differences from Greeks. Later in this book, however, solidarity with Greeks, which furthered Augustan geopolitical aims, will implicitly be affirmed through the Achaemenides episode.

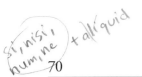

ne qua inter sanctos ignis in honore deorum
hostilis facies occurrat et omina turbet,
hunc socii morem sacrorum, hunc ipse teneto;
hac casti maneant in religione nepotes.
ast ubi digressum Siculae te admoverit orae   410
ventus, et angusti rarescent claustra Pelori,
laeva tibi tellus et longo laeva petantur
aequora circuitu; dextrum fuge litus et undas.
haec loca vi quondam et vasta convulsa ruina

406-7. **ne qua…:** the sight of anything ill-omened (*hostilis facies*) invalidated the sacrifice; analogously, silence was required lest any ill-omened word be heard. **in honore deorum:** "at" or "during" offerings to the gods.

408-9. **hunc…hunc…hac:** tricolon* with anaphora*, suitable to Helenus' elevated speaking style. **socii:** subject of the implied *tenento* (future imperative), cf. 388 n. **teneto:** future imperative occurs in general directions or precepts "serving for all time" (AG §449.2). **casti…:** free of ritual pollution.

410. **digressum:** i.e., "having departed" from Italy and re-embarking. **orae:** dative after compound.

411. **angusti rarescent claustra Pelori:** the "barriers of Pelorus" are the opposite headlands on the Sicilian (*Pelorus* is the cape at the northeastern tip of Sicily) and Italian sides. Between these is a narrow (*angusti*) strait. From a distance the land appears continuous, an actual barrier; on approach, the strait opens to view. *Raresco* is "to grow thin," "to lose density," but here, specifically, "to (appear to) diminish," i.e., "to open." Thus "the barriers of narrow Pelorus will begin to open" as the Trojans approach them. Note adjective before the caesura* modifying noun at verse end (see 108 n.).

412. **laeva tibi tellus:** the left or southern side of Sicily, around which Aeneas is to sail "*longo circuitu*" to avoid Scylla and Charybdis. Note the emphatic position of *laeva*, emphasized by its repetition later in the line. **petantur:** jussive subjunctive, lit. "let them be sought," i.e., the Trojans should make for these destinations.

413. **dextrum…litus:** once they are west of Italy's toe, the Trojans are to cross to Sicily, not go up the west coast of Italy. **fuge:** a motif, for which see Introduction and *passim*.

414–16. **loca…dissiluisse:** accusative and infinitive of indirect statement after *ferunt.* "They say these lands leaped apart…"

414. **haec loca** = *dextrum litus et undas,* "these lands," i.e., the lands on the right, just mentioned. **vasta convulsa ruina:** lit. "convulsed by vast ruin." The Romans believed that Sicily, once joined to Italy, had broken off (Diodorus Siculus 4.85.3; Ov. *Met.* 15.290; Pliny, *Nat. Hist.* 2.204). Rhegium is derived from Greek *rhegnumi*: break. Cf. Dougherty (1993) 24 with n. 49 *Ruina* may signify earthquake (Hardie (2007)).

(tantum aevi longinqua valet mutare vetustas)   415
dissiluisse ferunt, cum protinus utraque tellus
una foret: venit medio vi pontus et undis
Hesperium Siculo latus abscidit, arvaque et urbes
litore diductas angusto interluit aestu.
dextrum Scylla latus, laevum implacata Charybdis   420
obsidet, atque imo barathri ter gurgite vastos
sorbet in abruptum fluctus rursusque sub auras
erigit alternos, et sidera verberat unda.

---

415. **tantum...:** "so much," "such an effect," a parenthetical reflection (i.e., given great extent of time, significant changes can occur). The perhaps pedestrian nature of this reflection may contribute to characterization of Helenus. **valet:** with meaning *potest* (Horsfall *ad loc.*) and complementary infinitive, *mutare.*

416–17. **cum...foret:** archaic for *esset*, concessive clause, "although they were one...." **cum protinus...:** *protinus*, with *una*, here describes space ("one continuous expanse"), not time. Thus "although the two lands were one continuous (expanse), the sea came with violence in the midst." **medio:** ablative, local or of extension; *vi* "with violence" = "violently." **undis** : ablative of means.

418–19. **Hesperium...latus:** the western side (of Italy). **Siculo:** sc. *latere*: "from the Sicilian side." **arvaque...diductas:** the sea washes between (*interluit*) "the separated fields and cities...." Formerly the fields and cities were (1) not separated and (2) inland; now they are (1) separated and (2) on the sea-shore (*litore*).

420. **implacata:** = *implacabilis*, "unplacatable" or "unplacated," unattested before Vergil and possibly a Vergilian coinage. See Williams *ad 420* on such forms. For Latin speakers, such neologisms (if they are such) or rare words would be heard as poetic.

421. **obsidet:** subjects are both *Scylla* and *Charybdis*, though only Charybdis is subject of *sorbet* (422). Homer's Scylla is a man-eating monster with six heads, which she pokes out of her cave, fishing for dolphins or dogfish or anything bigger (*Od.* 12.94-6). She eats one man from each ship that passes (*Od.* 12.73-100, 222-59). Vergil's is a later version (see below); Charybdis is the whirlpool.

Circe tells Odysseus to avoid Charybdis absolutely and to sail instead close to Scylla on the cliffside, the loss of six men being preferable to loss of all (as would occur if they were sucked down by Charybdis). By Vergil's time Scylla and Charybdis were traditionally located in the Straits of Messina. (There is a Scilla today on the Italian side.)

421–3. **barathri:** "abyss" of land or sea, used of the underworld in Lucr. 3.966; cf. *Aen.* 8.245; lit. "and three times (a day) with the bottomless (*imo* [loose trans.]) whirlpool of her abyss she sucks vast waves (*vastos...fluctus*) into the sheer deep (*in abruptum*), and hurls them up again in turn to the skies (*sub auras*) and whips the stars with sea." **ter...:** "three times" (a day), cf. Hom. *Od.* 12.105. **sorbet:** subject is Charybdis. **in abruptum:** the neuter of the participle used as a noun. **sidera verberat unda:** exceptional hyperbole*.

at Scyllam caecis cohibet spelunca latebris
ora exsertantem et navis in saxa trahentem.   425
prima hominis facies et pulchro pectore virgo
pube tenus, postrema immani corpore pistrix
delphinum caudas utero commissa luporum.
praestat Trinacrii metas lustrare Pachyni
cessantem, longos et circumflectere cursus,   430
quam semel informem vasto vidisse sub antro
Scyllam et caeruleis canibus resonantia saxa.
praeterea, si qua est Heleno prudentia vati,
si qua fides, animum si veris implet Apollo,

424–8. Note the exaggerated sound effects appropriate to a monster, marked by assonance*
and alliteration*.

425. **ora…:** cf. Hom. *Od.* 12.94 where Homer makes Scylla pick off a sailor with each of her
heads, but Vergil makes her "drag ships into the rocks," i.e., into the rocky cavern where
she lurks. **exsertantem:** "always darting out," participle formed from the rare frequentative
of *exserere*, in parallel order of objects and participles (*ora exsertantem…navis…trahentem*).

426–7. "On top (*prima*) her appearance is human (*hominis facies*), and she is a young woman
with beautiful breast (*pulchro pectore virgo*) as far as the groin (*pube tenus*), behind a fish-
monster…"

426. **prima…:** referring to Scylla's topmost part versus *postrema* (427), her bottommost
part. **hominis facies:** "the face of a human" instead of *homo facie*: "human as to her face."
pulchro pectore: ablative of description; supply *est* in both clauses.

427. **tenus:** follows its noun, which is in the ablative (or sometimes genitive). **postrema:** sc.
facies est. **pistrix:** also found in the form *pistris* or *pristis*, the latter used at 5.116 as the
name of a ship bearing this monster as its figure-head.

428. **delphinum…:** "having tails of dolphins joined together with her belly of wolves."
caudas: accusative of respect, lit. "joined together as to her tails." Cf. 47, 65, 81, 405 for
other body-part accusatives of respect. **commissa:** passive participle of *committo* ("join
together with").

429. **metas:** goals around which racers had to turn, here applied to the headland of Pachynus
around which the Trojans are to turn.

430. **cessantem:** "lingering," "delaying," i.e., not taking the speediest route. Modifies an
implied *te*, the accusative subject of *lustrare* in indirect statement introduced by *praestat*
(429). **circumflectere:** perhaps a Vergilian coinage (Horsfall); see 420 n.

431. **quam:** after *praestat* (429) which has comparative force: "it is better than to have seen…"

432. **caeruleis canibus:** "sea-colored sea-dogs" practically the same as the *lupi* (428); *caeruleus*
"sea-colored" is a regular epithet of all sea creatures, cf. 194 n.

433–4. **si qua est…:** "if there is any foresight in Helenus, if any faithfulness in the seer, if…."
The rhetorical use of *si* or *si forte* with the indicative does not imply doubt, but the reverse.

unum illud tibi, nate dea, proque omnibus unum   435
praedicam et repetens iterumque iterumque monebo,
Iunonis magnae primum prece numen adora,
Iunoni cane vota libens dominamque potentem
supplicibus supera donis: sic denique victor
Trinacria fines Italos mittere relicta.   440
huc ubi delatus Cumaeam accesseris urbem
divinosque lacus et Averna sonantia silvis,

Helenus means "as surely as I do have foresight…" (By contrast, for genuine doubt expressed by *si qua* with subjunctive, see *Aen.* 1.18, 6.882.) The substitution of *Heleno* and *vati* for the personal pronoun suits the oracular high style. **veris**: the neuter plural used as a substantive.

Note *tricolon* abundans** with *si*-clauses is emphatic, even hyperbolic*; note further emphasis through repetition: *si qua…si qua…si, unum…unum, iterumque…iterumque, Iunoni…Iunoni.*

435. **unum illud:** "this one thing": *ille* points with emphasis to something which *follows* and should be translated by "this." *Iunoni…donis* (438-9) explain what "this" is. **proque omnibus unum:** "yes, this one thing instead of all beside," i.e., this one thing which is as important as all other counsels put together. **unum:** also emphatic, framing the line.

436. The line is elegantly framed with two first person futures, from different conjugations. Note emphatic repetition of *iterum* and the doubled *-que* (see 72 n.)

437–8. **Iunonis…Iunoni:** again, emphatic placement and repetition. Juno's wrath initiates the action of the poem, i.e., the storm that brings the Trojans to Carthage. *Iunonis… Iunoni…dominamque...* form another tricolon*; in conjunction with 433-4 above, this part of the prophecy has the rhetorical character of a peroration*. **cane vota libens:** "utter (i.e., perform) your vows gladly." *Libens* is conventional in the paying of vows; V L S (*votum libens solvit*) is common in inscriptions. For *cano* used of a sacred utterance, cf. 155.

439. **supera:** "vanquish," a strong word, "with suppliant sacrifices" (*supplicibus donis*), a seeming paradox; the metaphor is sustained in *victor*. **sic denique victor:** "thus (i.e., when you will have vanquished her hatred) at last victorious…." In fact, as Feeney (1984) shows, Juno does not become reconciled to the Romans until after the Second Punic War, centuries after the dramatic date of the *Aeneid*.

440. **Trinacria…relicta:** elegantly frame the line. **mittere:** second singular future passive, emphasizing divine guidance.

441. **Cumaeam…urbem:** again, elevated adjective for genitive noun, cf. 117 n.

442. **divinosque lacus:** i.e., the Lucrine, nearer the sea, and the Avernian, more inland and separated from the Lucrine by a narrow strip of land. Though both are mentioned, only Avernus is associated with the entrance to the underworld, see 386 n. The lakes are *divinos* because they are sacred to gods of the underworld. **Averna sonantia silvis:** lit. "Avernus sounding with its woods." The sibilants of *sonantia silvis* may suggest an other-worldly presence, conjuring the awesomeness of gloomy groves (*nemorum tenebrae* 6.238) that surrounded the lake. **Averna:** a plural place-name, formed on the analogy of *Pergamum, Pergama.* **silvis:** ablative of means.

insanam vatem aspicies, quae rupe sub ima
fata canit foliisque notas et nomina mandat.
quaecumque in foliis descripsit carmina virgo.   445
digerit in numerum atque antro seclusa relinquit:
illa manent immota locis neque ab ordine cedunt.
verum eadem, verso tenuis cum cardine ventus
impulit et teneras turbavit ianua frondes,
numquam deinde cavo volitantia prendere saxo   450
nec revocare situs aut iungere carmina curat.
inconsulti abeunt sedemque odere Sibyllae.
hic tibi ne qua morae fuerint dispendia tanti,
quamvis increpitent socii et vi cursus in altum
vela vocet, possisque sinus implere secundos,   455

443. **insanam vatem:** "an inspired (or "frenzied") prophetess." Helenus, by contrast, is not described as *insanus*. The Sibyl is perhaps more "possessed" by the god than Helenus. She communicates differently from Helenus, as he describes, below. The *vates* is the Sibyl of Cumae who guides Aeneas through the underworld in *Aen.* 6. Dante makes Vergil himself his guide through the Underworld, see 43 n. **rupe sub ima:** "deep within the rock."

444-5. **fata…:** "announces destiny and entrusts her signs and symbols to leaves." The Sibyl writes her prophecies in verse (*carmina* 445, cf. *canit* 155) on leaves, then "arranges the leaves in order" (*digerit in numerum*), so that the prophecy, read consecutively, can be understood. When the wind disturbs the leaves, however, she does not restore them to proper order. Cf. Dante, *Paradiso* 33.65-6 (the final canto of the *Divine Comedy*) alludes to the light leaves and the loss of the Sibyl's responses. **notas et nomina mandat:** suggests some form of writing. **carmina:** the Sibyl's responses as well as Aeneas' shield dedication (287) are in meter.

446. **(in) antro:** = *rupe ima* as above.

447. **locis:** supply *in.*

448. **verum:** "but." **eadem…:** accusative plural agreeing with *volitantia carmina* (450-1); the object of *prendere…curat* in 450-1. **verso…cardine:** of a door (*ianua* 449).

449. **impulit:** "has set in motion," "disturbed," enjambed.

452. **inconsulti:** "unadvised" "uncounseled": people come to the Sibyl for *consulta,* the "decrees" of the gods (cf. *Aen.* 6.151 *dum consulta petis*), but depart without them. Elsewhere *inconsultus* is "ill-advised" in the sense of "foolish." **odere:** = *oderunt.*

453. **hic tibi…:** completed by *quin* clause (in 456) instead of by *ut non*, as would be usual in a result clause. **ne…fuerint:** jussive subjunctive, perfect tense in a prohibition. In sum, "let no costs (consisting of delay, although your men object…., be (*fuerint*) of such importance (*tanti*) that you not (*quin*) approach the prophetess …and not ask…" **morae…dispendia**: lit. "the expenditure of delay," "the loss consisting of delay." **tanti:** genitive of value, "of such importance," or "worth," introducing a result clause. The expression of this thought is particularly laborious.

454–5. **increpitent…vocet, possis:** concessive subjunctives after *quamvis.* **sinus:** of the sails. **secundos:** epithet transferred (from implied "winds") to the sails that the wind blows. "The voyage invites the sails into the deep" (Conington).

quin adeas vatem precibusque oracula poscas,
ipsa canat vocemque volens atque ora resolvat.
illa tibi Italiae populos venturaque bella
et quo quemque modo fugiasque ferasque laborem
expediet, cursusque dabit venerata secundos.   460
haec sunt quae nostra liceat te voce moneri.
vade age et ingentem factis fer ad aethera Troiam.'
Quae postquam vates sic ore effatus amico est,

456. **quin:** *quin* is the archaic ablative *qui* + *ne* (lit. "by which not"); it follows negative verbs of preventing or refusing and takes a subjunctive verb (here, *adeas...poscas*); thus it would be regular after *nihil impediat* ("let nothing hinder"). Here, the *ne...tanti* construction = *nihil impediat*. AG §558, 559. For translation see 453 n.

457. **ipsa canat:** "that with her own lips she utter her oracles," i.e., Aeneas is to ask that she speak her answer to him, not entrust it to leaves; at 6.74 Aeneas makes the prescribed request. **canat...resolvat**: subjunctives in indirect command after *poscas*, in parataxis*. **volens:** "graciously," a word customary in prayers, cf. Hor. *Carm.* 3.30.16 *lauro cinge volens, Melpomene, comam;* Livy 7.26 *precatus...volens propitius adesset.* Note alliteration* of *v* sounds.

459. **fugiasque ferasque…:** (alliterating) subjunctives in indirect question after *expediet* (460). **que...que:** construe disjunctively, i.e., "flee" or "endure," cf. 6.892. On doubled-*que*, see 72 n. Note marked alliteration* of *qu*'s.

460. **cursus...secundos:** a familiar metrical pattern, ending the verse on a positive note. **venerata:** deponent participle, here passive in meaning (cf. 125, 475); it modifies the Sibyl, *illa* in 458.

461. **haec sunt quae…liceat:** *liceat* is subjunctive in relative clause of characteristic, "these are things of the sort about which it is permitted that I may warn you."

462. **ingentem…:** proleptic*: "by your deeds raise great (*ingentem*) Troy to the heavens" for "…raise Troy which will be great…" *Ingens*, here meaning "great," "powerful," "glorious," contrasts with the *parva Troia* (349) of Aeneas' description of Buthrotum. The pattern of *ingentem…Troiam* replicates that in 460, but with the adjective preceding the noun, thereby concluding the entire prophecy with "Troy." This is the only allusion in Helenus' speech to the future empire.

463–505. *Helenus and Andromache give farewell gifts to the Trojans. Aeneas contrasts their quietude with his continuing search for "the fields of Italy ever receding." He prays that their cities may one day be one Troy in spirit.*

The farewell scene of the Buthrotum episode is tense with things unsaid: despite Anchises' expressed impatience to depart (472-3), Helenus talks at some length, as he is aware (480-1), repeating instructions already given to Aeneas. Helenus hails Anchises as lucky in the *pietas* of his son (480). (Helenus and Andromache have no children.) Andromache, in the opening scene, mourned her dead husband; in this closing she mourns her dead son, whom she sees reflected in Aeneas' son Ascanius. Her words imply that she will never meet Ascanius or Aeneas again. Aeneas, however, looks to the future in his prayer for their two cities, exhorting Helenus and Andromache to live "fortunate," since they have achieved "quietude," to which he contrasts his own fate of continued seeking and striving (494-7).

463. **Quae:** connective relative equivalent to *et ea*.

dona dehinc auro gravia sectoque elephanto
imperat ad navis ferri, stipatque carinis   465
ingens argentum Dodonaeosque lebetas,
loricam consertam hamis auroque trilicem,
et conum insignis galeae cristasque comantis,
arma Neoptolemi. sunt et sua dona parenti.
addit equos, additque duces,   470
remigium supplet, socios simul instruit armis.
Interea classem velis aptare iubebat
Anchises, fieret vento mora ne qua ferenti.
quem Phoebi interpres multo compellat honore:

---

464. **auro gravia ac secto elephanto:** "heavy with gold and sawn ivory" may refer to plates
of ivory, used for inlaying (as in Hom. *Od.* 18.196, 19.564). **gravia:** the manuscript reading
gravia sectoque elephanto, which requires lengthening of final *a* of the neuter plural, has no
parallel in Vergil. The emendation *gravia ac secto elephanto* is accepted by Williams and
Horsfall, although it entails unusual hiatus.

465. **ferri:** for infinitive see 134 n.

466. **ingens argentum:** "huge (amount of) silver." **Dodonaeos:** i.e., like those hung from the
oaks at Dodona; see 117 n. on such adjectival forms. Priests struck these hanging kettles
and then interpreted the sounds. In mentioning Dodona, Vergil alludes to Dion. Hal.'s
version of the Aeneas legend, in which he does visit the famous oracle.

467. **loricam…:** "a breast-plate sewn together with links and triple-meshed with gold," i.e.,
chainmail (Horsfall). The first part of the phrase describes the *lorica* as a piece of chain-
armor; the second, the material of which it was made and the closeness of the pattern.

469. **sunt et sua dona parenti:** unusually, *sua* here is not reflexive, but means "for him,"
"suiting him." Thus "there are, too, his own special gifts for my father," i.e., not military
equipment.

470. **equos:** Buthrotum was in Epirus (cf. 503), a region celebrated for horses, cf. *Geo.* 1.59.
duces: "guides," "pilots," not typical parting gifts.

471. **remigium:** = *remiges,* cf. 296. **supplet:** to replace the men Aeneas had lost or left in
Crete (190).

473. **fieret…:** imperfect subjunctive in a negative purpose clause, "in order that there not
be a delay to the favorable wind." Note the postposition of *ne*; see 25 n. **vento:** dative of
reference. **ferenti:** lit. "bearing," the accusative *navis* being implicit, cf. 4.430 *ventosque
ferentis.*

474. **quem:** connective relative, equivalent to *et eum.*

‘coniugio, Anchisa, Veneris dignate superbo, 475
cura deum, bis Pergameis erepte ruinis,
ecce tibi Ausoniae tellus: hanc arripe velis.
et tamen hanc pelago praeterlabare necesse est:
Ausoniae pars illa procul quam pandit Apollo.
vade,’ ait ‘o felix nati pietate. quid ultra 480
provehor et fando surgentis demoror Austros?’
nec minus Andromache digressu maesta supremo
fert picturatas auri subtegmine vestis

475-6. **coniugio**: ablative after *dignate*. **Anchisa**: the Greek vocative form ends with an *eta* (long e). In 6.126 there is the same variation between *Anchisiade* and *Anchisiada*. **dignate**: vocative of perfect participle of a deponent with passive meaning (similarly *venerata*, cf. 460 n.). Servius *ad loc.* notes the more often active sense of *dignor*, as in *Aen.* 1.335. **deum**: genitive plural. **bis…**: Anchises had been saved both when Troy was destroyed by the Greeks, and also when it was sacked by Hercules, who had been defrauded by Laomedon, cf. 2.642-3. **Pergameis…ruinis**: with no main caesura*; see 117 n. A notably full address to someone hurrying to depart.

477. **tibi**: ethical dative; Helenus points towards the eastern shore of Italy and bids him "seize it with his sails": then, however, he explains that after all (*tamen*) the nearer shore (*hanc*) is to be avoided, for it is the distant western coast (*pars illa*) that is promised. **Ausoniae**: appositional genitive, see 293 n.

478. **praeterlabare**: second singular subjunctive of *praeterlabor* (= *praeterlabaris*) in a substantive result clause, functioning as the subject of *necesse est*. Cf. AG §568, 569.

479. **pars illa procul**: supply *est*.

480-1. **quid ultra…Austros?**: "why do I proceed further and, with talking, delay the rising breeze?" **fando**: gerund from *for, fari*. Helenus acknowledges delicately the length and repetitiousness of his prescriptions.

482. **nec minus Andromache**: Andromache shows "no less" (purpose or generosity) in the giving of gifts to Ascanius (see on 484 n.), i.e., than Helenus showed to Anchises. **digressu maesta supremo**: "mournful at the last parting." Both Andromache's speeches are filled with grieving, the first for her husband and the second for her son.

483. **picturatas…**: "figured with embroidery of gold." **subtegmine**: the gold thread "woven" or "worked into" the cloth.

et Phrygiam Ascanio chlamydem (nec cedit honore)
textilibusque onerat donis, ac talia fatur   485
'accipe et haec, manuum tibi quae monimenta mearum
sint, puer, et longum Andromachae testentur amorem,
coniugis Hectoreae. cape dona extrema tuorum,

---

484. **Phrygiam…chlamydem**: *chlamys* denotes a cloak pinned at the shoulder.
Conventionally worn by men, it had military and political associations. (Bender (2001)
150 suggests that when Dido wears a *chlamys* (4.137), it may be transgressive.) *Phrygian*
(=Trojan) may suggest only that the chlamys was purple. As Bender points out (151 n. 15)
Phrygio and *purpureo* appear interchangeable at 3.405 and 545. However, this *chlamys* is a
valuable gift made by Andromache and to be remembered. Therefore it would likely have
included bright colors, an ornate design, a border, gold trim or other ornamentation, as
detailed in other passages where a *chlamys* is given as a gift (5.250–7, 8.167). In *Aen.* 4.216-
17 Iarbas will insult Aeneas' Trojan dress. The future Romans will, of course, wear the toga
(*Aen.* 1.282), which will distinguish them from their Eastern neighbors. (Roman women
of the Republic and Early Empire wore outer garments (*stolae*) that were often dyed, but
not richly decorated and patterned (Symons (1987) 23)). **nec cedit honore:** probably "nor
does she (Andromache) yield (to Helenus) in honor," i.e., in the gifts which she bestows
on Ascanius. Grimm (1967) suggests that Andromache, as she speaks, puts the clothes on
Ascanius.

486. **monimenta:** in speaking of memorials and *dona extrema* (488 "last gifts"), Andromache
implies permanent parting. Note postposition of *quae*; see 25 n. and 114 for postponed
qua.

487. **sint…testentur:** subjunctives in a relative clause of purpose— "that they may be (*sint*)
to you memorials (*monimenta*) of my hands (*manuum…mearum*) and bear witness to the
enduring (*longum*) love of Andromache…." *longum* agrees strictly with *amorem*, but applies
also to *testentur*: the gifts are to bear enduring witness of an enduring love. The elision* of
longum draws out the meaning of *longum*. Andromache's reference to herself by name lends
pathos* to her speech.

488. **coniugis Hectoreae:** "the Hectorean spouse"; see 117 n. In identifying herself as the
wife of Hector (and in the presence of Helenus), Andromache echoes her earlier tending
of Hector's empty tomb (*Hectoreum…tumulum…inanem* 304) and her felt moral and
emotional status as an *univira*. In her own eyes Hector and Astyanax predominate: she
is still the wife of Hector, just as the dead Astyanax lives reflected in Ascanius. **dona
extrema:** "last" or "parting gifts" recall her offerings at Hector's empty tomb (*tristia dona*
301), as described by Aeneas at the opening of the Buthrotum episode.

o mihi sola mei super Astyanactis imago.
sic oculos, sic ille manus, sic ora ferebat; 490
et nunc aequali tecum pubesceret aevo.'
hos ego digrediens lacrimis adfabar obortis:
'vivite felices, quibus est fortuna peracta
iam sua: nos alia ex aliis in fata vocamur.
vobis parta quies: nullum maris aequor arandum, 495

489. **sola…super:** = *quae sola super es.* "O sole surviving image to me of my Astyanax."
Astyanax, the son of Andromache and Hector, is thrown from the walls of Troy by the
Greeks, as Andromache anticipates at Hom. *Il.* 24.734-6. (This murder is a subject of
Euripides' *Troades.*) Astyanax's death prefigures the deaths of other young men in the
poem, e.g., Nisus and Euryalus, Pallas, Lausus, Turnus, Marcellus.

Does Ascanius look like Astyanax? Such would be the case only if he looked like
his uncle Hector, not, e.g., like his own father Aeneas. (See Hexter (1999).) By contrast,
as Bettini observes, Dido sees in Ascanius an image of Aeneas: *illum absens absentem
auditque videtque/ aut gremio Ascanium genitoris imagine capta/ detinet, infandum si fallere
possit amorem* (4.83-5). In fact, Vergil gives no indications of what Aeneas (or Ascanius)
looks like (Griffith (1985) 309-19). See West (1983) 257-67 for comparison of the widows,
Andromache and Dido.

490. **sic oculos…ferebat:** "thus he showed (or "moved") his eyes.…" Cf. Hom. *Od.* 4.148-9
where Menelaus likens Telemachus to Odysseus in his hands, feet, hair, eyes. The tricolon*
abundans* with anaphora* (*sic…sic…sic*) is highly emotional.

491. **et nunc…pubesceret:** imperfect subjunctive in a present contrary to fact condition (with
the implied protasis* "if he were alive"), "and now he would be a youth of like age with
you." **aequali…aevo:** ablative of description.

493. **vivite felices…:** "live fortunate (as being people) whose destiny (lit. to whom their destiny) is
already accomplished." **quibus:** dative of reference. The fortunes of Helenus and Andromache
are settled; Aeneas and his followers are still "summoned from one destiny to another."

494. **iam sua:** note the diaeresis*, followed by asyndeton*(*nos alia ex aliis…*), making the
contrast emphatic. Note that the contrast Aeneas describes is between two states more
or less bad, not between happy and sad (Cova *ad loc*). Despite his (unvoiced) negative
responses to the perceived sterility of this imitation Troy, Aeneas makes a graceful,
affirmative speech in parting. Cf. Most (2001) 162.

494-5. **nos…vobis:** note the emphatic contrast. **vobis:** dative of reference. **parta quies:**
supply *est.* Given the melancholy nature of this *quies* in Buthrotum, readers might
legitimately see Aeneas' seemingly endless searching as preferable. "It is the fate only of
the dead to be finished" (Bettini (1997) 27). Cf. Bright (1981) 45 on *quies* as death (*Aen.*
10.745-6, 12.309-10). **aequor arandum:** gerundive expressing necessity; supply *est.*

arva neque Ausoniae semper cedentia retro
quaerenda. effigiem Xanthi Troiamque videtis
quam vestrae fecere manus, melioribus, opto,
auspiciis, et quae fuerit minus obvia Grais.
si quando Thybrim vicinaque Thybridis arva   500
intraro gentique meae data moenia cernam,
cognatas urbes olim populosque propinquos,
Epiro Hesperia (quibus idem Dardanus auctor
atque idem casus), unam faciemus utramque
Troiam animis: maneat nostros ea cura nepotes.'   505

496–7: **arva… | quaerenda:** that the fields are still "to-be-sought" is emphasized through hyperbaton* and enjambment*; for Aeneas, the fields not only are not getting closer, they seem ever farther away, *semper cedentia retro*. These famous verses are hauntingly expressive of the felt distance of the goal. **effigiem:** "you see an image." "The (Buthrotum) Trojans console themselves for their irreparable loss by contemplating the image of something that no longer exists" (Bettini (1997) 26-7).

498–9. **fecere:** alternative form of *fecerunt*. **melioribus…/auspiciis:** ablative of attendant circumstance "under better auspices…I pray (*opto*), and which will be (*quae fuerit*) less in the way of the Greeks," i.e., than Troy. **fuerit:** perfect subjunctive in a wish, after *opto*.

500–5. Very lit: "If ever I will have entered into (*intraro*, syncopated* future perfect) …and will see (*cernam*) the walls…then (*olim*)…we will make (*faciemus*) our kindred (*cognatas*) cities, our neighboring peoples (*populos propinquos*), in Epirus and in Hesperia, (cities/peoples) to whom (*quibus*) there is the same Dardanus (*idem Dardanus*) (as) founder (*auctor*) and the same misfortune (*casus*), each (one) one Troy in spirit (*animis*). May this care (i.e., the care to effect this) remain for our descendants."

500. **Thybrim…Thybridis:** polyptoton* of place name; cf. Creusa 2.781-2.

502. **cognatas…:** here begins the apodosis* of the condition whose protasis* comes in 500-1. *Cognatas urbes* and *populos propinquos* are governed by *faciemus* (504) and repeated in *utramque*, standing for *utrosque*, which is assimilated to the case of *Troiam*.

503-4. **quibus…casus:** they are united by both common descent and common disasters. The elision* between *Epiro* and *Hesperia* may exemplify the wished-for future unity.

505. **maneat:** used transitively, i.e., "await," "wait for."

Provehimur pelago vicina Ceraunia iuxta,
unde iter Italiam cursusque brevissimus undis.
sol ruit interea et montes umbrantur opaci.
sternimur optatae gremio telluris ad undam
sortiti remos passimque in litore sicco 510
corpora curamus: fessos sopor inrigat artus.
necdum orbem medium nox Horis acta subibat:
haud segnis strato surgit Palinurus et omnis
explorat ventos atque auribus aëra captat;
sidera cuncta notat tacito labentia caelo, 515

506–24. *The Trojans set sail again, skirting the Ceraunian rocks, and land at sunset. Before midnight, Palinurus, having studied the weather, gives the signal for immediate departure, and at dawn the Trojans sight Italy in the distance.*

The Trojans' landing at Castrum Minervae figures in the traditional Aeneas legend (Dion. Hal. 1.51.3). The transition from East to West has immense symbolic significance, as the Trojans enter a culturally different world, to be marked by the Roman (as opposed to Greek) custom of sacrifice that they there initiate. See 405 n.

506. **Provehimur:** note the passive verb, cf. 1-12 n. **pelago:** "on" or "along the sea," cf. 124 n. **vicina Ceraunia:** they sail northward because it is from the northern part of the Ceraunian mountain range that the distance between Greece and Italy is shortest. **iuxta:** in anastrophe*.

507. **iter Italiam:** the accusative follows the idea of motion contained in *iter*. **brevissimus:** modifies both *iter* and *cursus*, but, as often, agrees strictly only with the nearer noun.

508. **sol ruit:** "set" or "rushed on."

509. **sternimur:** middle, "we cast ourselves down." **ad undam:** "by" or "near the water."

510. **sortiti remos:** "having chosen the oars by lot." It was customary (in poetry at least) to decide by lot which of the crew would row in a particular position in the ship (Horsfall *ad loc.*). In this instance, the crew draw lots on landing in order to prepare for an anticipated sudden departure, as Palinurus indeed commands.

511. **corpora curamus:** "we take care of our bodies," the verb denoting any care of the physical self. **fessos:** again, exhaustion is a motif of the Trojans' wanderings. **inrigat:** "flows into," lit. "waters."

512. **orbem:** night is conceived as making a circuit through the sky, "driven by the hours" (*nox horis acta*), cf. 508. **orbem medium:** = midnight. Note the parataxis* of this and the following clause (513). In this particular instance, its effect of brevity has the special appropriateness of emphasizing the haste with which Palinurus acts.

513. **haud segnis:** "not slothful," i.e., very active (litotes*).

514. **auribus aëra captat:** "takes the air with his ears," i.e., "listens for the breeze," which is likely to change before midnight. Palinurus performs his task expertly. Note verbs framing the verse (*explorat...captat*) and their objects in chiastic* order.

Arcturum pluviasque Hyadas geminosque Triones
armatumque auro circumspicit Oriona.
postquam cuncta videt caelo constare sereno,
dat clarum e puppi signum: nos castra movemus
temptamusque viam et velorum pandimus alas.   520
Iamque rubescebat stellis Aurora fugatis
cum procul obscuros collis humilemque videmus
Italiam. Italiam primus conclamat Achates,

516. **Arcturum pluviasque Hyadas:** Arcturus is a star, and the Hyades, the Triones, and Orion are constellations, Orion being the only one in the southern sky. The Hyades is Gr. "the rainers" or "the raining ones." The Latin epithet *pluvias,* meaning "rainy," is thus an etymological play on the meaning of Hyades. (See 401-2 n. on *parva...Petelia.*) **geminosque Triones:** the twin "plowing oxen" or the Big and Little Bear, *Ursa Major* and *Minor.*

     This verse repeats *Aen.* 1.744 (from Iopas' didactic song in Dido's court), which is an almost precise citation of *Geo.* 2.477-8 (wherein the poet disclaims knowledge of *rerum causas*). In both instances, study of the stars exemplifies the didactic genre, a fundamental assumption of which is that nature's signs and patterns are regular, and that through attentive study of these signs, man can predict such things as, e.g., storms, and thereby respond to his world most advantageously. Neither passage mentions gods nor prescribes prayer, but relies instead on "science." In *Aen.* 3, pervaded as it is by divine presences, Palinurus' reliance on "science" or "technology" may be read as exceptional. Adler (2003) argues that Aeneas ultimately adopts a religious (as opposed to a scientific) understanding of human experience. On Palinurus see Adler (2003) 288-91.

517. **armatum...auro:** "armed with gold" because of the three brilliant stars that form his belt and sword. **circumspicit:** Palinurus "looks all around," i.e., both south (for Orion) and north (for the other constellations; see 516 n.). **Oriona:** Greek accusative form. Here the first three syllables are long, thus creating a spondaic fifth foot that emphasizes the line's Greek character.

518. **cuncta...constare:** "that all is uniform in the clear sky," i.e., there are no signs of disturbance.

519. **clarum...signum:** i.e., by a trumpet blast. **castra movemus:** a military technical term meaning "break camp."

520. **velorum:** the genitive of material describes that of which the wings consist. On pattern of line, see on 514 above. **alas:** the "wings" of the ship are the sails.

521. **rubescebat:** "began to redden," "was reddening," an inceptive (i.e., describing the beginning or process of an action) form not found before Vergil, perhaps a Vergilian coinage; on coinages, see 420 n. On *cum inversum* see 8 n. **stellis...fugatis:** "the stars having been put to flight."

522–4: **humilem...Italiam:** "low-lying" (Servius *ad loc.*), an ironically unimposing first view of the promised land. **Italiam. Italiam...Italiam:** the triple repetition represents

Italiam laeto socii clamore salutant.
tum pater Anchises magnum cratera corona   525
induit implevitque mero, divosque vocavit
stans celsa in puppi:
'di maris et terrae tempestatumque potentes,
ferte viam vento facilem et spirate secundi.'
crebrescunt optatae aurae portusque patescit   530
iam propior, templumque apparet in arce Minervae.
vela legunt socii et proras ad litora torquent.
portus ab Euroo fluctu curvatus in arcum,
obiectae salsa spumant aspergine cautes,

---

the men's celebratory shouting; elision* intensifies the excited effect. **Achates:** although not mentioned in previous versions of Aeneas' story, he is Aeneas' closest companion and frequent escort among the men in the *Aeneid* and the first to sight Italy. **clamore:** ablative of manner.

525–47. After Anchises offers libation, the Trojans come upon a harbor, which has a temple of Minerva on the heights behind it. Aeneas sees four white horses, an omen that Anchises interprets as foretelling war, but also peace. They sacrifice to Minerva and Juno.

525. **cratera:** Greek accusative.

527. **celsa:** because the stern (*puppi*) was raised above the other parts of the deck; the image of the ship's tutelary god was placed in the stern. The phrase *stans celsa in puppi* recurs of Augustus (8.680) at the battle of Actium, as depicted on the shield that Vulcan makes for Aeneas; cf. 10.261 of Aeneas with his troops.

528. **maris...terrae, tempestatum:** objective genitives with *potentes*, alluding to the tripartite division of the world into land, sea, and sky. Anchises makes the public prayer on first sight of Italy, naming all spheres in which there might be gods who should be invoked. On prayer forms, see 85 n.

529. **ferte viam vento facilem et spirate secundi:** note how the effect of smooth sailing is suggested by alliteration* of *v*'s, *f*'s, and *s*'s. **vento:** an ablative of means.

530. **crebrescunt:** unattested before Vergil, cf. 521. Vergil is creating (or using rare forms of) inceptive verbs for this scene. **portusque patescit:** "and a harbor nearer now opens (to our view)"; the harbor is at first concealed (535 n.) by the projecting headlands, but seems to open gradually as the Trojans approach. The harbor, *Portus Veneris*, is at the heel of Italy and close to *Castrum Minervae*.

532. **vela legunt:** a technical phrase, "furl the sails."

533-6. A brief ecphrastic* interlude, introduced by *(est) portus*.... See 13-16 n.

533. **ab Euroo fluctu curvatus:** the harbor "is curved out into a bow shape (*in arcum*) by the East-Wind waves." Supply *est*. *Euroi fluctus* are "East-Wind-driven waves." *Eurous, a, um* is a rare adjective. The alliteration* of *s* in 533-4 may suggest the sea (Williams).

ipse latet: gemino dimittunt bracchia muro   535
turriti scopuli refugitque ab litore templum.
quattuor hic, primum omen, equos in gramine vidi
tondentis campum late, candore nivali.
et pater Anchises 'bellum, o terra hospita, portas:
bello armantur equi, bellum haec armenta minantur.   540
sed tamen idem olim curru succedere sueti
quadripedes et frena iugo concordia ferre:

535. **ipse**: sc. *portus*. **gemino…muro:** ablative of quality "(on either side) tower-like crags extend their arms downward with (i.e., forming) a double wall." **dimittunt:** i.e., towards the sea.

536. **turriti:** "tower-like" or "towering," metaphorical. **refugit:** "flees," "backs away from" the shore, i.e., on a hill at the back of the harbor.

537. **quattuor…:** a chariot drawn by *white* horses was originally an attribute of gods and kings in Greece and Persia. In the Roman context it suggests the four-horse chariot of the triumphing Roman general. While horses used in Roman triumphs were usually dark, there were famous exceptions. Of these, real or alleged, Camillus' (fourth century BCE; cf. Livy 5.49.7 *parens patriae conditorque alter urbis*) stands out, as does Julius Caesar's, after his victory at Thapsus in 46 BCE (see Cassius Dio 43.14.3 and S. Weinstock (1971) 68-71). (See Prop. 4.1.32, Tib. 1.7.8, Ov. *Ars Am.* 1.214 for further instances of white horses.) Servius *ad loc.* says whiteness portends victory. Consequently, although the sight of the horses portends their use in war, Anchises foresees also, ultimately, triumph and peace. (Anchises interprets an omen also at *Aen.* 2.687 and, of course, an oracle at 103-17.) Cf. the horse head omen at *Aen.* 1.444, portending both bellicosity and wealth. Heinze (1993) 248-9 surveys briefly the range of omens and prodigies in the *Aeneid*. **primum omen:** Aeneas sees the first omen sighted in Italy, thus freighted with great (but ambiguous) significance, cf. *Aen.* 1.442.

538. **candore:** ablative of quality.

539-40. **et pater Anchises:** the verb *ait* comes at 543. **portas:** from *portare*, as of a messenger. "You carry a message of war." **bellum…bello…bellum:** emphatic triple repetition, replicating the triple repetition of *Italia* (523), along with assonance* of *armantur* and *armenta*, evoking oracular style. **bello:** dative of purpose.

541. **sed tamen…:** "but yet those same horses at other times are accustomed to submit to the chariot and to bear the harmonious (transferred epithet*) reins with the yoke." **idem:** nom. pl. masc., as scansion shows, with *sueti* and *quadripedes* (542). **curru:** dative after a compound. On infinitive of purpose with *sueti*, see AG §460b.

spes et pacis' ait. tum numina sancta precamur
Palladis armisonae, quae prima accepit ovantis,
et capita ante aras Phrygio velamur amictu,   545
praeceptisque Heleni, dederat quae maxima, rite
Iunoni Argivae iussos adolemus honores.
        Haud mora, continuo perfectis ordine votis
cornua velatarum obvertimus antemnarum

543. **spes (est) et:** "there is hope also of…" Anchises' interpretation of the omen opens with war (*bellum* 539) and ends with peace (*pacis* 543), as Horsfall notes *ad* 543; but these terms are not in perfect balance, as the genitive is the less emphatic case. The ambiguity of the sign, signifying both war and peace, is characteristic of divine signs, particularly as they appear in colonization narratives, cf. 537 n. For Williams (*ad loc.*), however, any ambiguity here is subsumed by the legitimacy of Rome's purpose: "This symbolizes the whole concept of the Roman mission: first war against the proud, then civilization for the subdued peoples." Contrast O'Hara (1990) 59.

544. **armisonae:** epic-type compound adjective, unattested before Vergil, cf. 75, 221, 553; the epithet evokes Minerva in her battle function. **ovantis:** sc. *nos*.

545. **capita…velamur:** middle, "we are veiled as to (i.e., we veil) our heads," accusative of respect with a body part.

546. **praeceptisque…:** ablative of cause in a "loose relationship to the sentence" (Williams *ad loc.*). Translate "and according to the prescriptions of Helenus, which (*quae*, i.e., *praecepta*) he had given as the most important (*maxima*)"; see 435-40.

547. **Iunoni Argivae:** recalls Juno in her manifestation as patron goddess of the Greeks at Troy, cf. *Aen.* 1.24. The unresolved hostility of Juno remains problematic for the Romans for centuries (see Feeney (1984)). **adolemus honores:** "we light up sacrifices."

548–87. *The Trojans sail past cities of southern Italy. Avoiding Scylla and Charybdis, they find safe harbor in Sicily at sunset. Nevertheless, terrifying sounds emanate from Mt. Etna, under which the giant Enceladus, rebel against Zeus, writhes in pain.*

The Trojans heed Helenus' full warning to avoid Scylla and Charybdis. Nevertheless, they encounter other expressions of the monstrous at the entrance to their new world. Mt. Etna is a terrifying force of nature, of the sort that, as Circe had pointed out to Odysseus, cannot be defeated by force of arms, but must be yielded to. In Vergil's version the rebel giant Enceladus, punished by Zeus' thunderbolt, lies buried, moaning and straining, under the volcano. Consequently Etna's eruptions may be read as reminders of hubris and divine punishment. Both natural and moral hazards menace the Trojans as they embark on their Italian mission. See Hardie (1986) 264 on the personification* (*viscera* 575, *eructans* 576, *gemitu* 577) of the "moralized volcano." See Nelis (2001) 45-8 for the relationship with Apollonius' *Argonautica*.

548. **Haud mora:** supply *est*. The parataxis* emphasizes the speed of the event.

549. **cornua…:** supply *vento* after *obvertimus* "we turn (into the wind) the tips ("horns") of the sail-bearing (*velatarum*) yards." To change direction, the men re-adjust the position of the yards (*antemnarum*) and reset the sails. The heavy spondaic line suggests the strain of the maneuver.

Graiugenūmque domos suspectaque linquimus arva.   550
hinc sinus Herculei (si vera est fama) Tarenti
cernitur, attollit se diva Lacinia contra,
Caulonisque arces et navifragum Scylaceum.
tum procul e fluctu Trinacria cernitur Aetna,
et gemitum ingentem pelagi pulsataque saxa   555
audimus longe fractasque ad litora voces,
exsultantque vada atque aestū miscentur harenae.
et pater Anchises 'nimirum hic illa Charybdis:
hos Helenus scopulos, haec saxa horrenda canebat.
eripite, o socii, pariterque insurgite remis.'   560

550. **Graiugenum**: epic compound, archaic genitive plural of *Graiugena, ae*.

551. **Herculei…**: "of Herculean (i.e., built by Hercules) Tarentum, if the story is true." There are many local legends and names connected with Hercules in southern Italy; Tarentum itself founded a colony named Heraclea in Lucania. On the adjective, see 117 n.

552. **diva Lacinia:** referring to the famous temple of *Iuno Lacinia* on Lacinium, a promontory on the Tarentine gulf, remains of which still exist; the promontory itself is called *Capo delle Colonne*.

553. **Caulonis:** dative of possession, governed by *arces*, "citadels of Caulon." **arces… Scylaceum:** compound subject; supply *se attollunt*. **navifragum**: an epic compound, "ship-breaking." **Scylaceum**: the name, which recalls and portends the monster *Scylla* (see Paschalis (1977) 147), scans as four syllables. As is characteristic of polysyllabic verse endings, it is a Greek noun (see Williams (1962) 328 n.).

554. **e fluctu:** "(rising) from the waves." The Trojans could not have seen Etna before seeing the straits of Messina; the Sicily episode, as we may infer also from its mythical monsters, does not aim at realism.

555. **gemitum:** the personification* here suggests the presence of spirits in nature, cf. *voces* (556). **pulsata**: by waves. Note the repetition of *s*-sounds in this and the following two lines.

556. **fractasque ad litora voces:** the waves "speak" (cf. *vox*) when breaking towards (*ad*) the shore.

557. **exsultantque…:** "the shallows leap up and the sands are swirled in the waves." Note elisions.

558. **et pater Anchises:** cf. 99 n. **nimirum…:** lit. "no wonder," "surely." **haec illa:** that (previously cited) Charybdis, i.e., of which Helenus warned us, see 420-3. On *hunc illum*, especially as used by an oracle or prophet, see Horsfall *ad* 3.558; 6.27; 7.128, 255, 272.

559. **canebat:** subject is *Helenus*; objects are both *scopulos* and *saxa*.

560. **eripite:** supply *vos* (lit. "snatch yourselves out (of danger)" or *nos* (Servius) or *navem* (Horsfall).

haud minus ac iussi faciunt, primusque rudentem
contorsit laevas proram Palinurus ad undas;
laevam cuncta cohors remis ventisque petivit.
tollimur in caelum curvato gurgite, et idem
subducta ad manis imos desedimus unda. 565
ter scopuli clamorem inter cava saxa dedere,
ter spumam elisam et rorantia vidimus astra.
interea fessos ventus cum sole reliquit,
ignarique viae Cyclopum adlabimur oris.
Portus ab accessu ventorum immotus et ingens 570

---

561. **haud minus ac…:** "no less than," "not otherwise than," cf. 236 n. **rudentem:** expresses
the "roar" of waves around the prow as Palinurus wrenches the boat to the left.

562. **laevas…laevam (563):** emphatic repetition, echoing Helenus' command (412). **laevam:**
leftwards.

563. **remis ventisque:** "with oars and sails"; also a regular phrase for "using every effort." Cf.
Cic. *Tusc.* 3.11. *res…omni contentione, velis, ut ita dicam, remisque fugienda.*

564–5. **tollimur…:** "we are lifted to the sky on the arcing sea (*curvato gurgite*) and then,
with the wave drawn down (*subducta…unda*), we are sunk to the deepest Shades." **idem:**
nom. pl., understand *nos.* **subducta…unda:** ablative absolute expressing cause. **ad Manis
imos:** i.e., to the deepest depths. **desedimus:** the "instantaneous perfect" (from *desidere*),
unexpected after the present *tollimur*; dramatizes the event through the contrast of tenses;
cf. 448.

566–7. **ter…ter:** anaphora*, emphatic, cf. 421 n. **clamorem:** further personification*; see 555
n. **dedere** = *dederunt.* **elisam:** "dashed upward"; *e* or *ex* may have the force of "upwards"
in compounds, cf. 557 *exsultant*, 576 *erigit eructans*, 577 *exaestuat.* **rorantia vidimus
astra:** "we saw the stars dripping" (i.e., with sea water, not with dew as *rorantia* ordinarily
connotes), another hyperbolic phrase.

568. **fessos:** a motif*; supply *nos.* **cum sole:** "the wind left (us) with the sun," i.e., at sunset. A
change of wind often occurs at sunrise or sunset.

569. **ignarique viae:** the phrase has both literal (unknowingly the Trojans have landed among
the Cyclopes) and philosophical or ethical significance, cf. *Geo.* 1.41 and 548-87 n. The
Trojans are entering a world animated by *monstra* (Scylla, Charybis, Etna, Polyphemus)
and moral challenge. **oris:** dative after compound.

570. **Portus…ingens:** a brief ecphrasis* of a harbor, largely generic; cf. harbor ecphrases
at Hom. *Od.* 10.87-91, *Aen.* 1.160-9, Ov. *Met.* 11.229-36. See also 333-6 and 13-16 n.
ab accessu: cf. 533 n. **immotus:** "unmoved by," i.e., "protected from the approach of the
winds." Note the ablative of impersonal agent with *ab*.

ipse: sed horrificis iuxta tonat Aetna ruinis,
interdumque atram prorumpit ad aethera nubem
turbine fumantem piceo et candente favilla,
attollitque globos flammarum et sidera lambit,
interdum scopulos avulsaque viscera montis   575
erigit eructans, liquefactaque saxa sub auras
cum gemitu glomerat fundoque exaestuat imo.
fama est Enceladi semustum fulmine corpus

571. **ipse:** emphatic, the harbor is "calm and large" and therefore a good harbor *in itself;* but (*sed*) this virtue is diminished or negated by the proximity of the volcano. This hyperbolic description of Mt. Etna is of a piece with those of other monstrous presences (Charybdis, Mt. Etna, and Polyphemus) in Book 3. All embody awesome, destructive forces that challenge courage and moral judgment; see notes on 548-87 and 578. Horsfall *ad* 570-87 lists possible sources of this description, including Plin. *Nat. Hist.* 2.234, 3.88 and Pind. *Pyth.* 1.15-28. See Hardie (1986) 263-5. **ruinis:** in senses of "downfall," "eruption" and also "destruction."

572. **atram...nubem:** cognate accusative* with *prorumpit:* "it explodes a black cloud to the sky." **aethera:** Greek accusative.

573. **turbine...piceo:** smoking "with pitchy spirals" and "whitening ash" (*candente favilla*). The chiastic* order, in this case of nouns and adjectives (AabB), corresponds to the intertwined colors described.

574. **sidera lambit:** "licks the stars," i.e., with its exploding tongues of fire. *Lambere* expresses the movement of fire as it begins to play around an object, cf. 2.683.

575. **scopulos avulsaque viscera montis:** "rocks and ripped away innards of the mountain," a kind of hendiadys* as the rocks *are* the innards of the mountain.

576. **erigit eructans:** observe the alliteration* and assonance*. **liquefactaque saxa:** "liquefied rocks," a striking phrase. *Eructans* occurs of the Cyclops as well (632), implicitly equating the two monstrous beings.

577. **cum gemitu glomerat:** "rolls with a roar." **fundo:** ablative of separation.

578. **fama est:** = *dicunt*, introduces an accusative and infinitive of indirect statement. **Enceladi:** Enceladus is one of the giants who strove to overthrow the gods in the myth of the Gigantomachy, i.e., the cosmic battle between the Gods (representing order) and the Giants (representing disorder). Hardie (1986), e.g., 259-67, tracing allusions to the Gigantomachy on the cosmic, political, and personal levels throughout the *Aeneid*, interprets the monstrous Charybdis, Etna, and Polyphemus as manifestations of the gigantomachic forces of disorder. These monsters, as he argues, have human counterparts (e.g., Mezentius), which it is the task of Aeneas, as "champion of cosmic order," and Rome to contain.

    Pindar (*Pyth.* 1.15-20) identifies the giant under Mt. Etna as Typhoeus. Scholars derive Enceladus from Gr. *en-kelados* ("within-noise" or "din") which could explain Vergil's choice of this version. See Paschalis (1997) 138.

urgeri mole hac, ingentemque insuper Aetnam
impositam ruptis flammam exspirare caminis,   580
et fessum quotiens mutet latus, intremere omnem
murmure Trinacriam et caelum subtexere fumo.
noctem illam tecti silvis immania monstra
perferimus, nec quae sonitum det causa videmus.
nam neque erant astrorum ignes nec lucidus aethra   585
siderea polus, obscuro sed nubila caelo,
et lunam in nimbo nox intempesta tenebat.

579–80. **ingentemque:** "and that huge Etna piled upon him breathes out flame from its ruptured furnaces." *Aetnam* is subject accusative of *exspirare*; *omnem…Trinacriam* is the subject accusative of *intremere* (581) and *subtexere* (582). The triple *in-* of *ingentem, insuper, inpositam* suggests great weight.

581–2. **mutet latus:** i.e., Enceladus (note the change of subject). *Mutet*, "turns over," is subjunctive in a subordinate clause in indirect statement (see on 578). Tremors and quakes are interpreted as the giant's writhings underground. **intremere omnem:** conflict of ictus* and accent* in the fifth foot perhaps suggests volcanic eruption. Note alliteration* of *m* in this and the following line. **omnem…Trinacriam:** the subject accusative of *intremere* 581, *subtexere* 582. **caelum subtexere fumo:** lit. "and under-weaves (*sub-texere*) the sky with smoke."

583–7. **causa…obscuro…caelo…nox intempesta:** there is no enlightenment (since the "cause" of sounds cannot be seen) nor (moon)light.

583. **inmania monstra:** the "awful portents" are Etna's menacing noises.

584. **causa:** cf. 32 *causas* with n.

585-6. **aethra | siderea:** ablative of cause. *Aethra* is the shining brilliance of the *aether* (Servius *ad loc.*).

587. **intempesta:** generally translated "unseasonble," i.e., "when no man can work." Others take it as meaning *intemperatus* "unmoderated," "profound."

588–612. At dawn a starved, ragged man emerges from the woods begging the Trojans for rescue or death. He is Achaemenides, a member of Odysseus' crew, inadvertently left behind on the Cyclops' island.

    The Achaemenides episode is a sequel to (or "correction" of [see Thomas 1986]) the *Odyssey*'s longest and most famous episode (9.105-566), wherein Odysseus narrates his ingenious escape from the Cyclops' cave and his costly boasting afterwards—

      "Cyclops, if any mortal man ever asks you who it was
      That inflicted upon your eye this shameful blinding,
      Tell him that you were blinded by Odysseus, sacker of cities" (9.502-4)—

that escalated his troubles. As noted in the Introduction, the meaning of Vergil's allusions to Homer inheres in their *differences* from Homer. In the Achaemenides episode Vergil creates a narrator who gives an account of events that diverges from Odysseus'/ Ulysses' own; i.e., a narrator who rivals and "corrects" Odysseus, as, in much the same way, the *Aeneid* and Vergil himself may be seen to rival and "correct" the *Odyssey* and Homer. Achaemenides retells Ulysses' account in such a way as to reveal that hero in a new—and lesser--light. While Ulysses' own narrative dazzles with his brilliant stratagems (the divine wine, the name of Nobody, the blinding of the Cyclops, the escape from the cave under the sheep), Achaemenides' narrative *omits* all these, involves fewer days, fewer men lost, a less dominant role for Ulysses overall, and culminates in his inadvertent abandonment of Achaemenides, one of his crew. Achaemenides' version, therefore, diminishes the magnitude and character of Ulysses' heroism. Assuming this revised perspective, Ulysses' adventures may seem overrated; there is room for a greater hero. Vergil shows Aeneas becoming this greater hero, whose defining virtue is not mere cleverness, but the moral consciousness implicit in *pietas*.

    Further, in preferring death at the Trojans' hands to death by the Cyclopes, Achaemenides emphasizes the monstrousness of these creatures, in the face of which he would prefer any human fate (e.g., 606). Thus the antagonism between Trojans and Greeks that has hitherto pervaded the narrative dissipates in the face of this larger threat to the human condition generally. The Trojans' compassion for Achaemenides and their joint flight from the Cyclopes portray Greek and Trojan as bound by their common humanity in the face of threats to that humanity. Thus, at the end of *Aeneid* 3, as Trojan and Greek together flee the Cyclopes, the Greeks are no longer the problem (as they were in *Aeneid* 2). In granting compassion (clemency) and rescue to Achaemenides, the Trojans demonstrate moral value superior to Ulysses' who left Achaemenides behind. The Achaemenides episode shows Vergil appropriating Homeric tradition to tell a new and Roman story.

    The attitude in this book toward Greeks is multi-dimensional. Vergil pursues three motifs simultaneously: differentiation of the Romans from the Greeks (as in their manner of sacrifice), subtle undermining of the value of the Greek victory at Troy (as with Aeneas' dedication of Abas' shield and allusions to the Greeks' variously disastrous *nostoi* (331-2 n.)), and finally, as here, compassionate solidarity with the (conquered, cf. 6.836-40) Greek world, a policy that, in Vergil's own time, furthers Augustan geopolitical aims.

    All commentators note the similarity between the Sinon episode of *Aeneid* 2 and this episode of *Aeneid* 3: similar wordings are 2.74 vs. 3.608-9; 2.57 vs. 3.590; 2.69 vs. 3.599; 2.75 vs. 3.608; 2.77 vs. 3.599; 2.81 vs. 3.617 (listed by Rammiger (1991) 56-7). Because of these similarities, some commentators assume that Vergil would have eliminated one or

Postera iamque dies primo surgebat Eoo
umentemque Aurora polo dimoverat umbram,
cum subito e silvis macie confecta suprema   590
ignoti nova forma viri miserandaque cultu
procedit supplexque manus ad litora tendit.
respicimus. dira inluvies immissaque barba,
consertum tegimen spinis: at cetera Graius,

the other of these episodes in revision. Others, however, read these two scenes –with the one alluding to the other— as emphatic demonstrations of Trojan/Roman compassion, despite the grievous outcome of Priam's compassion to Sinon in *Aen.* 2. Trojan clemency (first to Sinon at the opening of *Aeneid* 2, then to Achaemenides) forms the frame to Aeneas' self-deprecating narrative. Anchises' compassion to Achaemenides, unlike Priam's to Sinon, has positive results, since Achaemenides' consequent exhortation to flee is timely for the Trojans. Anchises is more fortunate than— or perhaps even superior to—Priam, allowing the inference that the Anchisiadae, not the Priamidae, are, in fact, the best of the Trojans (Khan (1998) 244). Khan's reading of Anchises here as superior to Priam would be consistent with the portrayal of Aeneas as superior to Helenus (see 374-462 n.).

For further discussions, see Lloyd (1957); Römisch (1976); Kinsey (1979); Putnam (1980) 11-14; G. W. Williams (1983); Harrison (1986); Rammiger (1991); Cova (1992); Heinze (1993) 77-85; McKay (1996); H. Akbar Khan (1998); Hexter (1999); Syed (2005) 201-4; Horfall *ad* 588-691.

588. **Eoo:** *Eous, a, um,* adjective here used as a noun, "the Eastern one," i.e., "The following day was rising with the first eastern (or dawn) star…." Note *iamque* in postposition* after *postera.*

589. **umentem…umbram:** "the damp shade (of night)."

590. **cum…procedit** (592): on *cum inversum*, see 8 n.

591. **nova:** "strange," not recognizably a human form. **miseranda:** shows sympathy. **cultu:** ablative of respect.

592. **supplexque manus…tendit:** stretching out the hands in supplication is a natural gesture as well as a formal feature of ritual supplication.

593–5. **respicimus**: asyndetic*, suggesting stopped action; the Trojans froze in place. The absence of a main verb from *dira inluvies* to *missus in armis* further expresses Aeneas' stunned incomprehension at the sight.

593. **respicimus:** the Trojans, on the shore preparing for departure, "look back." **immissaque barba:** "a wild-growing beard." Romans in Vergil's time generally did not have beards.

594. **consertum tegimen spinis:** supply *erat.* **cetera Graius:** lit. "as to other things, a Greek," *cetera* being an accusative of respect. Despite his degraded state, Achaemenides' Greekness is manifest.

et quondam patriis ad Troiam missus in armis.   595
isque ubi Dardanios habitus et Troia vidit
arma procul, paulum aspectu conterritus haesit
continuitque gradum; mox sese ad litora praeceps
cum fletu precibusque tulit: 'per sidera testor,
per superos atque hoc caeli spirabile lumen,   600
tollite me, Teucri; quascumque abducite terras:
hoc sat erit. scio me Danais e classibus unum
et bello Iliacos fateor petiisse penatis.
pro quo, si sceleris tanta est iniuria nostri,
spargite me in fluctus vastoque immergite ponto;   605
si pereo, hominum manibus periisse iuvabit.'

596. **isque:** closely connects what follows with what precedes, "we recognized him as a Greek *and he* quickly recognized us as Trojans." The Trojans are easily identified by their dress (*Dardanios habitus*) and arms (*Troia…arma*); cf. 306-7, 484. Distinctions between Trojan and Greek are clear. Contrast 606 n.

598–9. **sese tulit:** "he rushed."

599–600. **per sidera testor…per superos…:** anaphora* emphasizes earnestness (feigned or otherwise) in oath-making, cf. 2.141-4, 154-61; 4.314; 6.458-9. **testor:** the usual verb for calling witnesses to authenticate an oath (Hickson (1993) 123).

600. **hoc:** demonstrative. **caeli spirabile lumen:** "breathable light of the sky," a striking expression. See, similarly, *Geo.* 2.340 *cum primae lucem pecudes hausere* "when the first animals drank the light."

601. **tollite:** "take me (on board)." Contrast *Aen.* 6.370 *tecum me tolle per undas*, where Aeneas cannot accede to Palinurus' request. **quascumque…terras:** accusative of motion towards.

602. **scio:** only in *scio* and *nescio* does Vergil allow the shortening of the final *o* of a verb, especially in the phrase *nescio quis*. **scio me:** supply *esse*.

603. **bello…fateor petiisse:** *me* is omitted because there is no ambiguity, see 201 n. In confessing (*fateor*) to having fought against the Trojans at Troy, Achaemenides establishes credibility for his subsequent assertions, a type of *deprecatio* (Horsfall), a rhetorical strategy that anticipates and thereby wards off blame or distrust. Dido's *deprecatio* at 4.425-6 makes the opposite point (noted by Servius Dan., cited by Horsfall *ad loc.*).

605. **spargite me in fluctus:** "scatter me (i.e., after having torn me in pieces) on the waves"; cf. 4.600 where Dido declines to inflict this punishment on the Trojans.

606. **si pereo, hominum:** instances of hiatus* after a syllable in thesis* are not common in Vergil. Here, this vocal disruption expresses Achaemenides' emotional stress. **hominum:** is made strongly emphatic by hiatus, and cf. 626-7. Achaemenides bonds with the Trojans as fellow *homines*. The clear distinction between Greeks and Trojans (cf. 593-6 n.) pales in comparison to that between human beings and monsters.

dixerat et genua amplexus genibusque volutans
haerebat. qui sit fari, quo sanguine cretus,
hortamur, quae deinde agitet fortuna fateri.
ipse pater dextram Anchises haud multa moratus 610
dat iuveni atque animum praesenti pignore firmat.
ille haec deposita tandem formidine fatur:

607. **genibusque volutans:** "groveling at our knees," *genibus* is ablative of place. Supplication scenes are a convention of epic, Priam's supplication of Achilles for Hector's body being the most important of these. (See Rammiger (1991) 64-8 for examples). Procedurally, a supplicant clasps the knees of the person whose aid he seeks (Macleod (1982) *ad* 477-8.) Although supplications are often rejected (e.g. Hom. *Il.* 21.34-135), religious obligation does fall on the supplicated person to grant the request of a suppliant in this position. "Supplication also has a moral dimension, for it provides the one supplicated with an occasion for insight into the contours of mortal life—its vulnerability to circumstance and the seriousness of the claim another's suffering has to one's attention" (Crotty (1994) xi). Anchises therefore demonstrates his religious correctness (*pietas* broadly conceived) in granting mercy to the suppliant. For Roman readers this scene would evoke also the emperor's gesture of granting of clemency, the "primal Roman civilizing act" (Putnam (1980) 13), since Achaemenides rushes towards the Trojans with outstretched hands (592), a gesture that "in Roman art…usually indicated the subjection of defeated barbarians" (Rammiger 71 and 71 n. 59). See Khan (1998) 241 and Römisch (1976) esp. 210 f. Note that the granting of clemency, despite its surface humanity, serves to affirm power over the recipients. "The grace granted to the enemy is the symbol of [Roman] triumph over the Greek world" (Worstbrock (1963) 75 cited by Cova (1994) lxii).

608–9. **qui sit fari...quae fortuna..fateri:** the somewhat disjointed Latin imitates the Trojans' terse, urgent questioning—"Who are you? Say! Of what race? What ill-fortune…? Speak!" **qui...quo...quae:** a tricolon*. **sit...agitet:** subjunctives in indirect question. **deinde:** goes with *hortamur* (understood), "we first press him to say *who* he is…then to confess what ill-fortune…"; on *fateri* see 134 n.

610. **haud multa:** by litotes* means "very little." **multa:** cognate accusative* used adverbially. Anchises' grace or clemency to Achaemenides recalls Priam's to Sinon, both Greeks and followers of Ulysses. (See 613-54 n.) Thus, instances of Trojan clemency essentially frame Aeneas' narrative. Anchises appears to have better judgment about his suppliants than Priam.

611. **praesenti pignore:** the (alliterating) "present pledge" is the proffered hand.

'sum patria ex Ithaca, comes infelicis Vlixi,
nomine Achaemenides, Troiam genitore Adamasto
paupere (mansissetque utinam fortuna!) profectus.　　615
hic me, dum trepidi crudelia limina linquunt,
immemores socii vasto Cyclopis in antro

613–54. Achaemenides tells of joining Ulysses in the expedition against Troy and being accidentally left behind on the return voyage, when Ulysses and his other (uneaten) men escape from the Cyclops' cave. He entrusts himself to the Trojans and warns them to flee.

613. infelicis: sympathy would seem to inhere in this surprising epithet for Ulysses (reprised by Aeneas in 691), so that *durus Vlixes* (2.7) has become *infelix Vlixes*. For Cova (1994) lix-lxvii and some other recent scholars (e.g., Kinsey, Khan, Horsfall) Aeneas' use of this epithet suggests that he now experiences generous sympathy for all those who suffer loss, even enemies. This sympathy on his part would be consonant with the Trojans' compassion to suppliants and with the overall focus on humanity and reconciliation that closes this book. There are, however, other interpretive possibilities: Servius Dan. *ad loc.* took the epithet ironically, as an insult (*vituperatione*) that would, for example, undermine Odysseus' defining epithet in the *Odyssey*, Gr. *polutropos*, "resourceful." For G. W. Williams (1983) 262-78 the sympathy implicit for Ulysses here as well for the Cyclops (below) is deeply inappropriate in the mouth of Aeneas, although perfectly suited to the epic narrator. He therefore infers that the first-person narrative of *Aeneid* 3, as we have it, is an (imperfect) revision of an original third person narrative, wherein Vergil, as narrator, told the story.

614. nomine: ablative of respect. **Achaemenides**: this name and this character are unattested elsewhere, and are, therefore, likely Vergil's innovations. To be clear: this character occurs neither in the *Odyssey* nor in the Aeneas tradition. Greek elements in the name, *Achaios* = "Greek" and *meno* = "remain behind," suggest the meaning of "the left-behind Greek" (O'Hara (1996) 147). On the other hand, the name *Achaemenes* is characteristically Persian (see, e.g., Heinze (1993) 93 n. 43). Kinsey (1979) 112 suggests that "Achaemenides represents the world, and in particular the Greek world, in the [sc. subordinate] relationship it is to have to a Rome playing the role Anchises assigns to it in 6.847-53." See also Khan (1998) 259-63. **Troiam:** accusative of motion towards. **genitore...paupere**: ablative absolute.

615. mansisset: pluperfect subjunctive expressing a wish unfulfilled in past time, thus an intensely emotional interjection: "would that it had…," "if only it had…" **utinam:** in postposition*.

616. dum: regularly takes the present indicative even when referring to past time. **trepidi:** with *socii* in 617. **limina:** note the *omission* of Ulysses' stratagem of escaping the cave by clinging unnoticed to the underside of the sheep.

617. immemores: "unremembering" or "unmindful" (i.e., of Achaemenides). In Hom. *Od.* 9.105-541, the Cyclopes are one-eyed giants, and Polyphemus eats men (raw), although he is a shepherd.

deseruere, domus sanie dapibusque cruentis,
intus opaca, ingens. ipse arduus, altaque pulsat
sidera (di talem terris avertite pestem!)   620
nec visu facilis nec dictu adfabilis ulli;
visceribus miserorum et sanguine vescitur atro.
vidi egomet duo de numero cum corpora nostro
prensa manu magna medio resupinus in antro
frangeret ad saxum, sanieque aspersa natarent   625
limina; vidi atro cum membra fluentia tabo
manderet et tepidi tremerent sub dentibus artus —
haud impune quidem, nec talia passus Vlixes

618. **deseruere** = *deseruerunt*, emphatically enjambed, thus expressive of Achaemenides'
agitation. **sanie dapibusque cruentis:** ablatives of quality with *domus*. The expression,
asyndetic (see asyndeton*), ragged, lacking a verb, reflects Achaemenides' agitation. Strong
asyndeton* continues in the next line ("gloomy within, vast"), with ellipsis* of *est* or *erat*.

619. **ipse:** the intensive pronoun, commonly used absolutely as "the Master (of a house)." Both
senses are appropriate here: the Cyclops is "master" of his cave as well as "he himself," in
contrast to the house (*domus* 618). "He himself tall, strikes the stars." The rhetoric of this
verse is unusual: mostly adjectives, one verb (the first verb being omitted), followed by an
emotional interjection in 620, as also in 615. **pulsat:** stronger than *tangit*.

621. **nec visu facilis…:** lit. "not easy to look upon or speakable to in speech for anyone"; the
supines *visu* and *dictu* are ablatives of respect. Critics dispute whether this line is clever or
overly clever. **ulli:** dative of reference.

622. **visceribus…sanguine:** ablatives after *vescor*. "He feeds on the insides and black blood of
wretches."

623. **vidi egomet…vidi (626):** strongly emphatic: he is not speaking from hearsay.
duo…: contrast Hom. *Od.* 9.288-9, where the Cyclops three times repeats the act of
making a meal of two men. **cum…frangeret (625):** note *cum* in postposition*; *frangeret*
is subjunctive in a *cum* circumstantial or narrative clause, as are *natarent* (625) and
manderet…tremerent (627).

624. **resupinus:** "reclining," since in his hugeness he does not need even to rise to catch them.
Note alliteration* of *m*'s.

625. **frangeret ad saxum:** "smashed on a stone," with emphatic placement of *frangeret* (after
cum temporal in 623). **aspersa:** "spattered." As the blood spurted out, it spattered over the
threshold, which was then "swimming" (*natarent*) in blood.

626. **fluentia tabo:** "streaming with gore."

627. **tepidi:** "warm," i.e., still warm with life. Note the effective alliteration* of *t* and *d* in
tepidi tremerent sub dentibus artus.

628. **haud impune quidem:** "not unavenged (did he do this)." **passus:** supply *est*.

oblitusve sui est Ithacus discrimine tanto.
nam simul expletus dapibus vinoque sepultus   630
cervicem inflexam posuit, iacuitque per antrum
immensus saniem eructans et frusta cruento
per somnum commixta mero, nos magna precati
numina sortitique vices una undique circum
fundimur, et telo lumen terebramus acuto   635
ingens quod torva solum sub fronte latebat,
Argolici clipei aut Phoebeae lampadis instar,

---

629. **oblitusve…:** i.e., Achaemenides shows genuine admiration; Odysseus' (Ulysses') cleverness and courage (though different from Aeneas' defining virtues) demand respect. **sui:** genitive after *obliviscor*.

630. **simul:** = *simul atque*. Note chiastic* arrangement of adjective and noun pairs: *expletus dapibus: vinoque sepultus*. See 633 n. **expletus:** "gorged." **vino…sepultus:** "buried in (sleep brought on by) wine." –

631. **per:** "through," "throughout," finely suggesting the size of the monster; cf. 624 n.

632. **eructans:** the Cyclops resembles the volcano (576), both monstrous beings.

633. **mero:** Achaemenides makes no mention of Odysseus' brilliant foresight (Hom. *Od.* 9.213-5) in anticipating a need for the special, potent, divine wine (described at length in Odysseus' own narrative in *Od.* 9.205-15) from Maron, son of Euanthes, priest of Apollo. Achaemenides mentions merely *vino* (630)…*mero* (633).

634. **sortiti…vices:** "having cast lots (*sortiti*) for our tasks" (lit. "turns").

634–5. **una:** together. In Hom. *Od.* 9.331-5 Odysseus orders the men to draw lots to see which ones will join him in the blinding. In Achaemenides' account the various first-person plural verbs (*fundimur, terebramus, ulciscimur*) give agency to the men as a group. **circum | fundimur:** middle voice, either of the compound verb *circumfundere* (and therefore an instance of tmesis*) or the simple verb with the adverb *circum*. The sense is the same in either case, "we spread ourselves around." **lumen:** = "eye." **terebramus:** contrast Hom. *Od.* 9.375-95 where Odysseus elaborately describes how *he* sharpens an olive stake, hardens it over the fire, then uses it (with the help of four others) as a carpenter's "auger" to "bore" out the eye.

636. **ingens:** "huge," emphatic spondee*. **latebat:** "was hiding"; it was deep-set in his forehead, concealed by the "grim" (*torva*) and shaggy brow. From Achaemenides' perspective, the eye is deliberately hiding.

637. **Argolici…:** the "Argive shield," devised by the family of Abas, was round, large, and shining (Servius Dan. *ad loc.*)—thus the apt simile. Did Achaemenides chance to see this shield in Troy? (Cf. 278-93 n.) **Phoebeae lampadis:** the sun. **instar:** governs the genitives *clipei, lampadis*, and is in apposition to *lumen*.

et tandem laeti sociorum ulciscimur umbras,
sed fugite, o miseri, fugite atque ab litore funem
rumpite. 640
nam qualis quantusque cavo Polyphemus in antro
lanigeras claudit pecudes atque ubera pressat,
centum alii curva haec habitant ad litora vulgo
infandi Cyclopes et altis montibus errant.
tertia iam Lunae se cornua lumine complent, 645
cum vitam in silvis inter deserta ferarum
lustra domosque traho, vastosque ab rupe Cyclopas
prospicio sonitumque pedum vocemque tremesco.
victum infelicem, bacas lapidosaque corna,
dant rami, et vulsis pascunt radicibus herbae. 650
omnia conlustrans hanc primum ad litora classem

639–40. sed: Achaemenides interrupts his narrative to give urgent warning: *fugite...fugite*, a motif *of Book 3; cf. 44 and 398 n. **funem rumpite:** "break the cable" instead of the usual *solvite* "unloose," because the men are desperately rushing; so at 667 *incidere funem* "to cut the cable." This line is incomplete.

641–3. nam qualis quantusque...: "of what sort and of what size"; lit. "For such (i.e., hideous) and huge as Polyphemus (is, who) pens the cattle...(so hideous and huge are) the hundred other Cyclopes...."

642. lanigeras: compound adjective, archaic; found in Ennius (b. 239 BCE), *Saturae* 66; Lucr. *DRN* 2.318; *Geo.* 3.287.

643. haec habitant ad litora: "live along these shores."

644. Cyclopes: scanned as two longs and a short ultima (Gr. nominative plural as in 269). Opening spondees* convey the massive slowness of the giants. The rhythm of this line, with trochaic caesura* in third foot and no strong caesura* in fourth foot, is characteristically Homeric.

646–7. cum...traho: here *cum* means "during which time." The present tense *traho* indicates that Achaemenides has been and is still dragging out his (miserable) life (cf. 5.627 *septima...iam vertitur aestas cum ferimur*). *Cum* clauses take the indicative when the emphasis is on time specifically, not circumstance (AG §545). **lustra:** animals' dens. **Cyclopas:** here the first syllable is short, unlike in 644, 675. The inconsistency may reflect Achaemenides' agitation.

649. infelicem: "growing wild," "not cultivated." **lapidosa:** either "stone-hard" or "growing on stony ground."

650. dant: sc. *mihi.* **vulsis...radicibus:** ablative of means. **pascunt:** sc. *me.* Lit. "Grasses 'pasture' me with their torn-up roots" (as if Achaemenides were a herd animal).

651. hanc: demonstrative, "this fleet of yours."

Achaemenides > Greek left behind   μένω

victuals

I saw (the fleet) coming | *I vowed myself to this fleet, whatever it will have proved to be*

conspexi venientem. huic me, quaecumque fuisset,

Do you ? to be away

addixi: satis est gentem effugisse nefandam.

my life rather by any death

vos animam hanc potius quocumque absumite leto.'

he himself briefly said / we see at the top of the mountain

Vix ea fatus erat summo cum monte videmus   655

a vast shape moving

ipsum inter pecudes vasta se mole moventem

the shepherd / seeking the well-known shores

pastorem Polyphemum et litora nota petentem,

monstrum horrendum, informe, ingens, cui lumen ademptum.

from whom the light had been withdrawn

(Scylla)

---

652. **huic me…:** *huic* (sc. *classi*) repeats the *hanc* of the preceding clause. *Quaecumque fuisset*
is *quaecumque fuerit* (future perfect) in indirect statement in secondary sequence, the
direct quote being: "to this fleet, whatever it shall prove (lit. shall have proved) to be, I will
surrender myself." In secondary sequence: "I vowed myself to this fleet, whatever it might
have turned out to be." **quaecumque:** "whatever," i.e., whether belonging to friends or foes.

653. **addixi:** as a legal term, it occurs of the magistrate who "assigns" or "surrenders" a debtor
to be the slave of his creditor. **nefandam:** "lawless," "impious."

654. **vos:** emphatic in opposition to *gentem nefandam*, "do *you* rather take away my life by any
death." **animam hanc:** = my life.

655–91. As Achaemenides finishes speaking, Polyphemus, guiding his blind steps with a pine-
trunk, comes to shore to bathe his eye in the sea. Sensing the Trojans' presence, he cries out to
his fellows, who assemble on the shore, towering like trees, as the Trojans flee north with the
wind. Recalling the warnings of Helenus against Scylla and Charybdis, however, the Trojans
begin to reverse course, when the wind opportunely changes, carrying them past sites familiar to
Achaemenides from his prior journeying with Ulysses.

655–7. Note the alliteration* of *m*; elision over the caesura* (657), and rhymed endings in
656-7.

655. **cum…videmus:** on *cum inversum*, see 8 n.

656–7. **ipsum…moventem | pastorem…petentem:** these noun/adjective pairs framing
sequential lines emphasize the hugeness of the monster. **ipsum:** "himself," "in person,"
contrasting the actual sight of him with Achaemenides' description. Vergil's Cyclops
neither speaks nor is spoken to (Khan (1998) 252), although he has a shattering cry (672).

657. **litora nota:** the familiarity lends pathos* (Horsfall). Thomas (1996) 260-3 traces the
portrait, largely sympathetic, of Polyphemus back through Vergil's Corydon in *Ecl.* 2
to Theocritus *Id.* 11 as an example of genre transgression or transformation: Vergil is
integrating a figure from pastoral poetry into epic poetry and thereby transgressing or
transforming the genre of epic. If readers are indeed to recall the Polyphemus of *Ecl.* 2 and
Theoc. *Id.* 11, the finding of pathos* in the Cyclops' fate here would be legitimate.

658. **monstrum…:** a famous, very effective verse. Heaviness and immensity are suggested
by the spondees*, elision* of the first three words, alliteration* of *m*'s, and absence of
connecting particles. **cui:** dative of separation or, surely, disadvantage.

Theocritus

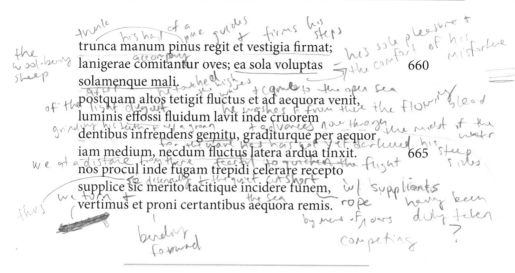

> trunca manum pinus regit et vestigia firmat;
> lanigerae comitantur oves; ea sola voluptas   660
> solamenque mali.
> postquam altos tetigit fluctus et ad aequora venit,
> luminis effossi fluidum lavit inde cruorem
> dentibus infrendens gemitu, graditurque per aequor
> iam medium, necdum fluctus latera ardua tinxit.   665
> nos procul inde fugam trepidi celerare recepto
> supplice sic merito tacitique incidere funem,
> vertimus et proni certantibus aequora remis.

659. **trunca manum pinus…:** new subject, "the trunk of a pine guides his hand and firms his steps"; that a pine-tree serves the blinded Cyclops as a staff suggests his great size. In Hom. *Od.* 9.319-24 the Cyclops has a club as big as "a mast of a cargo-carrying broad black ship of twenty oars." Though Achaemenides' narrative differs significantly from Odysseus', the latter's story of the blinding in *Od.* 9.371-400 is now confirmed.

660–1. **lanigerae:** epic compound adjective, see 642 n. **ea sola voluptas | solamenque mali:** "his sole pleasure and solace of his misfortune." See 613, 657 nn. on the pathos* here. **ea:** antecedent is *oves*; the pronoun is attracted in gender and number to the predicate nominative, *voluptas*.

661. One of the seven incomplete verses in this book.

662. **postquam altos…:** the Cyclops, being so immense, must wade to deep waves and open sea beyond (*aequora*) to bathe his wound: for a man of normal height, shallow water would suffice.

663. **effossi:** "dug out," very graphic. **lavit:** here third conjugation instead of first, as at 6.219, 12.722. Such variation in paradigms is archaic, recalling an earlier stage in the development of the language (Williams *ad loc.*). **inde:** "thence," i.e., with water from the sea.

664-5. **dentibus infrendens gemitu:** "grinding his teeth (and) with a groan"; *dentibus* is ablative of means, *gemitu* ablative of manner, expressing…pain, despair, rage? **graditurque…:** "and advances now through deep sea (*aequor…medium*), (for) the wave has not yet darkened his steep sides"; *medium mare* is regular Latin for deep sea.

666-8. Note the dactyls suggesting speed.

666-7. **celerare:** an historical infinitive, used particularly to convey swift, sharp action; similarly *incidere* (667). **recepto | supplice:** ablative absolute. **merito:** adverb, "deservedly," "rightly" to be taken on board (*recipi*) because, as a suppliant, he deserves mercy (see 607 n. on clemency) or because of his crucial help in warning the Trojans to flee or because the Trojans, understanding "the tears of things" (*lacrimae rerum*, 1.462), are compassionate. **taciti:** cf. 4.289. **incidere:** because of the need for haste.

668. **vertimus et:** postposition of *et*, poetic. **remis:** ablative of means.

sensit, et ad sonitum vocis vestigia torsit.
verum ubi nulla datur dextra adfectare potestas   670
nec potis Ionios fluctus aequare sequendo,
clamorem immensum tollit, quo pontus et omnes
contremuere undae, penitusque exterrita tellus
Italiae curvisque immugiit Aetna cavernis.
at genus e silvis Cyclopum et montibus altis   675
excitum ruit ad portus et litora complent.
cernimus astantis nequiquam lumine torvo
Aetnaeos fratres caelo capita alta ferentis,

669. **sensit...torsit**: subject is *Polyphemus*, these verbs framing the line. **Sensit**: not, of course, *vidit*, lends pathos*; emphatically placed and in asyndeton*. **ad sonitum vocis...torsit**: "turned towards the sound of the voice (of oars moving through the water)," another pathetic detail. For *vocis* cf. 556.

670. **adfectare**: sc. object *nos*. *Adfectare* is used as frequentative of *adficio* ("lay hold of") to express the repeated attempts to seize the ships; complementary to *potestas* as an infinitive follows *possum* or *potis* (e.g., 671).

671. **nec potis...**: an archaic, thus poetic form; "nor is he able, in pursuing, to equal the Ionian waves." The wind (cf. 683) and waves are with the Trojans, carrying them away faster than the Cyclops can follow.

672. **quo**: ablative of cause.

673. **contremuere**: = *contremuerunt*. **penitus...exterrita**: "profoundly terrified."

674. **Italiae**: appositional genitive, "the land of Italy" = "Italy." See 293 n. **curvisque...**: "and Etna roared (*immugiit*) within its winding caverns."

676. **ruit...complent**: *ruit* is singular to agree with *genus*, but, given that the *genus* encompasses many individuals, the plural verb is then used.

677. **nequiquam**: "in vain" because the Trojans have already fled to a safe distance. **lumine torvo...**: ablative of description; each Cyclops has only one eye. The Trojans flee the Cyclopes without incident—a most anticlimactic conclusion by contrast to the dramatic verbal exchange (Odysseus' hubristic boast and the Cyclops' curse) and rock-throwing of its Odyssean model (Hom. *Od.* 9.473-535). The anticlimax is a daring strategy on Vergil's part, as he risks being read simply as boring rather than as polemical. Yet here, as throughout this book, we see Vergil implicitly highlighting Odysseus' triumphs of cleverness and audacity in contrast to Aeneas' purposeful dedication to mission despite failure, exhaustion, and loss. Through ironic allusion to his Homeric model, Vergil allows this fundamental character of the Trojan/Roman achievement to emerge.

678. **Aetnaeos fratres**: either the Cyclopes of Aetna are all related or *frater* here means something like "colleague" or "fellow-inhabitant"; on adjective, see 117 n. **caelo...**: "to the sky," dative of direction; i.e., they are so tall that their heads reach the sky (presumably hyperbolic). **capita alta ferentis**: lit. "bearing their heads high."

concilium horrendum: quales cum vertice celso
aëriae quercus aut coniferae cyparissi 680
constiterunt, silva alta Iovis lucusve Dianae.
praecipitis metus acer agit quocumque rudentis
excutere et ventis intendere vela secundis.

679-81. concilium horrendum: a "fearsome assembly," *concilium* connoting especially an "assembly for consultation," although, ironically, no custom of consultation exists among the Cyclopes, cf. Hom. *Od.* 9.106-15. **quales cum…:** "such as when…airy oaks or cone-bearing cypresses stand, tall forest of Jove or grove of Diana." **vertice celso:** "with their high tops" or "on a high peak" (see Williams *ad loc.*). **coniferae:** an archaizing compound adjective. **constiterunt:** "have stood" and still stand; the gnomic perfect, corresponding to the Greek gnomic aorist (AG §475). The penult is short. *Silva alta Iovis* corresponds with *aëriae quercus*, oaks being sacred to Jupiter, and *lucus Dianae* (in her manifestation as *Hecate*, goddess of the underworld) corresponds to *coniferae cyparissi*, cypresses being especially associated with death.

Judgments of the quality of this simile, the only one in the book, are mixed. While Williams *ad 679 f.* terms it "a fine pictorial simile" with "powerful impact," G. W. Williams (1983) 264 says "the serene poeticism of the simile" does not suit either the fearfulness of the assembled monsters or the perspective of Aeneas. See 613 n. Certainly the simile points to the hugeness of the Cyclopes—as big as the tallest trees. Yet, in speaking of tall trees and gods, it points also to the majestic, rooted, natural, and sacred—certainly a surprising perspective on the Cyclopes for either Aeneas or a hypothetical third-person narrator.

This is the only simile in book 3, and no other book has so few similes. Some scholars argue that this is a proof of the book's significant incompleteness. It is assumed that Vergil would have added similes during his anticipated revisions. And yet, on the other hand, perhaps he would have taken this one out. *Aeneid* 2, Aeneas' first book as narrator, has nine similes, of varying length. The fact that similes did not occur to Vergil's imagination during the composition of this book may mean that similes did not serve his vision here. Odysseus concludes his narrative to the Phaeacians by calling his words a (Gr.) *muthos*, a story, that he has told conspicuously well (Hom. *Od.* 12.450-3). Aeneas, unlike Odysseus in the *Odyssey*, is not characterized as a self-conscious story-teller who delights in poetic devices.

682–3. agit…excutere: "drives (us) to shake out (*excutere*) the sheets (*rudentis*) no matter where, i.e., in any direction (*quocumque*). On this construction with infinitive, see 4-5 n.

contra iussa monent Heleni, Scyllamque Charybdinque
inter, utrimque viam leti discrimine parvo,   685
ni teneam cursus; certum est dare lintea retro.
ecce autem Boreas angusta ab sede Pelori
missus adest: vivo praetervehor ostia saxo

684–6. contra iussa monent…: Both the text and the translation of these famously difficult lines are disputed. The narrative situation is that the Trojans find themselves, in their haste to escape from the Cyclopes, sailing north with the wind towards Scylla and Charybdis. Recalling Helenus' warnings to avoid these, however, they decide to reverse course, when suddenly a wind comes *from* the north and they easily resume their destined journey. I have adopted Horsfall's text (for his full discussion, see his notes on 684-6).

Translate: "but, the orders (*iussa*) of Helenus warn (*monent*) that I not hold the course (*ni teneam cursus*) between Scylla and Charybdis (*Scyllamque Charybdinque | inter*), on both sides (*utrimque*) a way of death (*viam leti*) with little difference" (*discrimine parvo*). This translation assumes *teneam* where Hirtzel's text prints *teneant*, and *utrimque* for *utramque*; *viam* is to be taken in apposition to *cursus* (accusative, object of *teneam*) and *inter* in anastrophe with *Scyllam* and *Charybdin*.

684. contra: here, "but," "on the other hand."

685. inter: in anastrophe* with preceding objects *Scyllam atque Charybdinque*, cf., e.g., *Aen.* 1.218 *spemque metumque inter.* **utrimque:** from both sides. **discrimine parvo:** ablative of quality or description, pertaining to *viam*, the path being one "of little difference of death" between the one and the other.

686. ni: archaic for *ne*; cf. Servius *ad loc.* (*antiqui "ni" pro "ne" ponebant*). **teneam:** subjunctive in indirect command. **certum est:** sc. *nobis* or *mihi*.

687. Boreas: the north wind, cold, wintery, gusty. Cf. 4.442.

688. missus: perfect passive participle, modifying Boreas. The sender of the wind is not specified. **vivo…ostia saxo | Pantagiae (689):** "the mouth of the Pantagias (river) (formed) of living rock"; the mouth of the river formed a natural harbor. *vivo* means "living," i.e., "natural," "uncut," with *saxo*, ablative of description. **praetervehor:** of travel, "drive," "ride," or, as here, "sail by." The Trojans thus simply come nowhere near Scylla and Charybdis, another deliberate anticlimax by comparison to the Odyssean model, wherein Scylla grabs and devours six of Odysseus' men despite their struggling limbs (Hom. *Od.* 12.244-57) and Odysseus must twice survive Charybdis, the second time by hanging onto a fig tree until the whirlpool vomits up his raft (Hom. *Od.* 12.431-44). On anticlimax, see 677 n. Be it noted that at this point Odysseus has lost all his men. His mission has become for himself alone.

Pantagiae Megarosque sinus Thapsumque iacentem.
talia monstrabat relegens errata retrorsus   690
litora Achaemenides, comes infelicis Vlixi.

---

689. **Megaros:** adjective with *sinus*. **iacentem:** "low-lying." Megara and Thapsus are towns
north of Syracuse on Sicily's east coast. The integration of three place names in this one
verse is both ingenious and evocative (cf. Williams *ad loc.*).

690-1. **talia:** "such places," i.e., these and other similar places. **relegens errata retrorsus |
litora (691):** "retracing again (lit. backwards) the shores by which he had wandered," i.e.,
when he had come north with Ulysses from the land of the Lotus Eaters. **errata:** passive
participle meaning "traversed" or "passed in wandering." **infelicis Vlixi:** again, for G. W.
Williams (1983) 263 the epithet, since inappropriate to be spoken by Aeneas' character,
betrays an earlier third-person version. Servius Dan. *ad loc.*, anticipating the reading of
many current scholars, notes that this adjective is "incongruous," unless Aeneas, famous
for his *pietas*, pities even an enemy (*etiam hostis miseretur*) who suffers similar wanderings;
cf. notes on 613, 660. Pity is elicited several times in the portrait of the Cyclops; pity for
Ulysses would be consistent with that perspective, whether it is Aeneas' or an original
third-person narrator's.

692–711. The Trojans sail to Ortygia, where the Greek river Alpheus is said to emerge, after passing under the sea, at the fountain Arethusa; they pass Helorus, Pachynus, Camarina, Gela, Agrigentum, Selinus, Lilybaeum, arriving finally at Drepanum, where Anchises dies.

These lines allude to the genre specifically of the *periplus* (a "sailing-around"), popular in the Hellenistic period. Epic models of sea travel are, of course, the *Odyssey* and the *Argonautica*; the more narrowly conceived *periplus* or sea travelogue, here containing numerous place names, exemplifies the Hellenistic taste for learning (aetiologies*), word play (etymologies*), catalogs, and self-conscious poetic style (apostrophe* to *Arethusa* 696, *Selinus* 705; carefully balanced structure). See 401 n. on the poetic importance of such learned display. Characteristic (if not unique to the genre) formulae of the *periplus* appearing in this passage and cited by Horsfall (*ad loc.*) are: *iacet insula* 692, *contra* 692, *hinc* 699, *apparet...procul* 701.

The learning and mannered style of these lines is felt by some scholars to be inappropriate for Aeneas as narrator (G. W. Williams (1983) 265). Further, in looking ahead to the founding of Syracuse (Camarina was a colony founded from Syracuse in 598 BCE), Aeneas exceeds the bounds of what he (in 1200 BCE) could have known. This anachronism would seem to undermine the authenticity of Aeneas as narrator. In Book 2, by contrast, the consistency of Vergil's characterization of Aeneas as narrator is maintained throughout (G. W. Williams (246-62), Johnson (1999)). Horsfall (*ad* 692-707), however, affirms the appropriateness of this passage: "V. cares little that here he is not writing *ex sua persona*, or that his detail, on Aeneas' lips, opens him to criticism.... If his characters speak sometimes more like Alexandrinising scholars than Homeric heroes, that does not trouble him much...."

As it stands, whatever its rhetorical appropriateness, what purpose(s) does this travelogue interlude serve? The consensus view is that it has a transitional function. As Williams *ad* 689 puts it: "V. makes great use of the poetic possibilities of proper names of places" to effect a transition from mythical monsters to history and the realities of colonization and city-founding. Similarly, it has been suggested that the disjunction between the style of the travelogue and the rest of the book makes a theme of the passage of time itself: from Aeneas' mythical time to Augustus' historical time, from Homer's formulaic style to the contemporary (to Vergil) Roman taste for Hellenistic refinements (Nelis (2001) 64).

The passage is elaborately structured: five verses for Syracuse (692-6), the opening entry, and five for Drepanum (707-11) in closing; one for Selinus (705), two for Acragas (703-4), three for Camarina and Gela together (700-2). Each of the three opening lines begins with a geographical place name. Greek prosody is used for Greek names (i.e., lengthened *e* in *Alpheum* (694), lengthened *a* in *Gela* in 702). See Geymonat (1993) 323-31; Lacroix (1993) 131-55; H-P Stahl (1998) 37-84. See Parke (1941) for Vergil's possible use of a source on the origins of Sicilian cities and their related oracles. A detailed (but not extant) account of cities of Sicily by Callimachus (cf. *Aet.* 2 fr. 43) may lie behind much of 687-714 (O'Hara (1996) 148). Nelis (2001) 58 emphasizes the echoes between this passage, with its description of calm sailing, its place names, guide, and aetiological tale, and the close of *Argonautica* 2.1231-85, i.e., the arrival of Jason and the Argonauts in Colchis, their (unexpectedly) threatening destination. Despite the surface calm of the travelogue, then, it functions as an ominous allusion, portending dangers for Aeneas analogous to those faced by Jason in Colchis (e.g., Medea's desires and magic poisons, her father's fire-breathing bulls).

Sicanio praetenta sinu iacet insula contra
Plemyrium undosum, nomen dixere priores
Ortygiam. Alpheum fama est huc Elidis amnem
occultas egisse vias subter mare, qui nunc   695
ore, Arethusa, tuo Siculis confunditur undis.
iussi numina magna loci veneramur, et inde
exsupero praepingue solum stagnantis Helori.
hinc altas cautes proiectaque saxa Pachyni

---

692. Sicanio praetenta sinu: "stretched in front of a Sicilian bay"; *sinu* is dative after a
compound verb. This Sicilian bay, destined to become the famous harbor of Syracuse,
is protected from the sea by the island of Ortygia on the north and the promontory of
Plemyrium on the south. **Sicanio** = *Siculo*, cf. 1.557. **iacet insula:** a formulaic expression in
the periplus (Horsfall *ad loc.*).

693. Plemyrium undosum: throughout this passage Vergil engages in bilingual etymological
wordplays, i.e., applying to Greek nouns Latin epithets that suggest the derivation of the
nouns. Here, therefore, *undosum* suggests the derivation from Greek *plemmyris* "flood-tide,"
"flood"; similar are *stagnantis Helori* (698), Greek *helos* being "a marsh," a "swamp" and
Helorus a river in SE Sicily; *arduus Acragas* (703), *arduus* being the Latin equivalent of *akros*
"lofty" in Greek. On all these instances, see O'Hara (1996) 148. **dixere:** *dixerunt* = "they
named." **priores:** "men of old."

694-5. Ortygiam: Aeneas cites *Ortygia* (694), since Syracuse had not yet been founded.
Ortygia was also an ancient name of Delos, birthplace of Diana (see 124 n.), a key figure in
the story of this other Ortygia. **Alpheum…:** the indirect statement (*amnem egisse*) which
follows *fama est* breaks off at *mare*; *qui…undis* (696) is direct speech. The Alpheus, a river
of the Peloponnese, twice passes underground in its course. The story is that the goddess
Diana (Gr. Artemis), to rescue the nymph Arethusa from the pursuit of Alpheus the river
god, changed her into the fountain Arethusa in Ortygia; but Alpheus pursued her under
the sea and mingled his stream with hers. Note how elision joins *Ortygiam* and *Alpheum*.
Cf. *Ecl.* 10.1-6. This aetiological* digression exemplifies Hellenistic style.

696. ore…tuo: note apostrophe* here and at 705, a trope that has occasioned varied readings.
For G. W. Williams (1983) 266 both instances are "inane" in the mouth of Aeneas as
narrator, while for Horsfall (*ad loc.*), Vergil uses apostrophe* effectively to humanize and
vary his catalogs.

697. iussi…: nominative plural; who had "commanded" them or who were the *numina magna
loci* (mighty deities of the place) is not specified.

698. exsupero: the mixing of this singular verb with the plural verbs *veneramur* (697) and
radimus (700) is thought un-Vergilian by some scholars, but defended by Horsfall (*ad loc.*).

699. hinc: temporal. **Pachyni:** a promontory of southeastern Sicily.

radimus, et fatis numquam concessa moveri   700
apparet Camerina procul campique Geloi,
immanisque Gela fluvii cognomine dicta,
arduus inde Acragas ostentat maxima longe
moenia, magnanimum quondam generator equorum;
teque datis linquo ventis, palmosa Selinus,   705
et vada dura lego saxis Lilybeia caecis.

700. **radimus:** "scrape," "graze;" the expression comes from chariot-racing, where the charioteers, as they round the *meta* marking the limit of the course, almost "graze" it, cf. 5.170; see 698 n. **fatis numquam concessa moveri:** "not (allowed) by the fates to be disturbed," as used in Greek of sacred things which it is sacrilege to disturb (Gr. *akinetos*, "umovable"). For infinitive of purpose, see AG §460b, 563a.

     According to Servius, there once was a pestilential marsh around Camerina, which the inhabitants wished to drain. An oracle, however, warned that Camerina should not be disturbed. After the inhabitants, disregarding the oracle, drained the marsh nevertheless, their enemies advanced over the dry ground and took the city. The story is first attested in Callimachus, *Aetia* fr. 64.1 f. (Horsfall *ad loc.*).

702. **immanisque Gela fluvii…:** the final syllable of Gela is lengthened, either because it imitates the Greek prosody of feminine nouns ending in long *a* (see 702-22 n.) or because it comes before the fricative/liquid combination of *fl*. The city is named for the river. The genitive of *fluvius* is uncontracted, although the contracted form was current during and prior to the Augustan age; alternatively, Vergil may have intended the word to be scanned as a spondee*, with the first -*i* consonantal. See AG §49b and Williams *ad loc.*

703. **arduus…Acragas:** was founded by early inhabitants of Gela; see 693 n. on etymological wordplay.

704. **magnanimum:** an epic compound adjective, in the archaic genitive plural, cf. *deum, divum, superum;* see 75 n. This adjective is used only here in Vergil for horses. **quondam:** "once," "of old," anachronistic, since when Aeneas visited Sicily none of the towns named existed; for G. W. Williams (1983) 266, another sign of an original third-person narrative. See 613 n.

705. **teque:** apostrophe*, see 696 n. **datis…ventis:** ablative absolute. **palmosa:** likely, "conferring the victor's palm"; thus, as an epithet of *Selinus*, another instance of etymological play. *Selinon* (Gr.), a kind of celery or parsley (= palm, in this context), figured on coins of Selinus and was used in the making of victors' crowns in athletic games, e.g., Pind. *Ol.* 13.33. See O'Hara (1996) 149-50, Williams *ad* 705.

706. **vada dura lego…:** "thread the Lilybeian shallows, dangerous with unseen rocks"; *lego* describes Aeneas "picking" his way through submerged rocks. **saxis:** ablative of cause with *dura*. See 117 n. for adjective *Lilybeia*.

hinc Drepani me portus et inlaetabilis ora
accipit. hic pelagi tot tempestatibus actus

707–15. At Drepanum, unexpectedly, Anchises dies. Aeneas ends his narrative.

Other sources place Anchises' death elsewhere (e.g., Pallene, the Thermaic Gulf, Arcadia, Italy itself). Anchises' death here serves Vergil's narrative purposes, as his presence would not have been admissible in the following Carthage episode (Servius Dan. *ad* 710). (Books 2, 4, 5, 6, 10, and 12 also end with death or loss.)

Vergil, as epic narrator, imposes a quiet ending on Aeneas' narrative (*conticuit…fine quievit* 718), leaving his hero — who thinks that in Carthage he has found safety — in a mood of resigned repose. Of course, other features of this close undermine the surface calm. Aeneas himself is at a low moment, expressing his sense of abandonment (*me deseris*) by his father and deception by prophets, both friend and foe, who omitted Anchises' death from their accounts. For Aeneas, Anchises' death calls into question the very value of the mission (Cova *ad loc.*). With his faith in the mission shaken and lulled by a false sense of security (*Solve metus: feret haec aliquam tibi fama salutem,* as he says to Achates in Carthage (*Aen.* 1.403)), Aeneas falls into a liaison with Dido, a significant wandering off-course (*digressum* 716). Above all, dramatic irony* undermines closure for Roman readers, who know that no (proto)-Roman can be safe in Carthage.

The effect of Aeneas' narrative on his primary audience, Dido, becomes clear with the first words of the following book. His story of undeserved (e.g., *immeritam* 3.2), as he states, misfortune engenders a powerful pathos*, defusing and overwhelming the implicit menace of his narrative —the prophesied imperial destiny of the future Romans. Dido might be best advised to eliminate Aeneas and the threat he poses, but instead she wants to marry him. On the narrative level, love for Aeneas burns in Dido because of the conspiracy of Juno and Venus; but, on reviewing Aeneas' whole narrative, we see that Vergil has given him such rhetoric as elicits pity and implies (seductive) weakness. Cf. Johnson (1999) on Aeneas' weakness implicit in his narrative of loss in *Aen.* 2. Cf. Cic. *Inv.* 1.55-6 on strategies for eliciting pity and, more briefly, [Cic.] *ad Her.* 2.50; see Most (2001) 162 on Dido's emotional "reading" of Aeneas.

The response of the Phaeacian audience to Odysseus' narrative is the inverse of Dido's. Alcinous, the Phaeacian king, despite his earlier desire that Odysseus remain to marry his daughter Nausicaa (*Od.* 7.311-16), now urges presents and conveyance home for Odysseus (*Od.* 13.4-15). The Phaeacians correctly read the subtle menace in Odysseus' narrative (as Most (1989) variously shows). The Trojans' own responses to the appeal of pity in the cases of Sinon and Achaemenides function as ambiguous models for Dido as reader of pathetic narrative.

707. **Drepani:** Drepanum is on the west coast of Sicily (Gr. *drepane* means sickle or reaping-hook); so named either because of the shore's curvature or because Saturn threw his sickle there after castrating Uranus (Servius Dan. *ad loc.*). **inlaetabilis:** a Vergilian coinage*, "unjoyful" (versus "sad," "grievous") because of Anchises' death, an unexpected loss, cf. 6.112. This instance of "understatement" (Horsfall) suggests Aeneas' proto-Roman control of his grief.

708–10. Information is revealed in stages, building suspense and emphasis, climaxing with *amitto Anchisen* (710), emphatically placed through enjambment*.

708-9. **hic…hic:** anaphora*, here intensifying pathos*, heightened emotion. (In 707-15 there are seven instances of *hic* in various cases.) Note alliteration* of *t* in 708. **heu:** interjection,

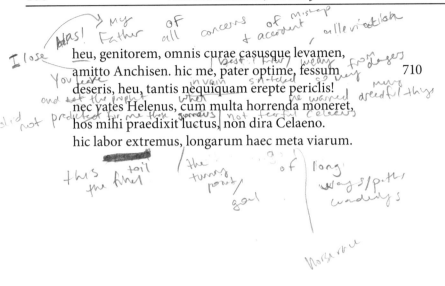

heu, genitorem, omnis curae casusque levamen,
amitto Anchisen. hic me, pater optime, fessum 710
deseris, heu, tantis nequiquam erepte periclis!
nec vates Helenus, cum multa horrenda moneret,
hos mihi praedixit luctus, non dira Celaeno.
hic labor extremus, longarum haec meta viarum.

repeated in 711, expressing a breaking-through of grief. **curae casusque:** alliteration* here intensifies the elegiac tone. **levamen:** lit. a lightening of grief.

710. **pater optime…erepte (711):** these vocatives to the deceased Anchises create authentic pathos* (as opposed to the mannered vocatives in 696, 705 above); in the *Aeneid* vocatives occur predominantly in addresses to the dead (G. Highet (1972) Appendix 2, 306). *optime* is formal, consistent with Aeneas' (Roman) decorum. (Cf. 4.291-2 *sese interea, quando optima Dido | nesciat et tantos rumpi non speret amores.*) **fessum:** again, the exhaustion motif.

711. **deseris:** emphatic through enjambment* and reproachful, cf. *Aen.* 2.741-6 for the "loss" of Creusa. Expressions of abandonment are conventional in lament. **tantis…periclis:** elegant disposition of adjective and noun, see 108 n. **nequiquam:** "in vain" because Aeneas had hoped to bring his father safely to Italy, lends pathos*; cf. *Aen.* 2.709-10 *quo res cumque cadent, unum et commune periclum, | una salus ambobus erit.* **erepte:** vocative for nominative by attraction to *pater optime*; see 710 n.

712–13. **nec vates Helenus…:** seers never tell the whole truth, as Helenus himself warned (379-80). The point is that Aeneas *mentions* the omission and that he feels deceived. His faith is shaken, leading him to question the whole enterprise. The lines are essentially framed with the names of the misleading prophets. **nec…non (713):** the negatives introducing two sequential clauses, like anaphora*, are intensifying. The second clause is as abrupt as the first is elaborated. **cum multa horrenda moneret:** *cum* temporal or concessive.

714-15. **hic labor…haec meta…hinc:** tricolon abundans* with anaphora*. This elegantly developing tricolon* contrasts with the two diminishing cola of 712-13. **labor extremus:** implying (ironically) that his arrival in Dido's kingdom constitutes safe haven, not in itself another *labor*. **meta:** the turning point at either end of a race course; therefore, it can mean either the end or the midway point of the journey. This ambiguity results in a fine instance of dramatic irony*: Aeneas is speaking of an *end* of his travails; but for readers, the allusions to Jason's arrival in Colchis portend a new beginning of travails in Carthage (see 700 n.).

hinc me digressum vestris deus appulit oris."   715
Sic pater Aeneas intentis omnibus unus
fata renarrabat divum cursusque docebat.
conticuit tandem factoque hic fine quievit.

---

715. hinc: connects with the narrative about Carthage that begins at *Aen.* 1.34. **digressum:** Aeneas states explicitly that he is off-course. **vestris deus appulit oris:** Aeneas addresses Dido and her people. As at 1.199 (*dabit deus his quoque finem*), Aeneas declines to specify which god (Servius Dan. *ad loc.*); readers, however, know that Juno instigated the storm that brought Aeneas to Carthage. "The irony is patent" (Nelis (201) 65). In saying that a god's will has bought him to Dido's shores, Aeneas commends himself to Dido (as Servius Dan. *ad loc.* notes), i.e., he implicitly—and ironically—yields himself to her protection and goodwill. For Dido as *internal* reader, Aeneas' narrative ends here; for the *external* readers (us) the account of the narrative ends at 718, below. The artful disposition of *vestris… oris* constitutes a formally elegant but substantively abrupt halt to Aeneas' own narrative. Contrast Hom. *Od.* 12.451-3

716–18. Vergil or (more strictly) the Aeneid *narrator resumes his role.*

716. pater Aeneas: Aeneas is called *pater Aeneas* both at the beginning of his narrative (*Aen.* 2.2) and here at the end, thus framing Aeneas' entire narrative. (On *framing* as a device for creating closure*, cf., e.g., Smith (1968), e.g., 2, 101-7 and Silk (1987) 38-9.) After his father's death, Aeneas is father of his people, in contrast to 343 where *pater* describes him as father only of Ascanius. **intentis omnibus unus:** "alone to the intent (audience)"; this phrase recalls the poet's introduction to Aeneas' narrative in *Aen.* 2.1 *conticuere omnes intentique ora tenebant*, and thus functions as another *framing* element for Aeneas' narrative as a whole. The antithesis between *omnibus* and *unus* contrasts Aeneas with his audience, emphasizing his isolation after Anchises' death (Roti (1983)).

717. fata…divum: Aeneas has been wholly forthcoming about the nature of his imperial mission. **renarrabat:** "recounted," not "told again."

718. tandem: acknowledges the length of Aeneas' narration. **factoque…fine:** (alliterating) ablative absolute. **quievit:** he rested from speaking, not "went to bed" ("intolerably low," Horsfall). Note the alliteration* of *t* and *f*. The coincidence of ictus* and accent* in the last two feet of the verse (thus a resolved metrical close) as well as the final word *quievit* contribute to strongly felt closure for the reader. (Words marking natural stopping places in life, e.g., rest, death, cold, or winter are among those that create the feeling of closure (cf. Smith (1968) 102).

Appendix A: Vergil's Meter[1]

Dactylic hexamater was the meter of Homer and later Greek epic. Once it was adopted by the influential Latin poet Ennius in his *Annales* (second century BCE),[2] it became the standard meter of Roman epic as well.

As the name indicates, "dactylic hexameter" literally describes a line that contains six (Gr. *hex*) measures or feet (Gr. *metra*) that are dactylic (– ‿‿).[3] In actual practice, however, spondees (– –) could substitute for dactyls within the first four feet,[4] and the line's ending was largely regularized as – ‿‿ / –x. The Latin dactylic hexameter can thus be notated as follows:

$$ – \underset{\smile\smile}{} / – \underset{\smile\smile}{} / – \underset{\smile\smile}{} / – \underset{\smile\smile}{} / – \smile\smile / – \times $$

(Here, "/" separates metrical feet; "–" = a long syllable; "‿" = a short syllable; and "x" = an *anceps* ("undecided") syllable, one that is either long or short.)

Very rarely a spondee is used in the fifth foot, in which case the line is called "spondaic."

The basic rhythm of the dactylic hexameter can be heard in the following line from the opening of Longfellow's *Evangeline*:

This is the fórest primévál. The múrmuring pínes and the hémlocks

---

1   For more on Vergil's meter, see Jackson Knight (1944) 232-42, Duckworth (1969) 46-62, Nussbaum (1986), and Ross (2007) 143-52.

2   The early Latin epics by Livius Andronicus and Naevius were composed in Saturnian verse, a meter that is not fully understood.

3   The word "dactyl" comes from the Greek word *dactylos*, "finger." A metrical dactyl with its long and two short syllables resembles the structure of a finger: the bone from the knuckle to the first joint is longer than the two bones leading to the fingertip.

4   More technically the two short syllables of a dactyl are "contracted" into one long; together with the first long syllable, they form a spondee.

Here five dactyls (búm-ba-ba) are followed by a final disyllabic foot. These metrical units (as with English verse more generally) are created through the use of natural word stress to create patterns of stressed and unstressed syllables. Thus a dactyl in English poetry is a stressed syllable followed by two unstressed syllables (e.g. "Thís is the" and "múrmuring"). In Classical Latin meter, however, metrical feet are based not on word *stress* but on the *quantity* of individual syllables (i.e. whether they are long or short). Thus, in Latin a dactyl contains one long syllable followed by two short ones (– ⌣⌣). A long syllable generally takes twice as long to pronounce as a short, and the first syllable of each foot receives a special metrical emphasis known as the *ictus*.

    To *scan* a line in dactylic hexameter (i.e. to identify how a line fits the metrical pattern of the dactylic hexameter), long and short syllables must be identified. A syllable can be *long by nature*, if it contains a vowel that is inherently long or is a diphthong;[5] or *by position*, if it contains a naturally short vowel followed either by a double consonant (*x* or *z*) or, in most cases, by two consonants.[6] In general, all other syllables are *short*. If, however, a word ending in a vowel, diphthong, or *–m* is followed by a word that begins with a vowel, diphthong, or *h*, the first vowel or diphthong is *elided* (cf. *laeti* in 1.35 below; elided syllables are enclosed in parentheses in the examples below). As a result the two syllables merge and are scanned as one—a phenomenon called *elision*. *Elision* occurs frequently in Vergil.

    By applying these rules, we may scan hexameter lines as follows:

          mūltă sŭ/pēr Prĭă/mō rŏgĭ/tāns, sŭpĕr / Hēctŏrĕ / mūltă

                                      (*Aen.* 1.750)

---

5   One can determine if a vowel is long by nature by looking the word up in a dictionary to see if it has a macron over it or by checking inflected endings in a grammar (for example, some endings, like the first and second declension ablative singular (*-a*, *-o*), are always long; others, like the second declension nominative neuter plural (*-a*), are always short).

6   An exception to this general rule: if a short vowel is followed by a mute consonant (*b, c, d, g, p, t*) and a liquid (*l, r*), the resulting syllable can be either short or long. Cf. 2.663 where *patris* and *patrem* are short and long respectively: *natum ante ora pătris, pātrem qui obtruncat ad aras*. It should also be noted that *h* is a breathing, not a consonant; it therefore does not help make a vowel long by position.

prōtrăhĭt / īn mĕdĭ/ōs; quae͞ / sīnt ĕă / nūmĭnă / dīvŭm

(Aen. 2.123)

vēlă dă/bānt lae͞/t(i) ēt spū/mās sălĭs / aere͞ rŭ/ēbānt

(Aen. 1.35)

The flow of a line is affected not only by its rhythm but also by the placement of word breaks. A word break between metrical feet is called a *diaeresis:*[7]

ēt iăcĭt. / ārrēc/tae͞ mēn/tēs stŭpĕ/făctăquĕ / cōrdă   *(Aen.* 5.643)

In this line, diaereses occur after *iacit* and after *stupefactaque;*[8] the former helps reinforce the syntactic pause after *iacit*. A word break *within* a metrical foot is called a *caesura*. When a caesura falls after the first syllable of a foot, it is called "strong" (as after the first *super* in 1.750 above); if it falls after the second syllable in a dactylic foot, it is called "weak" (as after the first *multa* in 1.750). The most important caesura in any given line often coincides with a sense break and is called the *main* or *principal caesura*.[9] It most frequently falls in the third foot, but also occurs not uncommonly in the second or fourth (or sometimes both). The slight pause implied in the main caesura helps shape the movement of each verse by breaking it into two (or more) parts. Here are the first seven lines of the *Aeneid*, scanned and with the principal caesurae marked ("‖"):

ārmă vĭ/rūmquĕ că/nō, ‖ Trō/iae͞ quī / prīmŭs ăb / ōrīs

Ītălĭ/ām fā/tō prŏfŭ/gūs ‖ Lā/vīniăquĕ* / vēnĭt

lītŏră, / mūlt(um) īl(le) / ēt tēr/rīs ‖ iāc/tātŭs ĕt / āltō

vī sŭpĕ/rūm, ‖ sae͞/vae͞ mĕmŏ/rēm Iū/nōnĭs ŏb / īrăm,

mūltă quŏ/qu(e) ēt bēl/lō pās/sūs, ‖ dūm / cōndĕrĕt / ūrbĕm

īnfēr/rētquĕ dĕ/ōs Lătĭ/ō, ‖ gĕnŭs / ūndĕ Lă/tīnŭm

---

7   When a *diaeresis* occurs just before the fifth foot, it is often called a *bucolic diaeresis* because this type of diaeresis was used frequently in pastoral poetry: e.g. *nos patriam fugimus: tu, Tityre, ‖ lentus in umbra (Ecl.* 1.4).

8   In the combinations *qu, gu, su* (e.g. –*que, sanguis, suesco*), note that the *u* is consonantal but that the combinations themselves count as a single consonant for the purpose of scansion.

9   Readers may differ on where (or even if) there is a main caesura in a given line.

Ālbā/nīquĕ pă/trēs ‖ āt/qu(e) āltā̄e / mōēnĭă / Rōmā̄e.

(*Note that *Laviniaque* is pronounced as four [not five] syllables, as if the second "*i*" were a consonant.)

In addition to metrical length, words also have a natural accent,[10] which may coincide or clash with the metrical stress (*ictus*), that falls on the first syllable of each foot. Coincidence of word accent and metrical stress produces fluidity in the verse; clashing of word accent and metrical stress creates tension. For example:

$$x \qquad x \qquad / \qquad x \qquad / \qquad /$$
īnfān/dūm, rē/gīnă, iŭ/bēs rĕnŏ/vārĕ dŏ/lōrĕm   (*Aen.* 2.3)

(Naturally accented syllables are in boldface; "/" = *ictus* that coincides with word accent; "x" = *ictus* that clashes with word accent.)

In this line, there are clashes in the first four feet where the word accent generally does not coincide with the verse accent (*ictus*), and coincidence in the final two feet.[11] In creating clashes, the placement of strong caesurae is particularly important. For example, "if a word of two or more syllables ends after the first long of a foot (that is, producing a strong caesura), there will be a clash between accent and *ictus* in that foot," because the final syllable of such words is not accented.[12] The strong caesurae in 2.3 (above) and in 2.108, 199 (below) display this principle well.

One of Vergil's artistic achievements was to manage the sequence of clash and coincidence of ictus and accent in such a way as to achieve a rhythmically varied and pleasing line. In general we find that Vergilian hexameters are characterized (to varying degrees) by the clash of *ictus* and word accent in the first four feet and by the coincidence of *ictus* and word

---

10   Disyllabic words have their accent on their initial syllable: *cáris, dábant, mólis*. If, however, words are three syllables or longer, the word accent falls: on the penultima (second to last syllable), if it is long (*ruébant, iactátos*) but on the antepenultima (the syllable preceding the penultima), if the penultima is short (*géntibus, mária, pópulum*).

11   Classical Latin speakers would presumably have pronounced the word accents in reading lines, while still maintaining the basic rhythm of the hexameter. Otherwise, the *ictus* would have transformed the basic sound of the word.

12   Ross (2007): 146. For word accentuation, see n. 10 (above).

accent in the last two feet, [13] which results in a pleasing resolution of stress at line end.

```
       /      x      x    x    /    /
     Saēpĕ fŭgām Dănăī Trōiā cŭpĭērĕ rĕlīctā          (2.108)

       /    x    x    x      /        /
     Hīc ălĭūd māiūs mĭsĕrīs mūltōquĕ trĕmēndŭm  (2.199)
```

This rhythmical innovation constituted an advance over Vergil's predecessors, who could write such lines as, e.g., Ennius' *spársis/ hástis/ lóngis/ cámpus/ spléndet et/ hórret*, which exhibits a monotonous coincidence of *ictus* and word accent throughout the entire line.

---

13 Vergil sometimes avoids such resolution for special effect, though he does so rarely. For example, in the following line, a clash between ictus and word accent occurs in the final foot: *sternitur/ exani/misque tre/mens pro/cumbit hu/mi bos* (5.481).

Appendix B: Glossary

Terms of Grammar, Rhetoric, Prosody, Poetics

Aetiology (Gr. *aition*, cause): the study of causes or origins. In the *Aeneid*, the aetiology of certain Roman rituals (e.g., sacrifice with head covered) is located in Aeneas' Trojan heritage or in his experiences on his voyage from Troy to Rome.

Alliteration: the repetition of words beginning with the same sound. *progredior portu, classis et litora linquens* (*Aen*.3.299) has alliteration of p and l.

Allusion: the deliberate evocation of a prior text by quotation precise enough to establish the source. The purpose may be to show adherence to a tradition (e.g., of epic or Hellenistic poetry); to display learning; and/or, by some change of context or content from the prior or model text, to suggest a meaning different from that in the model text, often a meaning that implies an ironic perspective on the model text. In the *Aeneid*, Vergil alludes to Homer's *Odyssey* in such as way as to 1) establish that he is writing an epic poem in the Homeric tradition and also to 2) illuminate differences between Odysseus and Aeneas. (Note: In this definition of allusion, there is an assumption of intention on the part of the alluding author. Other current definitions of allusion do not assume authorial intention or interpretable significance.)

Ambiguity: a quality of being open to more than one interpretation. In poetry ambiguity can be counted a virtue, since it serves to enrich or complicate the text by inviting readers to think through various interpretive possibilities. It is also a feature of oracular speech, e.g., *antiquam exquirite matrem* (*Aen*.3.96).

Anachronism: the representation of any person, place, or thing as existing in a time incompatible with, usually prior to, its possible existence. In *Aen*. 3.692-711 Aeneas names sites that were not founded until several hundred years after the presumed date of the Trojan war.

Anaphora: repetition of a word or phrase at the beginning of successive clauses; it may have the effect of achieving emphasis, emotional intensity, or rhetorical elevation; it is a feature of oracular speech, prophecy, and prayer:

> *"da propriam, Thymbraee, domum, da moenia fessis"* (3.85).

Anastrophe: an inversion of normal word order, which may have the effect of emphasizing the unusually placed words.

> *contra iussa monent Heleni, <u>Scyllamque Charybdinque</u>*
> <u>*inter,*</u> *utrimque uiam leti discrimine paruo, Aen.3.684-5*

The objects of the preposition inter are *Scyllamque Charybdinque*.

Apodosis: the main clause of a condition, stating what will or could or would result if the condition in the "if clause" (protasis) were met. At *Aen.*3.500-04, Aeneas says, "If ever I enter (*intraro*)…and see (*cernam*) the walls, then we will make (*faciemus*) one city.…" "Then we will make…" is the apodosis of this future more vivid condition.

Apostrophe (Gr. "a turning away"): a turning away from one addressee to address another; in practice, a direct address by a speaker to a dead or absent figure. A characteristic effect is of pathos. In the *Aeneid*, many instances of apostrophe occur in grieving speeches.

Archaism: a word, expression, or construction used in a prior phase of the language, but no longer current in the spoken language or prose. In the *Aeneid*, the effect of archaism is of remoteness, solemnity, elevation, evoking the epic tradition of, e.g., Homer or Ennius. Archaic features include alliteration, assonance, asyndeton, anastrophe, genitive in –ai, *tricola* as found in ancient *carmina* and legal and liturgical language. Cf. the archaic forms in "Our Father who art in Heaven, Hallowed be thy name."

Arsis: the unstressed syllables of a metrical foot, thus the second and third syllables of a *dactyl* and the second syllable of a *spondee*.

Asyndeton: juxtaposition of phrases or clauses without a joining particle or conjunction. Asyndeton may have the effect of abruptness, emphasis, antithesis, or archaism. As an example, Aeneas says farewell to Andromache and Helenus at *Aen.*3.493-4:

> *vivite felices, quibus est fortuna peracta*
> *iam sua: nos alia ex aliis in fata vocamur.*

One would expect a subordinating conjunction (e.g., "while", "although", or "since") before *nos*.

Caesura (Lat. "cut"): a word ending within a metrical foot. In dactylic hexameter the <u>main</u> caesura is defined as the break after the third ictus. If there is no main caesura, there is often instead a caesura after the fourth ictus, usually balanced by another caesura after the second ictus. Contrast diaeresis, which denotes the coinciding of a word and foot ending. In 3. 539:

et pater Anchises "bellum, o terra hospita, portas,"

the main caesura comes after *Anchises*.

Catalog: a poetic list, as of place names, military forces, crew members; a commonplace or *topos* of epic poetry. The naming of Sicilian cities in the travelogue at *Aen*.3.692-708 is a kind of catalog.

Chiasmus (Gr. chi or X.): a grammatical figure in which the order of words in one of two parallel clauses is inverted in the other; a diagonal ordering of elements, usually adjective-noun pairs: adjective a/ nounA/...noun B/ adjective b.

heu! fuge crudeles terras, fuge litus avarum! (*Aen*.3.44)

illustrates this pattern.

Closure: the end of a text; the patterns and formal features that bring a work to an end with a sense of finality. Thematically: a *strong* closure is achieved through resolution of major thematic elements; in so-called *weak* closure, major issues or themes feel unaddressed or unresolved; a feeling of finality is not achieved. Whether a closure is strong or weak is sometimes open to debate.

Cognate Accusative: an accusative of result following an intransitive verb to which it is related in meaning or etymology: *vitam duram vixi* "I have lived a hard life."

Quid non mortalia pectora cogis,
Auri sacra fames? (*Aen*. 3. 56-7)

has the meaning: "with what compulsion do you not compel, (you) cursed hunger for gold?"

Colon: member or clause of a sentence with a recognizable pattern. Tricola with asyndeton appear in Terence, c.190-159 BCE (*retinere amare omittere*) and Naevius, c.245-201 BCE (*urit populatur vastat*). See tricolon below.

Dactyl (Gr."finger"): a metrical foot consisting of a long syllable followed by two short syllables.

Diaeresis (Gr. "division" or "distribution"): the coinciding of a word ending with a metrical foot ending. In dactylic hexameter, the bucolic diaeresis (so called for its frequency in Theocritus) is the fourth foot diaeresis, a not infrequent feature of Homeric verse. Contrast with caesura, above.

Ecphrasis: a passage of description, usually of a work of art, that does not advance the narrative plot; a feature of epic poetry from Homer on, e.g., the shield of Achilles in *Iliad* 18, the cloak of Jason in *Argonautica* 1, the temple doors in *Aeneid* 1 and 6. Although not a plot element, an ecphrasis may relate to the framing story either through parallelism or contrast. Deciding how or whether an ecphrasis relates to the framing text can be a rewarding interpretive challenge.

Elision (Lat. "knock out"): the omission for purposes of metrical scansion of a vowel (or vowel + m) that ends a word before a following word beginning with vowel (or h+ vowel).

Ellipsis (Gr. "leaving out"): omission of one or more words (nouns, pronouns, objects, finite verbs, clauses) necessary to sense and that must be supplied by the listener or reader, as particularly frequent with forms of *esse*.

> *Nam Polydorus ego.* (*Aen.*3.45)

Enjambment (Fr. *enjamber* "to straddle"): a continuation of the sense of a verse into the next verse (as opposed to an end-stopped verse); the effect is to emphasize the enjambed word(s). In *Aen.* 3.1-2, Aeneas emphasizes the innocence of the Trojans through enjambment of *immeritam*.

> *Postquam res Asiae Priamique evertere gentem*
> *immeritam visum superis*

Epic or **compound adjective**: an adjective composed of more than one element, an essential feature of epic style. Compound adjectives ("swift-footed," "rosy-fingered") were a functional feature of the oral style of the Homeric epics, allowing the oral poet to fill out his line with the required metrical sequence. Compound adjectives figure in later, literate epics as allusions to Homeric epic, giving traditional epic character, as in *arquitenens* (3.75) "bow-holding" or *Troiugena* (3.359) "Trojan-born."

Epic simile: an extended comparison using "like" or "as" (*ac veluti*), a characteristic feature of epic style. In Homer, similes typically compare man to nature; in the *Aeneid*'s first simile (1.148-56), by contrast, nature is compared to the Roman political world. *Aeneid* 3 has only one epic simile, a fact often remarked on. (Contrast simile to *metaphor*, in which the comparison between two beings or entities is implicit, not explicit. In 3.439 Aeneas, described as *victor*, is thereby implicitly compared to a combatant in the "battle" to win over the goddess Juno.).

Epithet: an adjective or adjectival phrase consistently associated with a noun or proper name, as Homeric "swift-footed Achilles," "resourceful Odysseus." In oral poetry (such as the Homeric epics), epithets functioned largely to fill out metrical units of the dactylic hexameter line; in the *Aeneid*, they serve as allusions to Homer and other earlier epic poetry and establish epic tone. *Pius* Aeneas is the most famous example.

Etymology (Gr. *etumos* true, *logos* word): the derivation of a word, its original meaning. Etymologies (sometimes fanciful, sometimes correct by modern standards) were a favored trope of Hellenistic poets. See on *Aen*.3.127 for *sparsas* ("scattered"), implicitly linked with the *Sporades* (Gr. "scattered about"), thus alluding to the etymology of the islands' name.

Framing: a line marked by pairing of related words that enclose or frame the line, such as an adjective and noun in agreement, two verbs in the same person, two infinitives, two participles agreeing with the same noun.

> <u>ater</u> *et alterius sequitur de cortice* <u>sanguis</u>. (3.33)

> Also sometimes termed a Bronze line.*

Gnomic perfect: a generalizing use of the perfect tense, in which an action or event, having occurred, is assumed also to be continuing; usually to be translated as present. See on *constiterunt* (3.681).

Golden line: a line in the pattern adjective a, adjective b, verb, noun a, noun b (thus abVAB).

> *plena per insertas fundebat luna fenestras* (3.152)

> This pattern is felt to be particularly pleasing esthetically and appropriate to convey emphasis or to contribute to closure. Virgil's use of golden lines is less frequent in the *Aeneid* than in his earlier works. The chiastic* variant of abVBA is sometimes referred to as a Silver line*.

Hellenistic: in history, the period from 323-31 BCE. In poetry, a mannered, highly polished style, characteristically featuring etymologies, aetiologies, catalogs, and episodes that break the narrative line (if there is such). This style served to some degree as an aesthetic model for Roman poets of the late Republic and early Empire.

Hendiadys (Gr. "one through two"): the naming of one thing by two, usually two nouns joined by a conjunction, expressing the meaning of one noun modified by an adjective or genitive. See:

> *effigies sacrae divum Phrygiique Penates* (3.148)

> wherein the *effigies* "images" and the Penates are one and the same.

Hiatus: the coming together of two vowels without elision or contraction. There are two instances in the line below, one after *matri* and the other after *Neptuno*.

> *Nereidum matri et Neptuno Aegaeo* (3.74).

> Note that this is a spondaic line, defined below.

Hypallage: *see* transferred epithet.

Hyperbaton (Gr. "a stepping over"): any displacement of words naturally going together, e.g., adjective and noun or subject and verb; thus a violation of normal prose word order. In 3.74-5 *revinxit* takes *quam...errantem* as its direct object.

> *quam pius arquitenens oras et litora circum*
> *errantem Mycono e celsa Gyaroque revinxit.*

Hyperbole (Gr. "overshooting"): an exaggeration, overstatement, as in 3.567, where the stormy waves are said to bedew the stars (*rorantia vidimus astra*).

Hypotaxis: *see* parataxis.

Ictus: the metrical foot accent; in dactylic hexameter, the ictus falls on the first syllable of the foot, whether a dactyl or a spondee. Counterpoint between ictus and accent* in the first four feet and resolution in the last two feet is characteristic of Vergil's hexameters, giving them both tension and harmony between foot and word accent.

> *Forte fuit iuxta tumulus, quo cornea summo* (3.22)

illustrates this rhythm.

Interlocking order (or synchysis): refers to the interwoven or alternating arrangement of nouns and their modifiers or epithets, wherein the order is adjective a, adjective b, noun A, noun B .

Irony: the effect resulting from a disparity or gap, as when a speaker means the contrary of what he says. *Dramatic irony* refers to the circumstance in which there is a disparity between what the spectator or reader knows and what the character knows; or in which the character believes something that the text shows not to be true. The various bad or fatal homecomings of the Greeks from the Trojan war constitute an ironic comment on the Greek victory in Troy by implicitly questioning its value. Aeneas' feeling that he is safe in Carthage (3.714-5) is an instance of dramatic irony.

Litotes: the affirmation of a thing by denial of its contrary; understatement. Thus it is the opposite of hyperbole, a *not un*interesting point. See

> *Haud segnis strato surgit Palinurus et omnis*
> *explorat ventos* (3.513-4)

where "not at all lazy" means "lively" or "energetic." (Note also alliteration of *s* in these verses.)

Metaphor: *see* epic simile.

Metonymy: the representation of one thing by another associated with it. In 3.275 *Apollo* is metonymic for the temple of Apollo. Closely related is synecdoche, i.e., the representation of the whole by a part or a part by the whole. In 3.191 *trabe* ("beam" or "timber") for *nave* ("ship") is termed metonymy by R.D. Williams, but might also be seen as synecdoche.

Motif: a dominant idea or feature recurring throughout a composition. In *Aeneid* 3, city founding (i.e., by Hercules, Idomeneus, Aeneas) and disastrous homecomings of the Greek victors at Troy are both motifs.

Neologism (or Coinage): a newly created word. Both new words as well as archaic words are strange in terms of a reader's contemporary language and thus contribute to poetic (non-ordinary) effects. In 3.420 *implacata*, modifying Charybdis, may be a Vergilian coinage, meaning "unplacatable" or perhaps "unplacated."

Ornamental epithet: *see* epithet

Parataxis: the juxtaposition of sequential main clauses without a subordinating conjunction, a feature of archaic and epic style; opposed to *hypotaxis*, in which there is subordination that explicitly clarifies the hierarchical or causal relationship between clauses.

> *Terra procul vastis colitur Mavortia campis*
> *(Thraces arant) acri quondam regnata Lycurgo.* (*Aen*.3.13-14)

> *Thraces arant* succeeds the main clause with no subordination.

Pathos: a quality or effect that elicits feelings of pity, sympathy, or sorrow; or the feeling of sympathy or pity elicited in the reader. Representation of unmerited suffering (Andromache's slavery), premature loss (the death of her young husband, Hector), or abuse of the helpless (the murder of her son, Astyanax), to cite three instances, may evoke feelings of pity in the reader.

Patronymic: a name derived from the name of the father or ancestor, especially by the addition of a suffix, e.g., *Priamides* = son of Priam. Its use is a feature of Homeric epic and subsequently of Latin epic from Livius Andronicus' (c.290-207 BCE) translation of the *Odyssey* on.

Peroration: the concluding part of a speech or discourse, in which the speaker emphatically reviews or summarizes the preceding crucial points. An effective peroration has a closural cadence: "…that government of the people, by the people, for the people shall not perish from the earth." The speech closes with authoritative heavy monosyllables. (Note also the tricolon abundans.)

Personification: the representation of inanimate things as if they were human, endowing them with human characteristics and feelings, e.g., 3.555 where the sea "groans".

Polyptoton: a figure wherein two or more cases of the same word occur in proximity.

Si quando Thybrim vicinaque Thybridis arva (3.500).

Postposition: the placement of conjunctions after the first word of the clause that they introduce or of prepositions after their object; "poetic" because such practice does not occur in ordinary speech or prose.

conatus, ramis tegerem ut frondentibus aras (*Aen.* 3.25)

features *ut* in postposition (instead of *ut tegerem*).

Prolepsis: the introduction of an epithet in advance of when it is appropriate, thus anticipating an outcome that has not yet occurred.

Mihi frigidus horror
membra quatit gelidusque coit formidine sanguis (*Aen.* 3.30).

Gelidus is proleptic, because Aeneas' blood does not freeze until—not before—he is paralyzed with fear.

Protasis: the "if" or subordinate clause of a condition, the possible or potential fulfillment of which is expressed in the apodosis.

Simile: *see* epic simile.

Spondaic line: a line in which the fifth foot of the dactylic hexameter is a spondee. The effect may be emphatic, heavy, archaic, or Greek, as in 3.74:

Nereidum matri et Neptuno Aegaeo.

Synchysis: *see* Interlocking

Syncope or **Syncopation**: omission of a letter or short syllable from within a word, e.g., *repostus* for *repositus* or *intraro* for *intravero*. Syncopation is to be distinguished from contraction, which is the use of one long syllable for two short syllables.

Synecdoche: *see* Metonymy

Thesis: the syllable of a metrical foot that carries the ictus; in dactylic hexameter, always the first syllable of the foot. Contrast to *arsis*.

Tmesis (Gr. "cutting"): the separation of the two parts of a compound verb or, put otherwise, the original independence of a preposition from the base verb to which it subsequently became joined in post-epic language. *Circum* and *fundimur* in 3.634-5 may constitute an instance of tmesis. Or perhaps we should imagine that the preposition and base verb have not yet come together, as they ultimately did, to form *circumfundere*.

Topos: a commonplace, a conventional feature of a genre, as catalogs, prophecies, ecphrases are *topoi* of epic.

Transferred epithet: the grammatical agreement of an adjective with a noun which it does not modify in sense. The effect may be to draw attention to the terms involved.

> *fare age (namque <u>omnem</u> cursum mihi <u>prospera</u> dixit*
> *religio (3.362-3)*

> Here both epithets are "transferred," the actual meaning of the verse being that all the oracles foretold a prosperous voyage.

Tricolon abundans: a sequence of three cola in which the last is the longest, thus the most emphatic. An example from Lincoln's Gettysburg Address: "We cannot dedicate, we cannot consecrate, we cannot hallow this ground." This is a tricolon abundans with anaphora.

Zeugma: yoking of different words or phrases in one construction, the joining of two words in a construction that applies strictly only to one.

> *Troiugena, interpres divum, qui <u>numina</u> Phoebi,*
> *Qui tripodas, Clarii <u>laurus</u>, qui <u>sidera sentis</u>*
> *Et volucrum <u>linguas</u> …fare age. (Aen.3.359-61)*

> *Sentis* ("you feel" or "sense") strictly governs only *numina* ("the divine presence"), but is applied also to *tripodas, lauros, sidera, linguas,* and *omina.*

Sources:

J.B.Greenough et al. (1931); C. Lewis and C. Short (1962); H. Liddell and R. Scott (1968); R. Murfin and S. Ray (2003); L. Palmer (1954); A. Preminger and T. Brogan (1993); L.P. Wilkinson (1970).

Appendix C: Places Named in *Aeneid* 3

Acragas/ Agrigentum 703-4
Acroceraunia 506
Actium 280
Aenus 13
Aetna 554
Alpheus 694-5
Antandros 5-6
Arethusa 694
Argos 283
Ausonia 171
Avernus 442

Buthrotum 293-4

Camerina, 701
Carthage
Castrum Minervae 401
Caulon 553
Ceraunia 506
Chaonia 293
Cnossos 115
Colchis 692
Corythus 170
Crete 104
Cumae 441
Cyclades 127

Delos 73-83
Dicte 171
Dodona 466
Donusa125
Drepanum 707
Dulichium 271

Epirus 292

Gela 701-2
Geticis arvis 35
Gyaros 76

Hellespont 13
Helorus 698
Hesperia 163
Hyblaea

Ida, Mount 105 in Crete
        112, in Troad 6
Ilium 3
Italiam 166
Ithaca 272

Lacinia 552
Leucate 274
Lilybaeum 706
Locri 399

Megarus 689
Myconos 76

Naryycii 399
Naxos 125
Neritos 270

Olearos 126
Oinotria 166
Ortygia 124= Delos, 692
        =Syracuse, Sicily

Pachynus 429,
Pantagias 689
Paros 126
Pelorus 411
Pergamum 120 133 190
Pergama 86
Petelia 402
Phrygia
Plemyrium 692-4

Rhegium 414
Rhoeteum 108

Sallentine plains 400
Same 270
Scylaceum 553
Selinus 705
Sicily
Simois 302
Sporades 127
Strophades 209
Syracuse 692

Tarentum 551
Thapsus 689
Thrace 14
Tiber 500
Troy 3

Xanthus 350

Zacynthus 270

Bibliography

Adler, Eve (2003) *Vergil's Empire: Political Thought in the* Aeneid. Lanham, MD.

Allen, A. W. (1951) "The dullest book of the *Aeneid*." *Classical Journal* 47: 119-23.

Allen, G. (2000) *Intertextuality*. London.

Anderson, W. S. (1969, repr. 1989; 2005 second edition) *The Art of the* Aeneid. Wauconda, Il.

Anderson, W. S. and Quartarone, L. N. (eds.) (2002) *Approaches to Teaching Vergil's* Aeneid. New York.

Armstrong, D., Fish, J., Johnston, P. A., and Skinner, M. (eds.) (2004) *Vergil, Philodemus, and the Augustans*. Austin.

Armstrong, R. (2002) "Crete in the *Aeneid*: recurring trauma and alternative date," *Classical Quarterly*, n.s. 52: 321-40.

Bailey, C. (1935, repr. 1969) *Religion in Virgil*. New York.

Barchiesi, A. (1984) *La traccia del modello: effetti omerici nella narrazione virgiliana*. Pisa.

_____(1994) "Rappresentazioni del dolore e interpretazione nell' *Eneide*." *Antike und Abendland* 40: 109-124.

_____(1996) Review of Heinze (1993). *Journal of Roman Studies* 86: 229–31.

Beard, M., North, J., Price, S. (1998) *Religions of Rome I: A History*. Cambridge.

Bender. H. (2001) "*De habitu vestis*: clothing in the *Aeneid*," in *The World of Roman Costume*, eds. J. Sebesta, L. Bonfante. Madison, WI: 146-52.

Bettini, M. (1997) "Ghosts of exile: doubles and nostalgia in Vergil's *Parva Troia* (*Aeneid* 3.294 ff.)," *Classical Antiquity* 16: 8-33.

Beye, C. R. (1982) *Epic and Romance in the* Argonautica *of Apollonius*. Carbondale, IL.

Bliss, F. R. (1964) *"Fato profugus,"* in *Classical, Medieval, and Renaissance Studies in Honor of Berthold Louis Ullman*, ed. C. Henderson. Rome: 99-105.

Briggs, W. W., Jr. (1981) "Virgil and the Hellenistic epic," *Aufstieg und Niedergang der römischen Welt* 2.31.2: 948-84.

Bright, D. F. (1981) "Aeneas' other *Nekyia*," *Vergilius* 27: 40-7.

Cairns, F. (1989) *Virgil's Augustan Epic*. Cambridge.

Camps, W. A. (1969) *An Introduction to Virgil's* Aeneid. Oxford.

Casali, S. (2005) "La vite dietro il mirto: Lycurgus, Polydorus e la violazione delle piante in *Eneide* 3," *Studi italiani di filologia classica* 35: 231-50.

Clausen, W. (1964) "An interpretation of the *Aeneid*," *Harvard Studies in Classical Philology* 68: 139-47; repr. with revisions in *Virgil: A Collection of Critical Essays*, ed. S. Commager. Englewood Cliffs, NJ (1966): 75-88.

_____(1987) *Virgil's* Aeneid *and the Tradition of Hellenistic Poetry*. Berkeley, CA.

_____(1994) *A Commentary on Virgil,* Eclogues. Oxford.

_____(2002) *Virgil's* Aeneid: *Decorum, Allusion, and Ideology.* Munich and Leipzig.

Coleman, R. (1977) *Virgil:* Eclogues. Cambridge.

Conington, J. and Nettleship, H. (eds.) (1858-83) *Vergili Maronis Opera.* 3 vols. London.

Conte, G. B. (1986) *The Rhetoric of Imitation: Genre and Poetic Memory in Virgil and Other Latin Poets,* tr. C. Segal. Ithaca, NY.

_____(1999) "The Virgilian paradox: an epic of drama and sentiment," *Proceedings of the Cambridge Philological Society* 45: 17-42.

Cova, P. V. (1992) "Per una lettura narratologica del libro terzo dell'*Eneide.*" *Letteratura latina dell'Italia settentrional:* 87-139.

_____(1994) *Virgilio. Il libro terzo dell'*Eneide. Biblioteca di Aevum Antiquum, 5. Milan.

Crook, J. (1996) "Political history: 30 B.C. to A.D. 14," in *The Augustan Empire: 43 B.C. – A.D. 69. The Cambridge Ancient History, vol. X.* Second edition, eds. A. Bowman, E. Champlin, and A. Lintott. Cambridge: 70-112.

Crotty, K. (1994) *The Poetics of Supplication: Homer's* Iliad *and* Odyssey. Ithaca.

Culler, J. (1997) *Literary Theory: A Very Short Introduction.* Oxford.

DiCesare, M. (1974) *The Altar and the City.* New York.

Dougherty, C. (1993) *The Poetics of Colonization.* New York and Oxford.

Duckworth, G. (1969) *Vergil and Classical Hexameter Poetry: A Study in Metrical Variety.* Ann Arbor.

Dyson, J. (2001) *King of the Wood: The Sacrificial Victor in Virgil's* Aeneid. Norman, OK.

Eagleton, T. (1983) *Literary Theory: An Introduction.* Minneapolis, MN.

Edmunds, L. (2001) *Intertextuality and the Reading of Roman Poetry.* Baltimore.

Farrell, J. 1991. *Vergil's* Georgics *and the Traditions of Ancient Epic: The Art of Allusion in Literary History.* New York and Oxford.

_____(1997) "The Virgilian intertext," in *The Cambridge Companion to Virgil,* ed. C. Martindale. Cambridge: 222-38.

_____(2005) "The Augustan Period: 40 BC-AD 14," in *A Companion to Latin Literature,* ed. S. J. Harrison. Oxford: 44-57.

Feeney, D. C. (1983) "The taciturnity of Aeneas," *Classical Quarterly* 33: 204-19; repr. in *Oxford Readings in Vergil's* Aeneid, ed. S. Harrison (1995): 167-90.

_____(1984) "The reconciliations of Juno." *Classical Quarterly* 34: 179-94; repr. in *Oxford Readings in Vergil's* Aeneid, ed. S. Harrison (1995). Oxford: 339-62.

_____(1991) *The Gods in Epic: Poets and Critics of the Classical Tradition.* Oxford.

_____(1998) *Literature and Religion at Rome: Cultures, Contexts, and Beliefs.* Cambridge.

_____(2004) "Interpreting sacrificial ritual in Roman poetry: disciplines and their models," in *Rituals in Ink,* eds. A. Barchiesi, J. Rüpke, S. Stephens. Potsdam: 1-22.

Fordyce, C. J. (ed.) (1973) *Catullus: A Commentary.* Oxford.

Fowler, D. P. (1997a) "On the shoulders of giants: intertextuality and classical studies," *Materiali e discussioni per l'analisi dei testi classici* 39: 13-34.

_____(1997b) "The Virgil commentary of Servius," in *The Cambridge Companion to Virgil,* ed. C. Martindale. Cambridge: 73-8.

Fratantuono, L. (2007) *Madness Unchained: A Reading of Virgil's* Aeneid. Lanham, MD.

Friedrich, P., and Redfield, J. (1978) "Speech as a personality symbol: the case of Achilles." *Language* 54: 263-88.

Gale, M. (2000) *Virgil on the Nature of Things: The* Georgics, *Lucretius and the Didactic Tradition.* Cambridge.

Galinsky, K. (1988) "The anger of Aeneas," *American Journal of Philology* 109: 321-48.

_____(1992) "Aeneas at Rome and Lavinium," in *The Two Worlds of the Poet: New Perspectives on Vergil,* eds., R. Wilhelm and H. Jones. Detroit: 93-108.

_____(1996) *Augustan Culture: An Interpretive Introduction.* Princeton.

_____(2003) "Greek and Roman drama and the *Aeneid,*" in *Myth, History, and Culture in Republican Rome: Studies in Honour of T. P. Wiseman,* eds. D. Braund and C. Gill. Exeter: 275-94.

_____(ed.) (2005) *The Cambridge Companion to the Age of Augustus.* Cambridge.

George, T. V. (1984) *Aeneid* VIII and the *Aitia* of Callimachus. *Mnemosyne Suppl.* 27. Leiden.

Geymonat, M. (1993) "Callimachus at the end of Aeneas' narration." *Harvard Studies in Classical Philology* 95: 323-31.

Glenn, J. (1972) "Virgil's Polyphemus." *Greece & Rome* 19: 47-59.

Gransden, K. W. (1984) *Virgil's* Iliad: *An Essay on Epic Narrative.* Cambridge.

Greenough, J. B. *et al* (eds.) (1931) *Allen and Greenough's New Latin Grammar.* Boston and New York.

Griffith, M. (1985) "What does Aeneas look like?" *Classical Philology* 80: 309-19.

Grimm, R. (1967) "Aeneas and Andromache in *Aeneid* III," *American Journal of Philology* 88: 151-62.

Gruen, E. (1982) "Augustus and the ideology of war and peace," in *The Age of Augustus: An Interdisciplinary Conference Held at Brown University,* ed. R. Winkes. Providence: 51-72.

_____(1992) "The making of the Trojan legend," in *Culture and National Identity in Republican Rome.* Ithaca: 6-51.

Gurval, R. A. (1995) *Actium and Augustus: The Politics and Emotions of Civil War.* Ann Arbor.

Hannah, B. (2004) "Manufacturing descent: Virgil's genealogical engineering," *Arethusa* 37: 141-64.

Hardie, P. R. (1986) *Virgil's* Aeneid: *Cosmos and Imperium.* Oxford.

_____(1991) "The *Aeneid* and the *Oresteia,*" *Proceedings of the Virgil Society* 20: 29-45.

_____(1993) *The Epic Successors of Virgil.* Cambridge.

_____(1997) "Virgil and tragedy," in *The Cambridge Companion to Virgil,* ed. C. Martindale. Cambridge: 312-26.

_____(1998) Virgil. *New Surveys in the Classics* 28. Oxford.

_____(2007) "Review of Horsfall *Virgil,* Aeneid 3: *A Commentary,*" *Bryn Mawr Classical Review.*

Harrison, E. L. (1985) "Foundation prodigies in the *Aeneid,*" *Proceedings of the Liverpool Latin Society* 5: 131-64.

_____(1986) "Achaemenides' unfinished account: Vergil, *Aeneid* 3.588-69," *Classical Philology* 81: 146-7.

Heinze, Richard. (1928, 1972) *Virgils epische Technik*. Darmstadt.

_____(1993) *Vergil's Epic Technique*. Trans. H. Harvey, D. Harvey, F. Robertson. Berkeley, CA.

Hexter, R. (1999) "Imitating Troy: a reading of *Aeneid* 3," in *Reading Vergil's* Aeneid: *An Interpretive Guide*, ed. C. Perkell. Norman, OK: 64-79.

Heyworth, S. J. (1993) "Deceitful *Crete: Aeneid* 3.84 and the Hymn of Callimachus," *Classical Quarterly* n.s. 43: 255-7.

_____(2005) "Pastoral," in *A Companion to Latin Literature*, ed. S. J. Harrison. Oxford: 148-58.

Hickson, F. V. (1993) *Roman Prayer Language: Livy and the* Aeneid *of Vergil*. Stuttgart.

Highet, G. (1972) *The Speeches in Vergil's* Aeneid. Princeton.

Hill, H. (1961) "Dionysius of Halicarnassus and the origins of Rome," *Journal of Roman Studies* 51: 88-93.

Hinds, S. (1998) *Allusion and Intertext: Dynamics of Appropriation in Roman Poetry*. Cambridge.

Hirtzel, F. A. (ed.) (1900) *P. Vergili Maronis Opera*. Oxford.

Horsfall, N. (1973) "Corythus: the return of Aeneas in Virgil and his sources," *Journal of Roman Studies* 63: 68-79.

_____(1979) "Some problems in the Aeneas legend," *Classical Quarterly*, n.s. 29: 372-90.

_____(1986) "The Aeneas legend and the *Aeneid*," *Vergilius* 32: 8-17.

_____(1987) "The Aeneas legend from Homer to Virgil," in *Roman Myth and Mythography. Bulletin of the Institute of Classical Studies of the University of London*, suppl. 52, eds. J. N. Bremmer, N. Horsfall. London: 12-24.

_____(1989) "Aeneas the colonist," *Vergilius* 35: 8-26.

_____(1995) *A Companion to the Study of Virgil*. Leiden.

_____(2000) *Virgil,* Aeneid 7: *A Commentary*. Leiden.

_____(2003) *Virgil,* Aeneid 11: *A Commentary*. Leiden.

_____(2006) *Virgil,* Aeneid 3: *A Commentary*. Leiden.

Howe, G. (1929) "The revelation of Aeneas' mission," *Studies in Philology* 19: 31-41.

Hunter, R. L. (2006) *The Shadow of Callimachus: Studies in the Reception of Hellenistic Poetry at Rome*. Cambridge.

Jackson Knight, W. F. (1944) *Roman Vergil*. London.

Jens, W. (1948) "Der Eingang des Dritten Buches der *Aeneis*." *Philologus* 97: 194-7.

Jocelyn, H. (1991) "Virgil and Aeneas' supposed Italic ancestry," *Sileno* 17: 77-100.

Johnson, W.R. (1976) *Darkness Visible: A Study of Vergil's* Aeneid, Berkeley, CA.

_____(1999) "*Dis aliter visum*: self-telling and theodicy in *Aeneid* 2," in *Reading Vergil's* Aeneid, ed. C. Perkell. Norman, OK: 50-63.

_____(2005) "Introduction," in *Virgil*: Aeneid, trans. S. Lombardo, Indianapolis, IN: xv-lxxi.

Johnston, P. A. (1980) *Vergil's Agricultural Golden Age: A Study of the* Georgics. Leiden.

Jones, A. H. M. (1970) *Augustus*. London

Kennedy, D. (1992) "'Augustan' and 'Anti-Augustan': reflections on terms of reference," in *Roman Poetry and Propaganda in the Age of Augustus*, ed. A. Powell. Bristol: 26-58.

Khan, H. Akbar (1998) "Anchises, Achaemenides and Polyphemus: character, culture, and politics in *Aeneid* 3, 588 f.," in *Studies in Latin Literature and Roman History* 9, ed. C. Deroux. Brussels: 231-66.

Kinsey, T. E. (1979) "The Achaemenides episode in Virgil's *Aeneid* III," *Latomus* 38: 110-24.

Knauer, G. N. (1964a) *Die Aeneis und Homer: Studien zur poetischen Technik Vergils mit Listen der Homerzitate in der Aeneis*. Göttingen.

_____(1964b) "Vergil's *Aeneid* and Homer," *Greek, Roman and Byzantine Studies* 5: 61-84. Reprinted in *Oxford Readings in Vergil's* Aeneid, ed. S. J. Harrison (1990). Oxford: 390-412.

Lacroix, L. (1993) "Le périple d'Énée de la Troade à la Sicile: thèmes légendaires et réalités géographiques," *Antiquité Classique* 62: 131-55.

Laird, A. (1997) "Approaching characterisation in Virgil," in *The Cambridge Companion to Virgil*, ed. C. Martindale. Cambridge: 282-93.

Landis, S. (2007) "Aeneas as a reporter of speech in *Aeneid* 2-3," *Honors Thesis*, Emory University.

Lattimore, R. (trans.) (1951) *Homer: The* Iliad. Chicago.

_____(trans.) (1965) *Homer: The* Odyssey. New York.

Lewis, C. T. and Short, C. (eds.) (1962) *A Latin Dictionary*. Oxford.

Liddell, H. G. and Scott, R. (eds.) (1968) *A Greek-English Lexicon*, rev. H. S. Jones and R. McKenzie with supplement. Oxford.

Lloyd, R. B. (1957a) "*Aeneid* III: a new approach," *American Journal of Philology* 78: 133-51.

_____(1957b) "*Aeneid* III and the Aeneas legend," *American Journal of Philology* 78: 382-400.

_____(1957c) "The character of Anchises in the *Aeneid*," *Transactions of the American Philological Association* 88: 44-55.

Lynch, J. (1980) "Laocoon and Sinon: Virgil, *Aeneid* 2.40-198," *Greece & Rome* 27: 170-9.

Lyne, R. O. A. M. (1987) *Further Voices in Vergil's* Aeneid. Oxford.

Mackie, C. J. (1988) *The Characterisation of Aeneas*. Edinburgh.

Macleod, C. W. (ed.) (1982) *Homer:* Iliad *Book XXIV*. Cambridge.

Mandelbaum, A. (trans.) (1971) *The* Aeneid *of Virgil*. New York.

Martindale, C. (1993) "Descent into Hell: reading ambiguity, or Virgil and the critics," *Proceedings of the Virgil Society* 21: 111-50.

_____(ed.) (1997) *The Cambridge Companion to Virgil*. Cambridge.

McKay, A.G. (1966) "The Achaemenides episode: Vergil, *Aeneid* III, 588-691," *Vergilius* 12: 31-8.

Michels, A. K. (1981) "The *insomnium* of Aeneas," *Classical Quarterly* 31: 140-6.

Miller, J. F. (1993) "The shield of Argive Abas at *Aeneid* 3.286," *Classical Quarterly* 43: 445-50.

_____ (2009) *Apollo, Augustus, and the Poets*. Cambridge.

Most, G. W. (1989) "The structure and function of Odysseus' *Apologoi*." *Transactions of the American Philological Association* 119: 15-30.

_____(2001) "Memory and forgetting in the *Aeneid*," *Vergilius* 47: 148-70.

Murfin, R. and Ray, S. M. (eds.) (2003) *The Bedford Glossary of Critical and Literary Terms* Boston and New York.

Mynors, R. A. B. (ed.) (1969) *P. Vergili Maronis Opera*. Oxford.

_____(ed.) (1990) *Virgil: Georgics*. Oxford.

Nappa, C. (2005) *Reading After Actium: Vergil's* Georgics, Octavian, and Rome. Ann Arbor.

Nelis, D. (2001) *Vergil's* Aeneid *and the Argonautica of Apollonius Rhodius*. Leeds.

Nelson, L. (1961) "Baudelaire and Virgil: a reading of 'Le Cygne'," *Comparative Literature* 13: 332-45.

Nugent, S. G. (1992) "*Aeneid* V and Virgil's Voice of the Women," *Arethusa* 25: 255-92.

_____(1999) "The women of the *Aeneid*: vanishing bodies, lingering voices," in *Reading Vergil's* Aeneid, ed. C. Perkell. Norman, OK: 251-70.

Nussbaum, G. B. (1986) *Vergil's Metre: A Practical Guide for Reading Latin Hexameter Poetry*. London.

O'Hara, J. J. (1990) *Death and the Optimistic Prophecy in Vergil's* Aeneid. Princeton.

_____(1996) *True Names: Vergil and the Alexandrian Tradition of Aetiological Wordplay*. Ann Arbor.

_____(1997) "Virgil's style," in *The Cambridge Companion to Virgil*, ed. C. Martindale. Cambridge: 241-58.

_____(2007) *Inconsistency in Roman Epic: Studies in Catullus, Lucretius, Vergil, Ovid, and Lucan*. Cambridge.

Otis, B. (1964) *Virgil: A Study in Civilized Poetry*. Oxford.

Page, T. E. (ed.) (1894, 1900) *The* Aeneid *of Virgil*, 2 vols. London.

Palmer, L. R. (1954) *The Latin Language*. London.

Panoussi, V. (2002) "Vergil's Ajax: allusion, tragedy, and heroic identity in the *Aeneid*," *Classical Antiquity* 21: 95-134.

Parke, H. W. (1941) "The sources of Vergil, *Aeneid* III, 692-705," *American Journal of Philology* 62: 490-2.

Paschalis, M. (1986) "Virgil and the Delphic Oracle," *Philologus* 130: 44-68.

_____(1997) *Virgil's* Aeneid: *Semantic Relations and Proper Names*. Oxford.

Pavlock, B. (1985) "Epic and tragedy in Vergil's *Nisus* and *Euryalus* episode," *Transactions of the American Philological Association* 115: 207-24.

Pelling, C. (1996) "The Triumviral period," in *The Augustan Empire: 43 B.C. – A.D. 69: The Cambridge Ancient History*, vol. X. Second edition, eds. A. Bowman, E. Champlin, and A. Lintott. Cambridge: 1-69.

Perkell, C. (1981) "On Dido and Creusa and the quality of victory in Vergil's *Aeneid*," *Women's Studies* 8: 201-23; repr. in *Reflections of Women in Antiquity*, ed. H. Foley. London: 335-77.

_____(1989) *The Poet's Truth: A Study of the Poet in Virgil's* Georgics. Berkeley, CA.

_____(1994) "Ambiguity and irony: the last resort?" *Helios* 21: 63-74.

_____(1996) "The 'Dying Gallus' and the design of *Eclogue* 10," *Classical Philology* 91: 128-40.

_____(ed.) (1999) *Reading Vergil's* Aeneid. Norman, OK.

Petrini, M. (1997) *The Child and the Hero: Coming of Age in Catullus and Vergil*. Ann Arbor.

Pöschl, V. (1950) *Die Dichtkunst Vergils: Bild und Symbol in der* Aeneis. Innsbruck.

_____(1962) *The Art of Vergil: Image and Symbol in the* Aeneid, tr. G. Seligson. Ann Arbor.

Powell, A. (ed.) (1992) *Roman Poetry and Propaganda in the Age of Augustus*. Bristol.

Preminger, A. and Brogan, T. (eds.) (1993) *The New Princeton Encyclopedia of Poetry and Poetics*. Princeton.

Putnam, M. (1965) *The Poetry of the* Aeneid. Cambridge, MA.

_____(1979) *Virgil's Poem of the Earth: Studies in the* Georgics. Princeton.

_____(1980) "The Third Book of the *Aeneid*: from Homer to Rome," *Ramus* 9: 1-21.

_____(1982) *Essays on Latin Lyric, Elegy, and Epic*. Princeton.

_____(1993) "The languages of Horace, *Odes* 1.24," *Classical Journal* 88.2: 123-35.

_____(1995) *Virgil's* Aeneid: *Interpretation and Influence*. Chapel Hill and London.

Quint, D. (1982) "Painful memories: *Aeneid* 3 and the problem of the past," *Classical Journal* 78: 30-8.

_____(1993) *Epic and Empire: Politics and Generic Form from Vergil to Milton*. Princeton.

Rammiger, J. (1991) "Imitation and allusion in the Achaemenides scene (Vergil, *Aeneid* 3. 588-691)," *American Journal of Philology* 112: 53-71.

Reckford, K. J. (1974) "Some trees in Virgil and Tolkien," in *Perspectives of Roman Poetry,* ed. G. K. Galinsky. Austin, TX: 57-91.

Römisch, E. (1976) *"Die Achaemenides-Episode in Vergils Aeneis," Studien zum antiken Epos: Beiträge zür klassischen Philologie* 72: 208-27.

Ross, D. O. (1987) *Virgil's Elements: Physics and Poetry in the* Georgics. Princeton.

_____(2007) *Virgil's* Aeneid: *A Reader's Guide*. Oxford.

Roti, G. (1983) "'*Omnibus unus*' (*Aeneid* 3.716.)," *American Journal of Philology* 33: 300-1.

Sanderlin, G. (1975) "Aeneas as apprentice—point of view in the Third *Aeneid*," *Classical Journal* 71: 53-8.

Saunders, C. (1925) "The relation of *Aeneid* III to the rest of the poem," *Classical Quarterly* 19: 85-91.

Scheid, J. (1998) "Roman sacrifice," in *Oxford Companion to Classical Civilization*, eds. S. Hornblower and A. Spawforth. Oxford: 629-31.

Scullard, H. H. (1982) *From the Gracchi to Nero: A History of Rome from 133 B.C. to A.D. 68*. Fifth edition. London.

Shotter, D. (2005) *Augustus Caesar*. Second edition. London.

Silk, M. (1987). *Homer: The* Iliad. Cambridge.

Skutsch, O. (ed.) (1985) *The* Annals *of Q. Ennius*. Oxford.

Small, S. (1959) "Virgil, Dante, and Camilla." *Classical Journal* 54: 295-301.

Smith, B. H. (1968) *Poetic Closure: A Study of How Poems End*. Chicago.

Southern, P. (1998) *Augustus*. New York.

Spence, S. (1988) *Rhetorics of Reason and Desire: Vergil, Augustine, and the Troubadours*. Ithaca, NY.

_____(1999) "*Varium et mutabile*: voices of authority in *Aeneid* 4," in *Reading Vergil's Aeneid*, ed. C. Perkell. Norman, OK: 80-95.

Speroni, C. (1965) "The motif of the bleeding and speaking trees of Dante's suicides," *Italian Quarterly* 9: 44-55.

Stahl, H-P. (1998) "Political stop-overs on a mythological travel route: from battling Harpies to the Battle of Actium (*Aen.* 3.268-93)," in *Vergil's* Aeneid: *Augustan Epic and Its Political Context*, ed. H-P. Stahl. London and Swansea, Wales: 37-84.

Stocker, A. F. and Travis, A. H. (eds) (1965) *Servianorum in Vergilii Carmina Commentariorum*. 3 vols. Editio Harvardiana. Oxford.

Stubbs, H. W. (1998) "In defense of the troughs: a study in *Aeneid* III and V," *Vergilius* 44: 66-84.

Suzuki, M. (1989) *Metamorphoses of Helen: Authority, Difference, and the Epic*. Ithaca.

Syed, Y. (2005) *Vergil's* Aeneid *and the Roman Self: Subject and Nation in Literary Discourse*. Ann Arbor, MI.

Syme, R. (1939) *The Roman Revolution*. Oxford.

Symons, D. (1987) *Costume of Ancient Rome*. London.

Thomas, R. F. (1986) "Vergil's *Georgics* and the art of reference," *Harvard Studies in Classical Philology* 90: 171-98; repr. in Thomas (1999): 114-41.

_____(1988) *Virgil. Georgics*. 2 vols. *Cambridge Greek and Latin Classics*. Cambridge.

_____(1988) "Tree violation and ambivalence in Virgil," *American Journal of Philology* 118: 261-74.

_____(1996) "Genre through intertextuality: Theocritus to Virgil and Propertius," *Hellenistica Groningana* 2: 226-46; repr. in Thomas (1999): 246-66.

_____(1999) *Reading Virgil and His Texts: Studies in Intertextuality*. Ann Arbor, MI.

_____(2001) *Virgil and the Augustan Reception*. Cambridge.

Tracy, H. L. (1953) "The gradual unfolding of Aeneas' destiny," *Classical Journal* 48: 281-4.

Traill, D. (1993) "Between Scylla and Charybdis at *Aeneid* 3.684-86: a smoother passage," *American Journal of Philology* 114: 407-12.

Van Sickle, J. (1992) *A Reading of Virgil's Messianic* Eclogue. New York.

Vernant, J.-P. and Vidal-Naquet, P. (1988) *Myth and Tragedy in Ancient Greece*, tr. J. Lloyd. New York.

Versnel, H. S. (1998) "Prayer," in *Oxford Companion to Classical Civilization*, eds. S. Hornblower and A. Spawforth. Oxford: 570.

Volk, K. (ed.) (2008a) *Vergil's Eclogues*. Oxford.

_____(ed.) (2008b) *Vergil's Georgics*. Oxford.

Wallace-Hadrill, A. (1993) *Augustan Rome*. London.

Warmington, E. H. (1935-40) *Remains of Old Latin*. Revised edition. Four volumes. Cambridge, MA.

Weinstock, S. (1971) *Divus Julius*. Oxford.

West, D. (1994) "In the wake of Aeneas (*Aeneid* 3.274-88, 3.500-5, 8.200-3)," *Greece & Rome* 41: 57-61.

West, G. S. (1983) "Andromache and Dido," *American Journal of Philology* 104: 257-67.

_____(1985) "Chloreus and Camilla," *Vergilius* 31: 22-9.

White, P. (1993) *Promised Verse: Poets in the Society of Augustan Rome.* Cambridge, MA.

_____(2005) "Poets in the new milieu: realigning," in *The Cambridge Companion to the Age of Augustus*, ed. K. Galinsky. Cambridge: 321-39.

Wigodsky, M. (1972) *Vergil and Early Latin Poetry.* Wiesbaden.

Wilhelm, R. M. and Jones, H. (eds.) (1992) *The Two Worlds of the Poet: New Perspectives on Vergil.* Detroit.

Wilhelm, R. M. (1992) "Dardanus, Aeneas, Augustus, and the Etruscans," in *The Two Worlds of the Poet: New Perspectives on Vergil*, eds., R. Wilhelm and H. Jones. Detroit: 129-45.

Wilkinson, L. P. (1963, repr. 1970+). *Golden Latin Artistry.* Cambridge.

_____(1969) *The* Georgics *of Virgil: A Critical Survey.* Cambridge.

Williams, G. W. (1983) *Technique and Ideas in the* Aeneid. New Haven.

Williams, R. D. (ed.) (1962) *Virgil*: Aeneid *III.* Oxford.

_____(ed.) (1972-73) *The* Aeneid *of Virgil.* 2 vols. London.

Wiseman, T. P. (1974) "Legendary genealogies in Late-Republican Rome," *Greece & Rome* 21.2: 153-64.

Witton, W. F. (1960) "Two passages in the Third Book of the *Aeneid*," *Greece and Rome* 7: 171-2.

Wlosok, A. (1999) "The Dido tragedy in Virgil: a contribution to the question of the tragic in the *Aeneid*," in *Virgil: Critical Assessments of Classical Authors*, vol. 4, ed. P. Hardie. London: 158-81; transl. of Wlosok (1976) "*Vergils Didotragödie: ein Beitrag zum Problem des Tragischen in der Aeneis*," in *Studien zum antiken Epos*, eds. H. Görgemanns and E. A. Schmidt. Meisenheim: 228-50.

Zanker, P. (1988) *The Power of Images in the Age of Augustus*, tr. A. Shapiro. Ann Arbor.

List of Abbreviations

abl.	= ablative
acc.	= accusative
adj.	= adjective
adv.	= adverb
cf.	= confer, i.e. compare
comp.	= comparative
conj.	= conjunction
dat.	= dative
dep.	= deponent
f.	= feminine
gen.	= genitive
i.e.	= id est, that is
indecl.	= indeclinable
indef.	= indefinite
interj.	= interjection
intr.	= intransitive
interrog.	= interrogative
m.	= masculine
n.	= neuter
nom.	= nominative
num.	= numeral
opp.	= opposed
part.	= participle
pass.	= passive
perf.	= perfect
pers.	= personal
pl.	= plural
poss.	= possessive
prep.	= preposition
pron.	= pronoun
rel.	= relative
sc.	= scilicet, i.e. understand, supply
sing.	= singular
subst.	= substantive
superl.	= superlative
tr.	= transitive
v.	= verb
viz.	= videlicet, namely

Vocabulary

The words in brackets either indicate the derivation of a word or are closely akin to it.

ā, ăb, prep. with abl. *from, by*; **a puppi,** 130, *astern*

Ăbas, ntis, m. a king of Argos, 286 n.

abdūco, ěre, xi, ctum, *lead* or *carry away*

ăběo, īre, īvi or ĭi, ītum, *go away*

ablātus, see **aufero**

abrumpo, ěre, rūpi, ruptum, *break off* or *apart*

abruptus, a, um, part. of **abrumpo** as adj., *broken off; precipitous; bursting* clouds, 199; **in abruptum,** 422, *sheer downwards*

abscindo, ěre, scĭdi, scissum, *tear off* or *away*

abscondo, ěre, di or dĭdi, dĭtum, *hide; cause to disappear,* i.e. *see disappear,* 291 n.

absūmo, ěre, mpsi, mptum, *devour; destroy, consume*

ac, see **atque**

accēdo, ěre, cessi, cessum, *go to* or *near; approach*

accessus, ūs, m. *approach*

accĭpĭo, ěre, cēpi, ceptum, *receive, welcome*

ācer, cris, cre, adj., *sharp, keen, fierce*

Ăchaeměnĭdes, ae, m., *a Greek companion of Ulysses,* 614, 691

Ăchātes, ae, m., friend of Aeneas, 523

Ăchilles, is and **i, m.,** son of Pēleus and Thětis; the best fighter among the Greeks at Troy, 87

Ăchillēus, a, um, adj., *belonging to Achilles,* 326

Ăcrăgās, ntis, m., *Agrigentum,* a city on the S. coast of Sicily, 703

Actĭus, a, um, adj., *of* or *belonging to Actium,* site of the battle of Actium in 31 BCE, 282

ăcūtus, a, um, adj., *sharp*

ăd, prep. with acc., *to, towards; close to, near, at, by*; **ad saxum,** 625, *on a stone*; **ad litora,** 556, *shorewards*

Ădămastus, i, m., a Greek, 614

addīco, ěre, xi, ctum, *assign to, adjudge, surrender,* 653

addo, ěre, dĭdi, dĭtum, *add, join to*

ăděo, īre, īvi or ii, ĭtum, *go up to, visit*

ăděo, adv., *to such an extent; indeed*: **tres adeo soles,** 203 n., *three whole days*

adfābĭlis, e. adj., *that may be spoken to or addressed*

adfecto, āre, āvi, ātum, *try to obtain; keep grasping, clutching,* 670 n.

adfěro, ferre, adtŭli, adlātum, *bring to*; **sese adferre,** *advance, present oneself*

[adfor], ārī, ātus sum, *defective, speak to, address*

137

adgnosco, ĕre, gnōvi, gnĭtum,
   recognize
adgrĕdĭor, i, gressus sum, *advance*
   to, advance; attack, approach;
   approach with words, address, 358
ădĭmo, ĕre, ēmi, emptum, *take away*
adlābor, i, lapsus sum, *with* dat. *glide*
   to, float to
ādmŏvĕo, ēre, mōvi, mōtum, *move to;*
   bring to
adnītor, i, nīsus or nixus sum, *lean*
   upon; use effort, strive
ădŏleo, ēre, ŭi, ădultum, *grow up; set*
   alight, 547
ădŏpĕrio, īre, ŭi, ŏpertum, *cover up, veil*
ădōro, āre, āvi, ātum, *pray to; entreat*
adpāreo, ēre, ŭi, ĭtum, *appear, seem*
adpello, ĕre, pŭli, pulsum, *drive, move,*
   or bring to or toward
adspicio, ĕre, spexi, spectum, *look on,*
   behold, see
adsto, āre, stĭti, no sup. *stand by or*
   near; stand ready to hand
adsum, esse, fui, *be present, be at hand;*
   come; be favorable; **adest,** 688, *is*
   upon us
advĕho, ĕre, vexi, vectum, *carry to;* in
   pass. *sail, voyage, or ride to*
adversus, a, um, adj., *turned towards;*
   opposite, opposing; **postibus**
   adversis, 287, *on the doors facing*
ădȳtum, i, n. *the innermost shrine of a*
   temple (the place unentered)
Aeăcĭdes, ae, m., patronymic, *son*
   or descendant of Aeacus king of
   Aegīna, 296
Aeaeus, a, um, adj., *belonging to Aea* in
   Colchis, 366
Aegaeus, a, um, adj., *Aegean (sea)*
aeger, gra, grum, adj., *sick, suffering*
Aenĕădes, ae, m., patronymic, *son* or
   follower of Aeneas, 18

Aenēas, ae, m., 41, 97 etc.
aequālis, e, adj., *of equal size* or *age;*
   equal (aequus)
aequo, are, āvi, ātum, *make equal;*
   equal, rival, match
aequor, ŏris, n., *level surface, open sea,*
   sea (aequus)
āēr, āĕris, acc. **āĕră** or **-em, m.,** *air*
āĕrĭus, a, um, adj., *rising into the air,*
   lofty, heaven-reaching
aes, aeris, n., *bronze; bronze trumpet,*
   240; **aera,** *bronze cymbals,* 111
aestas, ātis, f., *summer*
aestus, ūs, m., *heat; boiling movement*
   of the sea, surge, swell
aethēr, ĕris, acc. **ĕra, m.,** *bright upper*
   air, sky, heaven
aethra, ae, f., *pure brightness, bright*
   light, radiance
Aetna, ae, f., a volcanic mountain in
   Sicily, 554 etc.
Aetnaeus, a, um, adj., *belonging to*
   Aetna, 678
aevum, i, n., *age, time*
Ăgămemnŏnĭus, a, um, adj., *belonging*
   to Agamemnon, the leader of the
   Greeks against Troy, 54
ăger, ăgri, m., *field*
aggĕro, ĕre, gessi, gestum, *carry to,*
   heap up
ăgĭto, āre, āvi, ātum, *keep moving;*
   hunt, pursue (freq. of **ăgo**)
ăgo, ĕre, ēgi, actum, *go; drive; impel;*
   advance; in imperat. **age, agite,**
   come! come now!
agrestis, e, adj., *of the country, rural* (ăger)
aio, v. defective, *say;* 3rd pers. sing. **ăit**
āla, ae, f., *wing*
Alba, ae, f., *the mother city of Rome*
albus, a, um, adj., *white*
ălĭus, a, ud, adj., *another, other;* **alius...**
   alius, *one...another*

almus, a, um, adj., *nourishing; kindly; propitious* (ălo)

ălo, ĕre, ŭi, ĭtum and **tum**, *nourish, bring up*

Alphēŭs, i, m. the chief river of Peloponnesus: rises in Arcadia and flows through Elis, 694

alter, tĕra, tĕrum, adj., *one of two, another, a second*

alternus, a, um, adj., *alternating, by turns*

altrix, īcis, f., *one who nourishes, nurse* (ălo)

altus, a, um, adj., *high; deep; on high* 678; **altum, i, n.** *the deep sea, the deep*

ambĕdo, ĕre, ēdi, ēsum, *eat round, gnaw round* (ambi + edo)

ambĭgŭus, a, um, adj., *doubtful; uncertain* (amb-igo, ago)

āmens, ntis, adj., *out of one's mind; frantic; hysterical*

ămictus, ūs, m., *clothing, covering*

āmīcus, i, m., *friend*

ămīcus, a, um, adj., *friendly*

āmitto, ĕre, mīsi, missum, *let go; lose*

amnis, is, m., *stream*

ămo, āre, āvi, ātum, *love, cherish*, 134

ămor, ōris, m., *love, passion, longing*

amplector, i, plexus sum, *embrace*

amplius, comp. adv., *more, further, any longer*

amplus, a, um, adj., *large, spacious*

ăn, conj., *whether, or*

anceps, cĭpĭtis, adj., *with two heads, double; wavering, doubtful, uncertain*

Anchīses, ae, voc. **ā, m.**, *Anchises, father of Aeneas*

ancŏra, ae, f., *anchor*

Andrŏmăchē, es, f., wife of Hector, 297 etc.

angustus, a, um, adj., *narrow*

ănĭma, ae, f., *breath, life, spirit, ghost*

ănĭmal, ālis, n., *living being; animal*

ănĭmus, i, m., *mind, heart, courage*

Ănĭus, i, m., king of Delos and priest of Apollo, 80

annus, i, m., *year, circuit, circle*, 284

Antandros, i, f., a town on the coast of the Troad at the foot of Mt. Ida, 6

antĕ, adv. and prep. with acc., *before; in front of; beyond, first;* **ante...quam**, *sooner than, before* with ind. or subj.

antemna (also **antenna**), ae, f., *sail-yard*

antīquus, a, um, adj., *ancient, of old; hereditary*, 342

antrum, i, n., *cave*

ăpĕrio, īre, ŭi, ertum, *open, open out;* **aperitur**, 275, *comes in sight*

Ăpollo, ĭnis, m., the sun-god, brother of Diana, god of divination, 79 etc.: for *Temple of Apollo*, 275

appăreo, see **adpăreo**

apto, āre, āvi, ātum, *make fit; adjust; prepare*

ăqŭilo, ōnis, m., *the North wind*, 285

āra, ae, f., *altar*

arbor or **arbos, ŏris, f.**, *tree*

Arcĭtĕnens, ntis, m., *he who holds the bow*, epithet of Apollo, 75

Arctūrus, i, m., the brightest star in the constellation Boötes, *the Bear-keeper*, 516

arcus, ūs, m., *bow*

ardŭus, a, um, adj. *high, lofty, steep, tall, towering aloft*

āreo, ēre, ŭi, no sup. *be dry, parched*

Ărĕthūsa, ae, f., a nymph; a famous fountain in Ortygia, near Syracuse, 696

argentum, i, n. *silver; silver plate*, 466

Argīvus, a, um, adj. *belonging to Argos; Argive; Greek*, 547; **Argŏlĭcus, a, um**, adj.=**Argivus**, 283, 637

arma, ōrum, n. plur. *arms, war*, 164

armentum, i, n., *herd* (aro)

armĭsŏnus, a, um, adj. *sounding with arms*

armo, āre, āvi, ātum, *furnish with arms; arm*

ăro, āre, āvi, ātum, *plough, till*

arrĭpĭo, ĕre, rĭpŭi, reptum, *seize upon* (ad + rapio)

artus, ūs, m., *joint;* in plur. *limbs*

arvum, i, n., *ploughed land, field* (aro)

arx, arcis, f., *place of defense, citadel, height* (arceo)

Ascănius, ii, m. son of Aeneas and Creūsa, also called Iūlus, 339, 484

Ăsĭa, ae, f. *Asia* Minor, or the W. coast near Troy

aspectus, ūs, m. *sight, appearance* (aspicio)

aspergo, ĭnis, f., *sprinkling; spray* (ad + spargo)

aspĕro, āre, āvi, ātum, *make rough, roughen*

aspĭcĭo, ĕre, spexi, spectum, *see, behold*

ast, see **at**

astrum, i, n., *star*

Astўănax, ctis, m., son of Hector and Andromache, hurled by the Greeks from the walls of Troy, 489 (Gr.'*Lord of the City*')

at, ast, conj., *but*

āter, tra, trum, adj., *black, gloomy; funereal*, 64

atquĕ or **ac**, conj., *and also, and;* **haud secus ac**, *not otherwise than;* similarly **haud minus ac**, 561

attollo, ĕre, no perf. or sup., *lift, raise up, elevate, lift on high*

attŏnĭtus, a, um, adj., *thunderstruck, amazed*

auctor, ōris, m., *creator, maker; ancestor; founder*, 503 (augeo)

audio, īre, īvi or **ĭi, ītum**, *hear, listen;* **audita**, 107 *things heard, the story*

aufĕro, ferre, abstŭli, ablātum, *carry off; remove, rob of* (ab+fero)

augŭrĭum, ĭi, n., *omen, augury; any kind of divination or prophecy*

aula, ae, archaic gen. **aulāï**, 354, f. *court, hall*

aura, is, f., *air, breeze*

auris, is, f., *ear*

Aurōra, ae, f., *the goddess of the dawn; morning*, 521, 589

aurum, i, n., *gold*

Ausŏnĭa, ae, f., *the land of the Ausones in the W. of Italy near Campania*, 477, 479, 495

Ausŏnĭus, a, um, adj., *belonging to Ausonia*, 171, 378, 385

auspex, ĭcis, m., *one who watches the flight of birds, diviner; protector, guardian*, 20 (avis + spĕcio)

auspĭcĭum, ĭi, n., *divination by observing flight of birds, auspices; augury; a sign or omen*

Auster, tri, m., *the South wind*, 357, 471; simply *wind*, 61, 70

aut, conj. *or*

autem, conj. *but*

auxĭlĭum, ĭi, n., *help*

ăvārus, a, um, adj., *greedy* (ăveo)

āvello, ĕre, velli or **vulsi, vulsum**, *tear away, tear out*

Ăvernus, i, m., *a lake near Cumae;* also used as adj., *belonging to L. Avernus*

Ăverna, ōrum, n. plur. *the district around L. Avernus*

āverto, ěre, ti, sum, *turn away; avert; remove from*, 620
ăvĭdus, a, um, adj., *desiring; eager* (ăveo)
ăvuncŭlus, i, m., *maternal uncle* (dim. of ăvus)

bacca, ae, f., *berry*
bacchor, āri, ātus sum, *revel, celebrate Bacchic rites*; perf. part. used passively, **bacchatam**, 125, *traversed by Bacchic revels*
Bacchus, i, m., *god of wine; wine*, 354
bărathrum, i, n. *abyss, pit*
barba, ae, f., *beard*
bellum, i, n., *war*
bĭs, num. adv., *twice*
bŏnus, a, um, adj., *good*; comp. **mĕlior**, see below; superl. **optīmus**
Bŏrěas, ae, m., *Boreas, the North wind*, 687
bōs, bŏvis, m. and f., *ox, cow*
brachium, ĭi, n., *arm*
brěvis, e, adj., *short*; comp. **brevior**, superl. **brevissimus**
Būthrōtum, i, n., *maritime town in Epirus*, 293

căcūmen, ĭnis, n., *summit*
cădo, ěre, cěcĭdi, cāsum, *fall*; of sails, *come down*, 207
caecus, a, um, adj., *blind; dark; secret, hidden*
caedes, i, f., *slaughter, murder* (caedo)
caedo, ěre, cěcīdi, caesum, *cut, cut down, slay*
caelĭcŏla, ae, m. and f., *heaven-dweller; heavenly being* (caelum + colo)
caelum, i, n., *heaven, sky*
caerŭlěus or caerŭlus, a, um, adj. *dark-colored, sea-colored; dark blue, dark, gloomy*; neut. pl.

caerŭla, ōrum, *the blue sea*, 208
caespes, ĭtis, m., *turf*
cālīgo, ĭnis, f., *fog, mist, thick darkness, gloom*
cālor, ōris, m., *heat, warmth* (căleo)
Cămărīna, ae, f. a Greek city on the S.W. coast of Sicily, founded by Syracuse B.C.E. 599, 701
cămīnus, i, m., *a smelting furnace* or *forge; the forge of the Cyclopes under Mt. Etna*, 580
candeo, ēre, ŭi, no sup. *be white, brilliant, glowing; be glowing hot* (cānus)
candor, ōris, m., *whiteness*
cănĭs, is, m. and f. *dog, hound*
căno, ěre, cěcĭni, cantum, *sing*; of prophetic utterance, *declare, announce, utter, prophecy*, 155
căpesso, ěre, essīvi or essĭi, essītum, *seize eagerly, seize* (freq. of căpio)
căpio, ěre, cēpi, captum, *take, seize; lay hold of; take captive*
căprĭgěnus, a, um, adj. *goat-born, born from a goat*, 221
captīvus, a, um, adj. *taken prisoner, captive* (căpio)
capto, āre, āvi, ātum, intens. *endeavor to seize, seek to catch* (freq. of căpio)
căput, pĭtis, n. *head*
carbăsus, i, f., *Spanish flax; sail*; heteroclite plur. **carbasa**, ōrum, n.
cardo, ĭnis, m., *pivot, hinge of door or gate*
cărīna, ae, f., *keel*
carmen, ĭnis, n., *song; oracle, verse; legend, inscription*, 287 (căno)
Cassandra, ae, f., *daughter of Priam and Hecuba*, 183, 187
castra, ōrum, n. plur., *fortified place; encampment; military camp*

castus, a, um, adj., *chaste, pure*
cāsus, ūs, m., *fall; chance, misfortune, danger* (cado)
cauda, ae, f., *tail*
Caulon, ōnis, m., a town founded by Achaeans on the E. coast of Bruttium, 553
causa, ae, f., *cause, reason, pretext*
cautes, is, f., *crag, rock*
căverna, ae, f., *hollow, cavern*
căvo, āre, āvi, ātum, *hollow out*
căvus, a, um, adj., *hollow*
cēdo, ĕre, cessi, cessum, *go away, retire, withdraw;* with dat. *yield to; pass into the hands of, fall to,* 297, 333
Cĕlaeno, ūs, f., one of the Harpies, 211 etc.
cĕlebro, āre, āvi, ātum, *crowd, throng; celebrate, make famous, honor*
cĕler, ĕris, ĕre, adj., *swift*
cĕlĕro, āre, āvi, ātum, *quicken, hasten*
celsus, a, um, adj., *lofty, high, raised high*
centum, num. adj., indecl. *hundred*
Cĕraunĭa, ōrum, n. plur. a mountain ridge in Epirus, 506
cerno, ĕre, crēvi, crētum, *distinguish with the eye, see*
certămen, ĭnis, n., *contest, rivalry*
certătim, adv., *eagerly; contending; competing with one another* (certo)
certo, āre, āvi, ātum, *strive, struggle*
certus, a, um, adj., *determined; sure, certain;* **facio certum,**179; *inform;* **certum est,** *it is resolved,* 686
cervix, īcis, f., *neck*
cesso, āre, āvi, ātum, *delay; cease from, stop*
[cētĕrus], a, um, adj., rare in sing., not found in nom. mas., *the other, the rest of;* n. pl. **cetera,** as subst., *the other things*

Chāon, ŏnis, m., a Trojan, 335
Chāŏnĭus, a, um, adj., *Chaonian,* 293, 334
Chāŏnia, ae, f. sc. *terra,* the land of Chaonia
Chărybdis, is, f., *Charybdis,* a whirlpool between Italy and Sicily, opposite from Scylla, 420, 558, 684
chlămys, ўdis, f., *broad woolen upper garment, cloak,* 484 (GR.)
cĭeo, ēre, cīvi, cĭtum, *rouse, stir up, call upon, summon*
cingo, ĕre, nxi, nctum, *surround; wreathe; surround the body with a girdle; gird on* (sword)
cĭnis, ĕris, m., *ashes; ashes of a corpse that is burned; the person after death*
Circē, ēs or ae, f., daughter of the Sun, possessed of magic powers, 386
circŭĭtus, ūs, m., *a going round, circuit* (circum + eo)
circum, adv. and prep. with acc., *around*
circumflecto, ĕre, flexi, flexum, *bend around*
circumfundo, ĕre, fūdi, fūsum, *pour around*
circumspĭcio, ĕre, spexi, spectum, *look around; look in a circle*
circumvolo, āre, āvi, ātum, *fly around*
circumvolvo, ĕre, no perf., **vŏlūtūm,** to *roll oneself around; to revolve,* 284
clāmor, ōris, m., *shout, cheer, roar, cry, shriek*
clangor, ōris, m., *sound, noise, scream*
Clărĭus, a, um, adj., epithet of Apollo, *belonging to Claros,* in Ionia, 360
clārus, a, um, adj., *clear, distinct, bright*
classis, is, f., *fleet*
claudo, ĕre, si, sum, *shut, shut in; of flock,* 642, *fold*

claustrum, ī, n., *barrier* (claudo)

clĭpĕus, i, m., *round shield*

cŏeo, īre, īvi or ĭi, ĭtum, *come together; grow solid; freeze*, 30

coepi, isse, ptum, defective, *begin*

cognātus, a, um, adj., *kindred, of one race* (cum + (g)natus)

cognŏmen, ĭnis, n. *a like name; an accompanying name*, 133; *name*, 163 etc. (cum + (g)nomen)

cognosco, ĕre, gnōvi, gnĭtum, *become acquainted with, learn* (cum + (g)nosco)

cōgo, ĕre, cŏēgi, cŏactum, *drive together, drive to; compel, force* (cum + ago)

cŏhĭbeo, ēre, ŭi, ĭtum, *hold together; hold in, restrain, confine* (cum + habeo)

cŏhors, tis, f., *enclosed place, mass of troops; fleet*, 563; *multitude*

collis, is, m., *hill*

collum, i, n., *neck*

cŏlo, ĕre, cŏlŭi, cultum, *inhabit; cultivate, till;* colitur, 73, *is inhabited,* almost *there is;* so too coli, 77, *be, remain*

cŏma, ae, f., *hair,* pl. *locks*

cŏmans, ntis, adj., *hairy, covered with hair;* cristas comantes, 468, *flowing crest*

cŏmĕs, ĭtis, m. and f., *companion, comrade*

cŏmĭtor, āri, ātus sum, *accompany*

commisceo, ēre, ŭi, mistum or mixtum, *mix together*

committo, ĕre, mīsi, missum, *join or put together; connect, join to*, 428

compello, āre, āvi, ātum, *address, accost*

complĕo, ēre, ēvi, ētum, *fill up, crowd*

compōno, ĕre, pŏsŭi, pŏsĭtum, *put together, build*, 387

concēdo, ĕre, cessi, cessum, *yield, grant, allow*

concĭeo, ĭēre, īvi, ĭtum or concio, īre, *rouse, stir up*

concĭlĭum, ĭi, n., *assembly, meeting; council*

conclāmo, āre, āvi, ātum, *cry out, cry out loudly*

concors, dis, adj., *with like heart; harmonious, in harmony*

condo, ĕre, dĭdi, dĭtum, *put together; lay up; hide; bury, lay to rest*

confĭcĭo, ĕre, fēci, fectum, *do thoroughly; bring to an end; wear away, wear out* (cum + făcio)

confīgo, ĕre, fixi, fixum, *pierce*

confundo, ĕre, fūdi, fūsum, *pour together with, mix with*

cōnĭfer, ĕra, ĕrum, adj., *cone-bearing, cone-laden* (conus+fero)

coniŭgĭum, ĭi, n., *wedlock* (cum+iungo)

coniunx, ŭgis, m. and f., *consort, husband, wife, bride* (cum+iungo)

conlustro, āre, āvi, ātum, *look around at, survey*

cōnor, āri, ātus sum, *endeavor, attempt*

consĕro, ĕre, sēvi, sĭtum, *sow, plant thickly, sow together*

consĕro, ĕre, sĕrŭi, sertum, *join, fasten together*

consīdo, ĕre, sēdi, sessum, *sit down, settle down*

consisto, ĕre, stĭti, stĭtum, *stand still; stand gathered*

conspĭcio, ĕre, spexi, spectum, *view, catch sight of, observe*

consto, āre, stĭti, stātum, *stand firm; be settled*

contactus, ūs, m., *touch* (cum+tango)

contemno, ĕre, mpsi, mptum, *despise, disdain, hold in contempt*

conterreo, ēre, ŭi, ĭtum, *alarm greatly; terrify*

contĭcesco, ĕre, cŭi, no sup., inceptive, *become silent, to cease speaking* (cum + tăceo)

contĭneo, ēre, ŭi, tentum, *hold together, keep in, check* (cum+teneo)

contĭnŭō, adv., *immediately, forthwith*

contorqueo, ēre, torsi, tortum, *twist or turn vigorously*

contrā, adv. and prep. with acc. *opposite; in reply to; in reply; on the other hand*

contrăho, ĕre, traxi, tractum, *draw together, assemble*

contrĕmisco, ĕre, mui, *begin to tremble greatly*

cōnūbium, ĭi, n., *marriage*

cōnus, i. f., *cone, peak of helmet,* 468

convello, ĕre, velli or **vulsi, vulsum,** *tear loose, tear up, rend apart*

cōram, adv., *face to face*

cornĕus, a, um, adj., *of cornel-wood*

cornu, ūs, n., *horn*

cornum, i, n., *cornel-berry, the fruit of the* **cornus, i, f.** *cornel-tree*

cŏrōna, ae, f., *garland, chaplet*

corpus, ŏris, n., *body*

corrĭpio, ĕre, ŭi, reptum, *snatch eagerly* (cum + rapio)

corrumpo, ĕre, rūpi, ruptum, *break up; spoil, taint,* 138

cortex, ĭcis, m. and **f.,** *bark*

cortīna, ae, f., *caldron,* in partic. the tripod of Apollo

Cŏrўbantĭus, a, um, adj., *belonging to the Corybantes* or priests of Cybele, 111

Cŏrўthus, i, m., a city of Etruria, perhaps the current Cortona, 170

crāter, ēris, m., *mixing-bowl*

crēber, bra, brum, adj., *frequent,* *numerous; many a,* 127

crēbresco, ĕre, ŭi, no sup., incept. *become frequent, increase; of wind,* 530, *pick up*

crēdo, ĕre, dĭdi, dĭtum, with dat. *believe, have faith in*

crĕpĭto, āre, no perf. or sup., *crackle, rustle; whisper,* 70 (freq. of crĕpo)

cresco, ĕre, crĕvi, crētum, *grow, spring,* 608

Crēta, ae, f., *Crete,* 104, 122, 129, 162

Crētaeus, a, um, adj., *Cretan, of Crete,* 117

crīnis, is, m., *hair*

crista, ae, f., *crest*

crūdēlis, e, adj., *cruel*

crŭentus, a, um, adj., *bloody*

crŭor, ōris, m., *blood* from a wound, *gore*

cŭbīle, is, n., *couch*

cultrix, īcis, f., *female inhabitant* or *dweller on,* 111 (cultor, cŏlo)

cultus, ūs, m., *cultivation; care, culture; dress, attire, apparel* (colo)

cum, conj., *when, while; since; although*

cum, prep. with abl., *with,* in combination with the personal pronouns *me, te, se, nobis, vobis,* e.g. **mecum**

Cūmaeus, a, um, adj., *Cumaean, belonging to Cumae* on the coast of Campania, an ancient Greek colony in Italy, 441

cūnābŭla, ōrum, n. plur., *cradle*

cunctus, a, um, adj., *all together, all the whole*

cupressus, i, f. or in its GR form **cyparissus,** 680, *cypress-tree*

cūra, ae, f., *care, affection; an object of care*

Cūrētes, um, m. plur., priests of Jupiter in Crete, often identified with the Corybantes, 131

cūro, āre, āvi, ātum, *take care of, care for, attend to,* 511 (cūra)

curro, ĕre, cŭcurri, cursum, *run;* with acc., *hasten over,* 191

currus, ūs, m., *chariot, car*

cursus, ūs, m., *course, voyage*

curvo, āre, āvi, ātum, *make round, bend, bow, curve;* **curvatus,** *arcing billow,* 564

curvus, a, um, adj., *bent, bending, curving, winding*

custos, ōdis, m. and **f.,** *guardian*

Cўbĕlus, i, m., a mountain in Phrygia, from which the goddess Cўbĕlē derived her name, 111

Cyclădes, um, f. plur., a group of islands lying round Delos, 127

Cyclops, ōpis, *the Cyclops,* the one-eyed giant blinded by Ulysses; later tradition describes the *Cyclopes* (plur.) as forging Jupiter's thunderbolts, 569 etc.

cymbĭum, ĭi, n., *small cup; basin, bowl,* 66

cўpărissus, see **cupressus,** 680

Dănăi, ōrum or **Dănăum, m.** plur., *the Greeks,* so called from Danaus, the founder of Argos, 87, 288; also as adj. *Greek,* 602

[daps] dăpĭs, not in nom. sing. f., *feast, banquet*

Dardănĭa, ae, f., *the city of Dardanus,* 52, 156

Dardănĭdae, ārum, m. plur., patronymic, *descendants of Dardanus, Trojans,* 94

Dardănĭus, a, um, adj., *connected with Dardanus, Dardanian*

Dardănus, i, m., *Dardanus,* son of Jupiter and founder of the royal line of Troy, 167, 503

dē, prep with abl., *from, down from; out of; according to;* **de more,** see *mos, moris*

dĕa, ae, f., *goddess*

dēbeo, ēre, ŭi, ĭtum, *owe;* **debitus,** *due* (de + habeo)

dēcĭpio, ĕre, cēpi, ceptum, *deceive* (de + capio)

dēdūco, ĕre, xi, ctum, *draw down;* of ships, *launch*

dēfĕro, ferre, tŭli, lātum, *bring down, carry to;* pass. *sail to,* 154

dēhinc, often as monosyllable, adv., *thereafter, then, next*

dĕindĕ, often **dein,** adv., *then, thereafter*

dēiĭcio, ĕre, iēci, iectum, *cast down* (de + iacio)

dēlābor, i, lapsus sum, *glide down, swoop down*

dēlātus, see **defero**

dēlĭgo, ĕre, lēgi, lectum, *choose out*

Dēlĭus, a, um, adj., *of Delos,* one of the Cyclades, birthplace of Apollo.

delphin, īnis, m., *dolphin*

dēmitto, ĕre, mīsi, missum, *send down, lower, extend downwards;* **dēmissus,** as adj., *brought down, lowered; low-lying; downcast*

dēmo, ĕre, mpsi, mptum, *take away*

dēmŏror, āri, ātus sum, *delay, detain*

dēnĭquĕ, adv., *at last*

dens, tis, m., *tooth*

densus, a, um, adj., *thick, many*

dēnuntio, āre, āvi, ātum, *announce, declare; menace, threaten*

dēpōno, ĕre, pŏsŭi, pŏsĭtum, *lay aside*

dērĭgesco, ĕre, rĭgŭi, incept., *become stiff; freeze*

dērĭpĭo, ĕre, ŭi, reptum, *tear off* or *from* (de + răpio)

descrībo, ĕre, psi, ptum, *write down,* 445

dēsĕro, ĕre, ui, sertum, *abandon, desert*

dēsertus, a, um, part. of desĕro as adj., *abandoned, desolate*

dēsīdo, ĕro, sēdi, no sup., *sink down*

dĕus, i, m., *god*; gen. pl. **deum** or **deorum**; **di** and **dis** are often used for **dei** and **deis** in plur.

dextĕr, tĕra, tĕrum or tra, trum, adj., *on the right*; **dextĕra** or **dextra**, sc. *manus*, as subst. f., *right hand*

Dĭāna, ae, f., daughter of Jupiter and Latona, sister of Apollo; often identified with the Moon and with Hecate, goddess of the underworld, 681

dīco, ĕre, xi, ctum, *point out, tell; say; call, name*

Dictaeus, a, um, adj., *belonging to Dicte*, a mountain in Crete; *Cretan*, 171

dictum, i, n., *word, saying* (dīco)

dīdūco, ĕre, xi, ctum, *draw apart, separate* (dis + duco)

dĭes, ēi, m. and f. in sing,; m in pl., *day*

diffīdo, ĕre, diffīsus sum, semi-dep with dat., *distrust*

dīgĕro, ĕre, gessi, gestum, *carry apart; distribute, arrange* (dis + gero)

dignor, ārī, ātus sum, *deem worthy*; perf. part. as pass. **dignātus**, *thought worthy of*, 475

dignus, a, um, adj., *worthy, worthy of,* with abl.; *deserved*

dīgrĕdior, i, gressus sum, *depart*

dīgressus, ūs, m., *departure, parting*

dimŏveo, ēre, mōvi, mōtum, *move apart, disperse* (dis + moveo)

Dĭōnaeus, a, um, adj. epithet of Venus, who was daughter of Dione, 19

dīrĭpio, ĕre, ui, reptum, *tear asunder; plunder* (dis + rapio)

dīrus, a, um, adj., *fearful, terrible, hideous*

discerno, ĕre, discrēvi, discrētum, *separate, part, divide*

disco, ĕre, dĭdĭci, no sup., *learn*

discrīmen, inis, n., *that which divides, separation; a critical time, hour, crisis* (dis + cerno)

dispendĭum, ĭi, n. *weighing out; expenditure, expense* (dispendo)

dispergo, ĕre, rsi, rsum, *scatter* (dis + spargo)

dispōno, ĕre, pŏsŭi, pŏsĭtum, *put in different places; arrange*

dissĭlio, īre, ŭi, no sup., *leap apart*

disto, āre, no perf. or sup., *stand apart; be separated*

dīva, ae, f., *goddess*

dīversus, a, um, adj., *opposite, contrary, diverse; distant; in different directions*; **ex diverso caeli**, 232, *from an opposite quarter of the sky*

dīvĭdo, ĕre, vīsi, vīsum, *divide, separate*

dīvīnus, a, um, adj., *belonging to the gods, divine; divinely inspired*

dīvus, i, m. gen. plur., **divum** or **divom**, *deity, god*

do, dăre, dĕdi, dătum, *give, grant, appoint*; **d. vela, d. lintea**, *spread* or *set sail*

dŏceo, ēre, ŭi, doctum, *teach; inform* or *tell about*

Dōdōnaeus, a, um, adj., *belonging to Dodona*, a city of Epirus with an ancient oracle of Jupiter, 466

dŏmĭna, ae, f., *mistress*; applied to a goddess, *queen*, 113 etc.

dŏmĭnor, ārī, ātus sum, *be lord and master; have dominion, rule, reign; govern* dŏmus, ūs, and i, 2nd and 4th decl., f., irregular; *house, home, habitation*

dōnum, i, n., *gift*

Dŏnūsa, ae, f., a small island in the Aegaean sea, E. of Naxos, 125

Drĕpănum, i, n., a promontory near Drepana, a town on the W. coast of Sicily, 707

dŭbĭto, āre, āvi, ātum, *doubtful, doubt, be doubtful about:* dubitandus, *to be regarded with doubt, doubtful*

dūco, ĕre, xi, ductum, *lead; draw out, drag on life,* 315

dulcis, e, adj., *sweet, dear*

Dūlĭchĭum, ĭi, n., an island in the Ionian sea, S.E. of Ithaca, 271

dum, conj., *while*

dŭo, ae, o, num. adj., *two*

dūrus, a, um, adj., *hard*

dux, dŭcis, m. and f., *leader, chief, guide, pilot* (duco)

e or ex, prep. with abl., *out of, from; rising from*

eccĕ, interj., *lo! behold!*

ecqui, quae or qua, quod, pron. interrog. adj., *is there anyone who* or *anything that?*

ecquis, quid, pron.interrog. subst., *is there any? anyone? anything?* ecquid? used as an adv., *does at all?* 342

ēdīco, ĕre, xi, ctum, *speak out; proclaim, give orders*

effĕro, ferre, extŭli, ēlātūm, *carry forth or out, raise up:* se extulit, 215, *rose*

effĭgĭes, ēi, f., *likeness, image* (ex + fingo)

effŏdio, ĕre, fōdi, fossum, *dig out*

effor, āri, fātus sum, *speak out, utter*

effŭgĭo, ĕre, fūgi, fŭgĭtum, *flee, escape or flee from*

effundo, ĕre, fūdi, fūsum, *pour forth*

ĕgŏ, pers. pron., *I*

ĕgŏmĕt, strengthened form of ego

ēgrĕdior, i, gressus sum, *step out; disembark*

ĕlĕphantus, i, m., *ivory*

ēlīdo, ĕre, si, sum, *knock, strike; dash or tear out*

Ēlis, ĭdos, f., a district on the coast of the Peloponnesus, 694

ēlŏquor, i, lŏcūtus sum, *speak out*

ēn, interj., *behold*

Encĕlădus, i, m., one of the giants who fought against Jupiter; slain with a thunderbolt and buried under Mt. Aetna; 578

ēnītor, i, nīsus or nixus sum, *make an effort, strive; bring forth, bear children*

ensis, is, m., *sword*

ĕo, īre, īvi or ĭi, ĭtum, *go*

Ēŏus, a, um, adj., *Eastern,* as subst., *he of the East,* i.e., Lucifer, the *day-star,* 588

Ēpīrus, i, f., a district in the North of Greece, 292, 503

ĕpŭlor, āri, ātus sum, *feast*

ĕquĭdem, adv., *indeed, truly*

ĕquus, i, m., *horse*

ergō, adv., *therefore; then*

ērĭgo, ĕre, rexi, rectum, *raise up, upheave*

ērĭpĭo, ĕre, ŭi, reptum, *snatch away, ravish,* 330; *save,* 560 (e + rapio)

erro, āre, āvi, ātum, *wander, drift:* litora errata, 690 *the wandered over shores,* i.e., *by which he had wandered*

error, ōris, m., *wandering, mistake*

ēructo, āre, āvi, ātum, *belch forth*

ĕrus, i, m., *master*, less correctly herus

ĕt, conj., *and; also, too;* et...et, *both...
and;* vix...et, 9, *scarcely...when*

ĕtĭam, conj., *also;* in indignant
questions, 247 *indeed, even*

Eurōus, a, um, adj., *connected with the
East wind, Eastern,* 533 (Eurus)

ēvādo, ĕre, si, sum, *go forth, pass
beyond, escape from*

ēverto, ĕre, ti, sum, *overthrow*

ex, e, prep. with abl., *out of*

exaestŭo, āre, āvi, ātum, *boil up*

excēdo, ĕre, cessi, cessum, with abl., *go
forth from, depart from*

excĭo, īre, īvi or ĭi, ītum and excieo,
ēre, ĭtum, *call or bring out; stir up,
excite, arouse*

excĭpio, ĕre, cēpi, ceptum, *receive in
turn; receive; lie in wait for, catch*
(ex + capio)

excĭto, āre, āvi, ātum, *arouse* (freq. of
excieo)

excŭtio, ĕre, cussi, cussum, *shake off,
dash away; shake loose, loosen,
fling loose,* of sails, 267, 683 (ex +
quatio)

exerceo, ēre, ŭi, ĭtum, *keep busy;
practice; harrass, try, vex*

exŏrĭor, īri, ortus sum, *arise; originate,
begin; rise*

exōro, āre, āvi, ātum, *win by entreaty,
pray earnestly for*

expĕdio, īre, īvi or ĭi, ītum,
*disentangle; make clear, explain,
set forth*

expleo, ēre, ēvi, ētum, *fill up, gorge*

explōro, āre, āvi, ātum, *search out*

exposco, ĕre, pŏposci, no sup., *demand
or beg earnestly*

exquīro, ĕre, quīsīvi, quīsītum, *search
out* (ex + quaero)

exsecror, āri, ātus sum, *curse strongly*

exserto, āre, āvi, ātum, *thrust forth
constantly* (freq. of exsero)

exsĭlĭum, ĭi, n., *exile, banishment; place
of exile,* 4

exspergo, ĕre, rsi, rsum, *scatter
abroad; splash,* 625 (ex + spargo)

exspīro, āre, āvi, ātum, *breath out or
forth*

exstrŭo, ĕre, struxi, structum, *build
up, pile high*

exsul, ŭlis, m. and f., *an exile*

exsulto, āre, āvi, ātum, *leap up*

exsŭpĕro, āre, āvi, ātum, *rise above;
surpass; pass*

externus, a, um, adj., *outward,
external; foreign, strange*

exterreo, ēre, ŭi, ĭtum, *frighten greatly;
terrify, startle, astound*

extrēmus, a, um, sup. adj., *outmost,
utmost, last;* extrema, 315, *utmost
dangers or difficulties*

exūro, ĕre, ussi, ustum, *burn up*

făcĭes, ēi, f., *face; appearance, form,
aspect*

făcĭlis, adj., *easy; smooth,* 529; nec visu
f., 621, *not easily to be looked upon*
(făcio)

făcio, ĕre, fēci, factum, *make; cause;
do;* passive fīo, fĭĕri, factus sum,
be made, become

factum, i, n., *deed*

falsus, a, um, adj., *false, counterfeit,
mock* (fallo)

fāma, ae, f., **report, rumor, story**

fămes, is, f., *hunger*

fămŭla, ae, f., *female servant,
bondwoman*

fămŭlus, i, m., *servant, bondman*

fas, n. indecl., *divine law; what is
lawful:* fas omne, 55, *every sacred
tie*

fastus, ūs, m., *pride, insolence*
făteor, ēri, fassus sum, *confess*
fātum, i, n., *that which is spoken;*
   destiny, fate
fātur, 3rd sing. pres. ind. of defect.
   verb, **fāri, fātus sum,** *speak; say*
fauces, ium, f. plur., *throat*
făvilla, ae, f., *hot ashes, embers*
fēlix, īcis, adj., *happy, favorable*
fĕnestrā, ae, f., *window*
fĕra, ae, f., *wild beast*
fĕrē, adv., *almost, about,* 135
fĕrio, īre, no perf. or sup., *strike*
fĕro, ferre, tŭli, lātum, *bear, bring,*
   carry, carry off; show, offer, 490;
   raise, lift, 462 etc.; *offer sacrifice,*
   19; *set* or *put end to,* 145; *bring*
   forth; bear, endure; say, report; **sese**
   tulit, 599, *he rushed,* **vento ferenti,**
   473, *favorable breeze*
ferrĕus, a, um, adj., *of iron*
ferrum, i, n., *iron; sword*
fessus, a, um, adj., *weary*
fētus, ūs, m., *offspring, young,* pl. *litter,*
   391
fĭdes, ĕi, f., *faith, belief; trust,*
   what causes faith, proof, 375;
   faithfulness, 434
fīdus, a, um, adj., *faithful, true*
fīgo, ĕre, fixi, fixum, *fix, fasten*
fingo, ĕre, finxi, fictum, *form, mold,*
   make, invent, devise
fĭnis, is, m. and **f.,** *end:* pl. *borders,*
   territories
fīo, see **facio**
fīrmo, āre, āvi, ātum, *make strong,*
   confirm, support
fistŭla, ae, f., *shepherd's pipe, Pan-pipe*
flamma, ae, f., *flame*
flammo, āre, āvi, ātum, *inflame, set*
   on fire
flētus, ūs, m., *weeping; tears* (fleo)

fluctus, ūs, m., *wave*
flŭĭdus, a, um, adj., *flowing*
flūmen, ĭnis, n., *river, stream*
flŭo, ĕre, fluxi, fluxum, *flow*
flŭvius, ĭi, m., *river*
fŏcus, i, m., *hearth*
foedo, āre, āvi, ātum, *make foul,*
   pollute, mar
foedus, a, um, adj., *foul*
fŏlium, ĭi, n., *leaf*
[for], see **fatur**
forma, ae, f., *form, shape*
formīdo, ĭnis, f., *fear, dread, terror*
formīdo, āre, āvi, ātum, *fear, dread*
fortĕ, adv., *by chance*
fortūna, ae, f., *chance; fortune, good*
   fortune, ill fortune, destiny,
   condition
frango, ĕre, frēgi, fractum, *break,*
   smash
frāter, tris, m., *brother*
frēnum, i, n., *bridle*
frĕtum, i, n., *strait of the sea, sea*
frīgĭdus, a, um, adj., *cold*
frondeo, ēre, no perf. or sup., *to put*
   forth leaves, to be in leaf
frons, dis, f., *leaf*
frons, tis, f., *brow, forehead*
frŭor, i, fructus sum, with abl., *enjoy;*
   enjoy the hospitality of, 352
frustrum, i, n., *piece, fragment of food*
fŭga, ae, f., *flight*
fŭgio, ĕre, fūgi, fŭgĭtum, *flee; flee*
   from; avoid, escape
fŭgo, āre, āvi, ātum, *put to flight*
fulmen, ĭnis, n., *thunderbolt*
fūmo, āre, āvi, ātum, *smoke*
fūmus, i, m., *smoke*
fundo, ĕre, fūdi, fūsum, *pour, pour*
   forth: **fundimur,** 635, *middle, we*
   spread ourselves
fundus, i, m., *bottom*

fūnis, is, m., *rope, cable*
fūnus, ĕris, n., *funeral*
Fŭrĭae, ārum, f., plur., *the Furies*; their names were Ālecto, Tīsĭphŏne, and Mĕgaera, 331. In general sense of Harpies, 252.
fŭro, ĕre, ŭi, no sup., *rave, rage*
furtim, adv., *by stealth*

gălĕa, ae, f., *helmet*
Gĕla, ae, f., a town of Sicily, called Gela from the name of its river, 702
gĕlĭdus, a, um, adj., *freezing, cold, chilled* (gelu)
Gĕlōus, a, um, adj., *belonging to Gela*
gĕmĭnus, a, um, adj., *twin, twofold, double*
gĕmĭtus, ūs, m., *groaning, roar*
gĕnĕrator, ōris, m., *producer; breeder*, 704
gĕnĭtor, ōris, m., *father*
gens, tis, f., *family, clan, race*
gĕnu, ūs, n., *knee*
gĕnus, ĕris, n., *race, family*
gĕro, ĕre, gessi, gestum, *bear, carry; wage war*
gestāmen, inis, n., *a thing borne or worn*, 286 (gero)
Gĕtĭcus, a, um, adj., *belonging to the Getae*, a people on the Danube; used loosely = *Thracian*
glăcĭālis, e, adj., *icy*
glĕba, ae, f., *clod, soil*
glŏbus, i, m., *ball*
glŏmĕro, āre, āvi, ātum, *roll together*
Gnōsĭus, a, um, adj., *belonging to Cnossos*, the capital of Crete; *Cretan*, 115
grădior, i, gressus sum, *walk, stride*
Grādīvus, i, m., epithet of Mars, meaning unknown. 35
grădus, ūs, m., *step*

Grāīus, a, um, adj., *Greek*. **Grāīi** or **Grāi** as subst., *Greeks*
Grāĭŭgĕna, ae, m., *Greek-born, a Greek*, 550
grāmen, ĭnis, n., *grass*
grātus, a, um, adj., *pleasing*
grăvis, e, adj., *heavy*
grĕmĭum, ĭi, n., *lap, bosom*
gŭbernātor, ōris, m., *steersman, pilot*
gurges, ĭtis, m., *whirlpool*
gutta, ae, f., *drop*
Gўăros, i, f., a small island in the Aegaean Sea, S.W. of Andros, 75

hăbeo, ēre, ŭi, ĭtum, *have, hold keep*
hăbĭto, āre, āvi, ātum, *inhabit; dwell* (freq. of hăbeo)
hăbĭtūs, ūs, m., *dress, garb*
haereo, ēre, haesi, haesum, with dat., *stick to, cling to, cleave to; stop, halt*
hāmus, i, m., *hook; link of coat of mail*, 467
hărēna, ae, f., *sand*
Harpўĭă, ae, f., *a Harpy*
hastīle, is, n., *spear-shaft, spear-like shoot*, 23
haud, adv., *not*
Hector, ŏris, m., leader of the Trojans, eldest son of Priam, husband of Andromache and father of Astyanax; slain by Achilles
Hectŏrĕus, a, um, adj., *belonging to Hector*, 304, 488
Hĕlĕnus, i, m., a son of Priam possessing the power of prophecy
Hĕlōrus, i, f., a town on the E. coast of Sicily, S. of Syracuse, at the mouth of the Helorus river, 698
herba, ae, f., *blade of grass, grass*; pl. *grass, herbage, herbs*
Hercŭlĕus, a, um, adj., *belonging to Hercules*, 551

Hermĭŏnē, ēs, f., daughter of Menelaus and Helen, 328
hēros, ōis, m., *hero*
Hespĕrĭa, ae, f., *the western land, Italy*
Hespĕrĭus, a, um, adj., *belonging to evening, to the land of the setting sun; western; Italian*
heu, interj., *alas!*
hīc, adv., *here; at this time or place; hereupon*
hĭc, haec, hōc, dem. pron., *this*
hĭemps, hĭĕmis, f., *winter; storm, winter tempest*
hinc, adv., *hence, from here, from this place, next*
hisco, ĕre, no perf. or sup., *open the mouth, yawn; gape; stammer*, 314
hŏmo, ĭnis, m., *man, human being*
hŏnor, ōris, m., *honor; dignity; an honoring; gift; sacrifice;* pl. *offerings* 264
hōra, ae, f., *hour; season*
horrendus, a, um, adj., *dreadful, dire; of terror*, 712
horreo, ēre, horrui, no sup., *shudder, shiver; stand bristling; shudder at, dread;* **horrens**, *quivering, trembling*
horresco, ĕre, horrŭi, or sup., *begin to shudder; shudder at, dread*
horrĭdus, a, um, adj., *making to shudder, horrible; bristling with*, 23
horrĭfĭcus, a, um, adj., *horrible*
horror, ōris, m., *shivering; shudder, terror, dread*
hortor, āri, ātus sum, *exhort, encourage, say encouragingly*
hospĭtĭum, ĭi, n., (1) *the relation between host and guest; hospitality;* (2) *place where hospitality is given or received;* **hospitium pollutum**, 61, *a land of hospitality profaned*

hospĭtus, a, um, adj., *of* or *relating to a host or guest; strange, unfamiliar* 377
hostīlis, e, adj., *belonging to an enemy, hostile*
hostis, is, m. and **f.**, *stranger; enemy*
hūc, adv., *hither, to this*
hŭmilis, e, adj., *low; low-lying*
hŭmus, i, f., *ground;* **humi**, *on the ground;* **humo**, *from the ground*
Hÿădes, um, f. plur., "*the rainers*," a group of seven stars in the constellation Taurus, 516
Hÿmĕnaeus, i, m., *god of marriage; marriage;* plur. *nuptials*, 328

Ĭăsĭus, ĭi, m., *Iasius*, 168
Īda, ae, f., a mountain close to Troy; also a mountain in Crete, 6
Īdaeus, a, um, adj., *of Ida*, 105, 112; see **Ida**
īdem, ĕădem, ĭdem, pron. adj., *the same*
Īdŏmĕnēūs, ei, acc., **-ēă, m.**, a king of Crete, who fought at Troy, 122, 401
ignārus, a, um, adj., *not knowing, ignorant;* with gen., *unacquainted with; in our ignorance of*, 569 (in + gnarus, cf. gnosco)
ignis, is, m., *fire, flame*
ignōtus, a, um, adj., *unknown* (in + (g)nosco)
īlex, ĭcis, f., *holm-oak*
Īlĭăcus, a, um, adj., *belonging to Ilium, Trojan*
Īlium, ĭi, n., a poetical name of Troy
ille, illa, illud, demonst. pron., *that; that one over there; that famous one*
ĭmāgo, ĭnis, f., *appearance, image*
imber, bris, m., *rain, storm-cloud*

immānis, e, adj., *immeasurable; huge; monstrous, awful*

immĕmor, ŏris, adj., *forgetful*

immensus, a, um, adj., *immeasurable, boundless, mighty*

immergo, ĕre, rsi, rsum, *plunge into*

immĕritus, a, um, adj., *undeserving, guiltless*

immītis, e, adj., *cruel*

immitto, ĕre, mīsi, missum, *send on* or *in; let grow:* inmissa barba, 593, *wild-growing beard*

immōtus, a, um, adj., *unmoved*

immūgio, īre, īvi or ĭi, no sup., *bellow* or *roar*

inmundus, a, um, adj., *unclean, filthy*

impello, ĕre, pŭli, pulsum, *drive onward, set in motion, stir*

impĕro, āre, āvi, ātum, *command*

implācātus, a, um, adj., *not appeased; implacable*

impleo, ēre, ēvi, ētum, *fill*

impōno, ĕre, pŏsŭi, pŏsĭtum, *place upon, pile upon*

impĕrĭum, ĭi, n., *military command; dominion, empire*

impūnĕ, adv., *without punishment*

īmus, a, um, sup. adj., *lowest, bottom of; uttermost bottom,* 577 (positive infĕrus, comp., infĕrior)

in, prep. with abl., *in, within, on;* with acc., *into, up to, to, upon, against, with regard to, for;* in abruptum, 422, *sheer downwards*

ĭnānis, e, adj., *empty*

incassum, adv., *in vain*

incautus, a, um, adj., *not careful, incautious, heedless*

incendo, ĕre, di, sum, *set on fire, make to blaze*

incertus, a, um, adj., *not sure, doubtful, indistinguishable*

incīdo, ĕre, cīdi, cīsum, *cut short, cut* (in + caedo)

incĭpio, ĕre, cēpi, ceptum, *begin* (in + căpio)

inconsultus, a, um, adj., *not advised, ill-advised, foolish*

incrēdĭbĭlis, e, adj., *not to be believed, incredible*

incrĕpĭto, āre, āvi, ātum, *keep making a noise at, chide*

incresco, ĕre, crēvi, crētum, *grow up in*

indĕ, adv., *from that place; from that time; thereafter, after that*

indīco, ĕre, xi, ctum, *proclaim publicly*

indŭo, ĕre, ŭi, ūtum, *put on; clothe, dress, wreathe with,* 526

infandus, a, um, adj., *unutterable, monstrous* (fāri)

infēlix, īcis, adj., *unhappy; unfruitful, barren,* 649; *ill-boding,* 246

infernus, a, um, adj., *belonging to the underworld; infernal*

infĕro, ferre, tŭli, lātum, *bring to; offer:* bellum inferre, *begin war, wage an aggressive war*

inflammo, āre, āvi, ātum, *set on fire, kindle, enflame*

inflecto, ĕre, flexi, flexum, *bend;* inflexus, 631, *drooping*

inflo, āre, āvi, ātum, *breathe into, blow out, swell out*

informis, e, adj., *shapeless, monstrous*

infrendo, ĕre, *gnash with the teeth,* dentibus infrendens, 664

ingĕmĭno, āre, āvi, ātum, *redouble; repeat; increase,* 199

ingens, tis, adj., *huge, monstrous, massy*

ingrĕdior, i, gressus sum, *advance; begin; land,* 17

ĭnhorreo, ĕre, ŭi, no supine, *stand on end, bristle; shiver,* 195

ĭnīquus, a, um, adj., *not level; adverse, hostile, cruel* (in + aequus)

iniūrĭa, ae, f., *wrong, injury, guilt*

inlābor, i, lapsus sum, with dat., *glide* or *steal into*

inlaetābĭlis, e, adj., *not joyous, joyless, desolate*

inlŭvĭes, ēi, f., *dirt, filth*

inrĭgo, āre, āvi, ātum, *bring water to, draw water, water, irrigate; pour upon, overflow, flow into,* 511

inruo, ĕre, rui, no sup., *rush into* or *upon*

insānus, a, um, adj., *mad, frenzied, inspired*

insĕquor, i, sĕcūtus sum, *follow on;* with inf., *press on to,* 32

insĕro, ĕre, ŭi, sertum, *put* or *place in, insert*

insignis, e, adj., *remarkable*

insomnis, e, adj., *sleepless*

insons, tis, adj., *guiltless, innocent*

inspērātus, a, um, adj., *unhoped for*

instar, n. indecl., *likeness,* 637

instauro, āre, āvi, ātum, *make to stand; renew*

instrŭo, ĕre, struxi, structum, *build up, set in order, equip*

insŭla, ae, f., *island*

insŭper, adv., *above, on the top*

insurgo, ĕre, surrexi, surrectum, *rise up:* with dat., *rise over*

intĕmĕrātus, a, um, adj., *unviolated, pure*

intēmpestus, a, um, adj., *unseasonable; of night,* 587

intendo, ĕre, di, sum and **tum,** *stretch out; stretch towards;* **intentis omnibus,** 716, *to the intent crowd*

inter, prep. with acc., *between, among, during*

interdum, adv., *sometimes;* **int....int.** 572, *at times...at times*

intĕrĕā, adv., *meanwhile*

interlŭo, ĕre, no perf. or sup., *go or flow between; wash* of rivers or the sea

interpres, ĕtis, m and **f,** *intermediary, agent; intermediary between gods and men, soothsayer,* 359

intrĕmo, ĕre, ŭi, no sup., *tremble*

intro, āre, āvi, ātum, *enter*

intŭs, adv., *within, from within*

invādo, ĕre, vāsi, vāsum, *go into, enter; go against, rush upon, attack*

invĕnio, īre, vēni, ventum, *come upon, discover*

invĭus, a, um, *pathless*

involvo, ĕre, vi, vŏlūtum, *roll in, envelop, surround; enshroud*

Ĭŏnĭus, a, um, adj., *belonging to the mare Ionium, the Ionian sea, Ionian,* 671

ipse, a, um, pron., *self; him-, her-, itself*

īra, ae, f., *anger, wrath*

ĭs, ĕă, ĭd, demonstr. pron., *that; he, she, it*

Ītălĭa, ae, f., *Italy*

Ītălus, a, um, adj., *Italian,* first syllable long, 185; short, 396, 440

ĭter, ĭtĭnĕris, n., *journey, way*

ĭtĕrum, adv., *a second time, again*

Ĭthăca, ae, f., a rocky island on the Ionian Sea, the kingdom of Ulysses, 272, 613

Ĭthăcus, i, m., *Ithacan;* the *Ithacan,* Ulysses, 629

iăceo, ēre, ŭi, ĭtum, *lie, lie down;* **iacens,** 689, **low-lying**

iăcio, ĕre, iēci, iactūm, *fling, throw*

iacto, āre, āvi, ātum, *keep flinging; toss about* (freq. of iacio)

iăcŭlum, i, n., *javelin* (iacio)

iam, adv., *already, by now, at last;* with negative, *any longer*

iānŭa, ae, f., *door, gate*

iŭbeo, ēre, iussi, iussum, *bid, order*

iŭgum, i, n., *that which joins; yoke, mountain-ridge* (iungo)

iungo, ĕre, nxi, nctum, *unite, join, yoke*

Iūno, ōnis, f., *daughter of Saturn, wife of Jupiter, queen of heaven, 380 etc.*

Iūppĭter, Iŏvis, m., *the greatest of the gods, Jupiter, 104 etc. (=Diu-pater; gen.=Diovis, cf. Zeus)*

ius, iūris, n., *right;* **iura**, *laws*

iussum, i, n., *command* (iubeo)

iŭvencus, i, m., *bullock, steer*

iŭvĕnis, is, m. and **f.**, adj. *young;* as subst., *youth*

iŭventūs, ūtis, f., *youth, body of young men*

iŭvo, āre, iūvi, iūtum, *assist;* **iuvat**, *impersonally, it delights, it is a joy to*

iuxtā, adv. and prep. with acc., *close at hand; near to*

lăbor, ōris, m., *toil, trouble, suffering*

lābor, i, lapsus sum, *glide, slip; fall down, fall*

lac, lactis, n., *milk*

Lăcĕdaemŏnĭus, a, um, adj., *Lacedaemian or Spartan*

lăcĕro, āre, āvi, ātum, *tear, rend, lacerate*

Lăcīnĭus, a, um, adj., *belonging to the promontory Lacinium, 552*

lăcrĭma, ae, f., *tear*

lăcrĭmābĭlis, e, adj., *mournful*

lăcrĭmo, āre, āvi, ātum, *weep*

lăcus, ūs, m., *lake*

Lāertĭus, a, um, adj., *belonging to Laertes, father of Ulysses, 272*

laetĭtĭa, ae, f., *joyfulness, joy*

laetus, a, um, adj., (1) *glad;* (2) *fruitful, fertile, fat*

laevus, a, um, adj., *on the left, left;* **laeva, ae, f.**, supply **manus**, *left-hand*

lambo, ĕre, i, no sup., *lick; play* (of fire)

lampas, ădis, f., *torch, lamp*

lānĭgĕr, gĕra, gĕrum, adj., *wool-bearing* (lana + gero)

Lăŏmĕdontĭădes, ae, m., patronymic, *descendant of Laomedon*, king of Troy, father of Priam; *Trojan, 248*

lăpĭdōsus, a, um, adj., *full of stones, stony* (lăpis)

lapsus, ūs, m., *gliding; gliding motion; swoop, 225*

lātē, adv. *far and wide, at large*

lătĕbra, ae, f., (rare in singular), *lurking place, retreat*

lăteo, ēre, ŭi, ītum, *lie hid, lurk*

lātus, a, um, adj., *broad*

lătus, ĕris, n., *side, flank*

laurus, i and **ūs, f.**, *laurel*

lăvo, āre, lăvāvi or **lāvi, lăvātum, lōtum** and **lautum**, *wash*

laxo, āre, āvi, ātum, *loosen; fling free, 267*

lĕbes, ētis, acc. pl. **-as, m.**, *basin of metal, used for the washing of hands at meals, caldron, 466*

Lēdaeus, a, um, adj., *of Leda, Leda's*, epithet of Hermione whose mother Helen was daughter of Leda, *328*

lĕgo, ĕre, lēgi, lēctum, *gather, collect; furl sails, 532; pick out; skim, pass over or by, 127; thread way through, 706*

lēnis, e, adj., *gentle, soft*

lento, āre, āvi, ātum, *make pliant, bend*

lentus, a, um, adj., *pliant, flexible, tough*

lĕo, ōnis, m., *lion*

lētĭfer, fĕra, fĕrum, adj., *death-bringing, deadly*

lētum, i, n., *death*

Leucātes, ae, m., a promontory on the island of Leucas; site of a famous temple of Apollo

lĕvāmen, ĭnis, n., *alleviation, solace*

lĕvo, āre, āvi, ātum, *make light, lighten; alleviate*

lĭbens, ntis, adj., *willing*

lībo, āre, āvi, ātum, *to pour out in honor of a deity, to make a libation*

lĭcet, ĕre, ŭit or lĭcĭtum est, impers., *it is lawful; it is permitted to*

Lĭlўbēĭus, a, um, adj., *belonging to Lilybaeum*, a town and promontory on W. of Sicily, 706

līmen, ĭnis, n., *threshold*

lingua, ae, f., *tongue*

linquo, ĕre, līqui, lictum, *leave*

lintĕum, i, n., *linen-cloth, sail*

lĭquĕfăcio, ĕre, fēci, factum, *make liquid, melt*

līquor, i, no perf., *be fluid, flow*

lītŏrĕus, a, um, adj., *of* or *relating to the shore*

lītus, ŏris, n., *shore, coast*

lŏco, āre, āvi, ātum, *place*

Lŏcri, ōrum, plur., *Locrians, inhabitants of Locris,* a district on the E. coast of Greece opposite Euboea, 399

lŏcus, i, m. plur. loci and loca, p*lace, region, land, position*

longaevus, a, um, adj., *long-lived, aged* (longus + aevum)

longē, adv., *afar*

longīnquus, a, um, adj., *distant*

longus, a, um, adj., *long; deep*

lŏquor, i, lŏcūtus sum, *speak, say*

lōrīca, ae, f., *breastplate*

lūcĭdus, a, um, adj., *shining, bright*

luctus, ūs, m., *grief* (lugeo)

lūcus, i, m., *grove*

lūdus, i, m., *play*; plur., *games*

lŭes, is, f., *pestilence, plague*

lūmen, ĭnis, n., *light; eye*

lūna, ae, f., *moon*

lŭpus, i, m., *wolf*

lustro, āre, āvi, ātum, *purify*; mid. pass *over or by, traverse;* lustramur, 279, *we purify ourselves; pass round*

lustrum, i, n., *a haunt or den of wild beasts; a wood or forest,* 647

lux, ūcis, f., *light; day*

Lyctĭus, a, um, adj., *belonging to Lyctus,* a city in Crete, 401

Lўcurgus, i, m., an ancient king of Thrace, who persecuted Dionysus, 14

măcĭes, ēi, f., *leanness*

macto, āre, āvi, ātum, *slay in sacrifice, slay*

măcŭlo, āre, āvi, ātum, *spot, pollute, strain*

maestus, a, um, adj., *mournful*

magnănĭmus, a, um, adj., *high-souled, generous*

magnus, a, um, adj., comp. maior, sup. maxĭmus, *great, mighty, powerful*

māla, ae, f., *jaw*

mălum, i, n., *evil, trouble, woe* (mălus)

mălus, a, um, adj., comp., peior, superl., pessĭmus, *bad; hostile,* 398

mando, āre, āvi, ātum, *entrust to, send to*

mando, ĕre, di, sum, *crush, chew*

măneo, ēre, mansi, mansum, *remain; await;* mansuram urbem, 86, *a continuing city*

Mānes, ium, m. plur., *the souls of the dead, the dead,* 63, 303; *the abode of the dead, hell,* 565

mănĭfestus, a, um, *palpable, clear, plain*

māno, āre, āvi, ātum, *flow, trickle*

mănus, ūs, f., *hand*

mărĕ, is, n., *sea*

mărītus, i, m., *husband*

Mars, tis, m., *god of War*

māter, tris, f., *mother*

Māvortĭus, a, um, adj., *belonging to Mavors or Mars*

mēcum, i.e., *cum me, with me*

mĕdĭus, a, um, adj., *middle, midst of;* as subst. aulai medio, 354, *in the midst of the hall;* medio venit, 417, *in the midst, between,* almost adv.

Mĕgărus, a, um, adj., *belonging to Megara,* a city N. of Syracuse in Sicily, 689

Mĕlĭbōĕŭs, a, um, adj., *belonging to Meliboea,* a town in Thessaly, 401

mĕlior, us, adj., used as comp. of *bonus, better, happier;* meliora, 188, *better counsels*

membrum, i, n., *limb, member*

mĕmĭni, esse, defect., *remember* (mens)

mĕmŏro, āre, āvi, ātum, *recall, relate, say, tell*

mens, tis, f., *mind*

mensa, ae, f., *table*

mĕrĕor, ēri, ĭtus sum, *deserve;* also mereo, ēre, ŭi, ĭtum

mĕrĭto, adv., *deservedly*

mĕrĭtus, a, um, part. of mereo, as adj., *deserved, due, deserving*

mĕrum, i, n., *pure wine*

mēta, ae, f., *mark or limit; goal or turning post for chariot races; goal,* 714

mĕtus, ūs, m., *fear*

mĕus, a, um, adj., *my, mine*

mīles, ĭtis, m., *soldier;* as a collective noun, *soldiery*

mĭnae, ārum, f. plur., *threats, menaces*

Mĭnerva, ae, f., Roman goddess identified with Pallas Athena, supporter of the Greeks in the Trojan War, 531

mĭnor, āri, ātus sum, *threaten*

mĭnus, adv., *less*

mīrābĭlis, e, adj., *wonderful, marvelous*

mīrus, a, um, adj., *wonderful, wondrous*

misceo, ēre, ŭi, mistum and mixtum, *mingle*

Mīsēnus, i, m., Trojan, the trumpeter of Aeneas, 239

mĭser, ĕra, ĕrum, adj., *wretched*

mĭsĕrandus, a, um, gerundive of miseror, as adj., *pitiable, piteous*

mĭsĕror, āri, ātus sum, *pity*

mitto, ĕre, mīsi, missum, *send, speed*

mŏdŏ, adv., *only*

mŏdus, i, m., *way, manner*

moenĭa, ium, n. plur., *walls, fortifications* (munio)

mōles, is, f., *mass, bulk*

mōlĭor, īri, ītus sum, *do* or *make with toil, build,* 6

mŏneo, ēre, ŭi, ĭtum, *warn; warn of*

mŏnĭmentum, i, n., *reminder, memorial,* 102 (moneo)

mons, tis, m., *mountain*

monstro, āre, āvi, ātum, *show*

monstrum, i, n., *omen; prodigy, monster, portent* (moneo)

mŏra, ae, f., *delay*

mŏrĭor, i, mortuus sum, *die*

mŏror, āri, ātus sum, *delay*

mors, tis, f., *death*

morsus, ūs, m., *biting, bite* (mordeo)

mortālis, e, adj., *belonging to death; mortal; human* (mors)

mōs, mōris, m., *custom;* mos sacrocorum, *ritual rule,* 408; de more, *according to custom*

mŏveo, ēre, mōvi, mōtum, *move; disturb, influence;* m. animo, 34, *ponder*

mox, adv., *soon*

mūgio, īre, īvi or **ĭi, ītum,** *bellow, roar*
multus, a, um, *much, many a;* in plur.
  many
mūnus, ĕris, n., *gift, offering*
murmur, ŭris, n., *murmur*
mūrus, i, m., *wall, rampart*
mūto, āre, āvi, ātum, *change*
Mȳcŏnos, i, f., one of the Cycladic
  islands, 76
myrtus, i, and **ūs, f.,** *myrtle*

nam, namque, conj., *for*
Nārȳcĭus, a, um, adj., *belonging to*
  Naryx or *Narycium* a town in S.ern
  Italy founded by the Opuntian
  Locrians and the mother city of
  the Italian Locri, 399
nascor, i, nātus sum, *be born;* **nate**
  deo, *goddess-born*
năto, āre, āvi, ātum, *swim*
nātus, i, m., *son;* in plur., *offspring*
  (nascor)
nauta, ae, m., *sailor*
nautĭcus, a, um, *belonging to sailors*
nāvĭfrăgus, a, um, adj., *ship-breaking,*
  causing shipwreck (navis+frango)
nāvis, is, f., *ship*
Naxos, i, f., the largest of the Cycladic
  islands, 125
nē, adv. with imper., *not do, not;* conj.
  with subj., *lest*
-nĕ, interrogat. particle appended to
  other words
nĕc, adv., see **neque**
necdum, adv., *nor yet,* and *not yet*
nĕcessĕ, neut. adj., *necessary;* **necesse**
  est followed by subj. or inf., *it is*
  necessary to
nec non, conj., *moreover,* see **nĕquĕ**
nĕfandus, a, um, adj., *unutterable;*
  impious (ne+fari)
nĕfas, n. indecl., *that which is contrary*

to divine law, unlawful, awful,
  abominable
nĕgo, āre, āvi, ātum, *deny, say not,*
  refuse
nĕmŏrōsus, a, um, adj., *full of groves or*
  forests, wooded
nĕmus, ŏris, n., *grove*
Nĕoptŏlĕmus, i, m., a name of
  Pyrrhus, son of Achilles 333, 469
nĕpos, pōtis, m., *grandson;* plur.,
  posterity, 158
Neptūnus, i, m., *god of the sea,* 74, 119
Neptūnĭus, a, um, adj., *connected with*
  Neptune; Neptune-built
nĕquĕ or **nĕc,** conj., *and not, nor,*
  neither; **neque…neque,** *neither…*
  nor; **nec non,** *nor not,* i.e., *and also,*
  moreover
nēquīquam, adv., *in vain*
Nĕrĕis, ĭdis, f., patronymic, *a daughter*
  of Nereus, a Nereid; a sea-nymph, a
  daughter of the Sea and Doris, 74
Nērītos, i, f., an island near Ithaca, 271
nī = nĭsĭ, conj., *unless*
nĭger, gra, grum, adj., *black*
nimbōsus, a, um, adj., *cloudy*
nimbus, i, m., *rain-cloud*
nīmīrum, adv., *undoubtedly, surely*
nīsus, ūs, m., *struggling, effort* (nītor)
nĭtens, tis, adj., *sleek, shining*
nĭteo, ēre, ŭi, no sup., *shine, glitter,*
  look bright
nĭvālis, e, adj., *snowy* (nix)
nĭvĕus, a, um, adj., *snowy; snow-white*
  (nix)
nōmen, ĭnis, n., *name*
non, adv., *not*
nondum, adv., *not yet*
nos, see **ĕgŏ**
noster, tra, trum, adj., *our*
nŏta, ae, f., *mark, sign*
nŏto, āre, āvi, ātum, *mark, observe*

nōtus, a, um, adj., *known, well-known*

Nŏtus, i, m., *the South wind,* 268

nŏvus, a, um, adj., *new, novel, startling, strange*

nox, noctis, f., *night*

nūbes, is, f., *cloud*

nūbĭla, ōrum, n. plur., *clouds*

nūdo, āre, āvi, ātum, *make naked, strip, denude*

nullus, a, um, adj., *not any, no, none* (ne+ullus)

nūmen, ĭnis, n., *divine will; the will or power of gods* (nuo)

nŭmĕrus, i, m., *number; rank, position; order,* 446

nunc, adv., *now;* nunc...nunc, *at one time...at another time*

nunquam, adv., *never*

nuntĭus, ă, m., *messenger*

Nympha, ae, f., *Nymph,* half divine being dwelling in seas, rivers, or forests, 34

O, interj., *oh!*

obĭcio, ĕre, iēci, iectum, *throw before* or *opposite;* obiectus, *opposite;* obiectae cautes, 534, *the barrier of rock* (ob; iăcio)

oblīviscor, i, oblītus sum, with gen., *forget*

obluctor, āri, ātus sum, with dat., *struggle against; tug against,* 38

ŏbŏrior, īri, ortus sum, *rise up* or *in front of*

obscēnus, a, um, adj., *filthy, disgusting*

obscūrus, a, um, adj., *dark, gloomy*

obsĭdĕo, ēre, sēdi, sessum, *sit down against, besiege, beset*

obsĭdĭo, ōnis, f., *siege, blockade*

obstĭpesco, ĕre, stĭpui, no sup., *become amazed or astounded*

obtrunco, āre, āvi, ātum, *lop off; slay, murder*

obverto, ĕre, ti, sum, *turn towards, set square to the wind,* 549

obvĭus, a, um, adj. with dat., *in the way of, exposed to*

occŭlo, ĕre, ŭi, ltum, *hide*

occultus, a, um, part. of occulo, as adj., *hidden, secret*

occŭpo, āre, āvi, ātum, *take possession of, occupy; take hold of*

occurro, ĕre, curri and cŭcurri, cursum, *run to meet, meet*

ŏcŭlus, i, m., *eye*

ōdi, isse, defective, *hate*

ŏdor, ōris, m., *smell, stench*

Oenōtrus, a, um, adj., *belonging to Oenotria,* a district in the extreme S.E. of Italy

Ōlĕăros, i, f., an island in the Aegaean sea, one of the Cyclades, 126

ŏlĕum, i, n., *oil*

ōlim, adv., *of past time, at that time, some time ago, formerly; of the future, one day, on a future day, hereafter*

ōmen, ĭnis, n., *omen, sign*

omnĭpŏtens, tis, adj., *all-powerful*

omnis, e, adj., *all, every, whole*

ŏnĕro, āre, āvi, ātum, *burden, load*

ŏpācus, a, um, adj., *shady, dark*

ŏpĕror, āri, ātus sum, *be busy;* with dat., *be at work on*

ŏpīmus, a, um, adj., *rich, sumptuous* (opes)

ops, ŏpis, f., defective, *aid, power;* mostly in plur., *wealth, power*

optĭmus, a, um, adj., used as a superl. of bŏnus, *best*

opto, āre, āvi, ātum, *wish for; choose, hope; eagerly seek,* 132

ŏpus, ĕris, n., *work, task*

ōra, ae, f., *coast, shore*

ōrācŭlum, or ōrāclum, i, n., *oracle*

orbis, is, m., *circle, round*

ordo, ĭnis, m., *arrangement, order; orbit,* 376

Ŏrestes, is, m., son of Agamemnon and Clytaemnestra, 331

Orīŏn, ŏnis, m., a constellation, whose setting is accompanied by storms

ŏrĭor, īri, ortus sum, *arise, spring*

Ortўgĭa, ae, f., (1) ancient name of Delos; (2) island in the Bay of Syracuse, 694 (*the island of quails*)

os, ōris, n., *mouth,* pl., *face, features*

os, ossis, n., *bone*

ostento, āre, āvi, ātum, *keep showing, display*

ostĭum, ĭi, n., *mouth of river*

ŏvis, is, f., *sheep*

ŏvo, āre, āvi, ātum, *exult, triumph*

Păchynus, i, m. and **f.,** the S.E. promontory of Sicily, 429, 699

pălaestra, ae, f., *wrestling-place, wrestling;* plur., *wrestling bouts,* 281

Pălĭnūrus, i, m., pilot of Aeneas

Pallas, ădis, f., Greek name of Minerva, goddess of war and wisdom, 544

pallĭdus, a, um, adj., *pale*

palma, ae, f., *palm of the hand; palm tree*

palmōsus, a, um, adj., *abounding in palms*

pando, ĕre, di, pansum or **passum,** *spread open*

Pantăgĭas, ae, m., a river in Sicily, 689

Parca, ae, f., one of the three *Fates;* their names were Clōtho, Lăchĕsis, and Atrŏpos, 379

parco, ĕre, pĕperci sometimes **parsi, parcĭtum** or **parsum,** with dat., *spare*

părens, ntis, m. or **f.,** *parent*

pāreo, ēre, ŭi, ĭtum, with dat., *obey*

părio, ĕre, pĕpĕri, partum, *bear, bring forth; acquire, gain*

părĭtĕr, adv., *equally; as one man,* 560 (par)

păro, āre, āvi, ātum, *make ready, prepare*

Păros, i, f., an island in the Aegaean sea, one of the Cyclades, celebrated for its white marble, 126

pars, tis, f., *part, share*

parvus, a, um, adj., comp. **mĭnor,** superl. **mĭmĭmus,** *small, tiny*

pasco, ĕre, pāvi, pastum, *feed*

passim, adv., *throughout*

pastor, ōris, m., *shepherd* (pasco)

păter, tris, m., *father;* **Pater,** *the Father,* i.e. Jupiter, 251

pătĕra, ae, f., *open saucer-like goblet* (păteo)

păternus, a, um, adj., *belonging to a father, paternal*

pătesco, ĕre, pătŭi, no sup., incept., *become open, open* (pateo)

pătĭor, păti, passus sum, *suffer; endure*

pătrĭa, ae, f., *fatherland, native land*

pătrius, a, um adj., *belonging to a father* or *fatherland, ancestral*

paucus, a, um, adj., *small;* in plur., *few*

paulum, adv., *a little; somewhat*

pauper, ĕris, adj., *poor*

păvor, ōris, m., *panic, terror*

pax, pācis, f., *peace*

pectus, ŏris, n., *breast, heart, bosom*

pĕcus, ŭdis, f., *cattle; sheep;* pl. *flocks*

pĕlăgus, i, n., *sea*

pello, ĕre, pĕpŭli, pulsum, *drive or drive away*

Pĕlōrus, i, m., the N.E. promontory of Sicily, now C. Faro, 411, 687

Pĕnātes, ium, m., *gods of the hearth* or *household*

pĕnītus, adv., *from within; thoroughly, deeply; from its depths,* 673

penna, ae, f., *wing*

per, prep. with acc., *through, over, among;* per somnum, 633, *in sleep*

pĕrăgo, ĕre, ēgi, actum, *go through, accomplish*

pĕreo, īre, īvi or ĭi, ĭtum, *pass through* or *away; perish*

perfĕro, ferre, tŭli, lātum, *bear to the end, endure*

perfĭcio, ĕre, fēci, fectum, *finish, accomplish* (făcio)

perfundo, ĕre, fūdi, fūsum, *wet, steep, bathe*

Pergăma, ōrum, n. plur., the citadel of Troy, hence *Troy*

Pergămĕus, a, um, adj., *belonging to Pergama*

pĕrīcŭlum or perīclum, i, n., *danger, peril*

permētior, īri, mensus sum, *measure through, traverse*

pēs, pĕdis, m., *foot; talons,* 233

pestis, is, f., *plague, pestilence*

Pĕtēlĭa, ae, f., a town of Brutium in S. Italy, 402

pĕto, ĕre, īvi or ĭi, ĭtum, *seek; attack;* p. terram, 93, *fall to the ground*

Phaeāces, um, m., *Phaeacians,* a mythical people, inhabitants of the island Scheria on the W. coast of Greece, visited by Ulysses in his wanderings, 291

Phĭloctētes, ae, m., a Greek leader, possessor of the bow of Hercules: left behind at Lemnos because of a foul wound in the foot, but brought to Troy by Ulysses

Phīnēĭus, a, um, adj. *belonging to Phineus,* king of Thrace, 212

Phoebēus, a, um, adj., *belonging to Phoebus,* 637

Phoebus, a, um, adj., an epithet of Apollo the sun-god, 80 etc.

Phrȳgĭus, a, um, adj., *of Phrygia* in Asia Minor, 6 etc.

pĭcĕus, a, um, adj., *of pitch, pitchy, pitch-dark*

pictūrātus, a, um, adj., *decked with pictures; embroidered*

pĭĕtas, ātis, f., *devoted loyalty to gods, country, and family*

pignus, ŏris, f., *pledge*

pīnus, ūs, f., *pine-tree*

pistrix, ĭcis, f., *sea-monster*

pĭus, a, um, adj., *dutiful; loyal, dedicated; pious*

plăcĭdus, a, um, adj., *calm, tranquil, peaceful*

plāco, āre, āvi, ātum, *make calm or tranquil, propitiate*

Plēmŭrĭum, ĭi, n., a promontory on the S. of the harbor of Syracuse, 693

plēnus, a, um, adj., *full*

plūma, ae, f., *feather*

plŭvĭus, a, um, adj., *rainy*

pōcŭlum, i, n., *cup, goblet*

pollŭo, ĕre, ŭi, ūtum, *defile, profane*

pŏlus, i, m., *the pole; sky*

Pŏlȳdōrus, i, m., son of Priam and Hecuba

Pŏlȳphēmus, i, m., one of the Cyclopes, blinded by Ulysses, 657

pondus, ĕris, n., *weight*

pōno, ĕre, pŏsŭi, pŏsĭtum, *place; set up; build*

pontus, i, m., *sea*

pŏpŭlus, i, m., *people, nation*

porta, ae, f., *gate*

portendo, ĕre, di, tum, *stretch forth; foretell; foreshadow*

portĭcus, ūs, f., *portico, colonnade,* 353

porto, āre, āvi, ātum, *carry, bring*

portus, ūs, m., *harbor, port*

posco, ĕre, pŏposci, no sup., *demand; ask eagerly for*

possum, posse, pŏtŭi, irreg., *be able* (*potis* or *pote+sum*)

postĕrus, a, um, adj., *that is behind, that follows, next;* comp. **posterior,** superl., **postrēmus,** see below

postis, is, f., *door-post;* pl., *portal,* 287

postquam, conj., *after, afterwards*

postrēmus, a, um, adj., superl. of **posterus,** *hindmost, last, behind*

pŏtens, tis, adj., *powerful, mighty;* with gen., *powerful over*

pŏtestas, ātis, f., *power*

pŏtĭor, īri, ītus sum, with abl., *possess, gain possession of; safely reach,* 278; *be lord of,* 296

pŏtis, e, adj., *rarely declined, able;* comp. **potior,** *preferable;* superl. **potissimus**

pŏtĭus, comp. adv. from *potior, rather*

prec-] *defective noun,* f., *not found in nom. or gen. sing.,* **prĕcem** and **prĕcī,** *rare,* **prĕce** and **prĕces,** pl. *common*

praecelsus, a, um, adj., *very high* or *lofty*

praeceps, cipĭtis, adj., *head foremost, headlong* (prae+caput)

praeceptum, i, n., *teaching, precept, rule* (praecĭpio)

praeda, ae, f., *booty*

praedīco, ĕre, xi, ctum, *foretell*

praepes, ĕtis, adj., *winged, flying* 361

praepinguis, e, adj., *very fat; over rich,* 698

praesens, tis, adj., *present, immediate; in full view,* 174

praesĭdeo, ēre, sēdi, sessum, with dat., *preside over*

praesto, āre, stĭti, stĭtum and stātum, *stand before, superior to;* **praestat,**
it is better

praetendo, ĕre, di, tum, *stretch in front*

praetĕrĕā, adv., *moreover, besides*

praeterlābor, i, lapsus sum, *glide past*

praetervĕhor, i, vectus sum, *be carried past; sail past*

[prex, précis] f., see [prec-]

prĕcor, āri, ātus, sum, v. dep. tr. *pray, beseech, pray for*

prĕhendo or prendo, ĕre, di, sum, v. tr. *lay hold of, grasp, catch*

prĕmo, ĕre, pressi, pressum, *press, weigh down;* **mentem pressus,** 47

prensus, see **prehendo**

presso, āre, āvi, ātum, *press, squeeze*

Prĭămēĭus, a, um, adj., *belonging to Priam*

Prĭămĭdes, ae, m., patronymic *son* or *descendant of Priam,* 295, 346

Prĭămus, i, m., king of Troy during the Trojan war, husband of Hecuba

prīmum, adv., *in the first place*

prīmus, a, um, sup. adj., *first, earliest, in front; above all,* 58; comp. **prior**

princeps, ĭpis, adj., *holding first place; first; chief;* as subst., m., *chief, leader*

princĭpĭum, ĭi, n., *beginning;* **principio** as adv., *in the first place,* 381

prĭor, us, comp. adj., *former;* as subst. **priores,** *men of old,* 693; superl. **prīmus**

prō, prep. with abl., *before, in return for, on account of, instead of*

prŏăvus, i, m., *great-grandfather, ancestor, forefather*

prōcēdo, ĕre, cessi, cessum, v. intr. *advance; of time, pass*

prŏcer, ĕris, m., *chieftain*

prŏcul, adv., *at a distance; at a little distance,* 13

prōdĭgĭum, ĭi, n., *portent, prodigy*

proelĭum, ĭi, n., *battle, combat*
prŏfĭciscor, i, prŏfectus sum, *set out*
prōgrĕdior, i, gressus sum, *advance*
prŏhībeo, ēre, ŭi, ĭtum, *forbid, hinder*
(hăbeo)
prōĭcio, ĕre, iēci, iectum, *cast forth;*
proiectus, 699, *jutting* (pro + iăcio)
prōles, is, f., *offspring*
prōlŭvĭes, ēi, f., *overflow, inundation;*
excretion, 217 (proluo)
prōnus, a, um, adj., *bending forwards*
prŏpĕ, adv. and prep. with acc., *near*
prŏpinquus, a, um, adj., *neighboring,*
close at hand
prŏpĭor, us, comp. adj., *nearer;* superl.
proxĭmus, *nearest* (prŏpe)
prŏprĭus, a, um, adj., *one's own;*
abiding, secure, 85
prōra, ae, f., *prow*
prōrumpo, ĕre, rūpi, ruptum, v. tr.
make to burst forth; fling forth
prosĕquor, i, sĕcūtus sum, v. dep. tr.
accompany, attend on the way
prospĕrus, a, um, adj., *fortunate,*
favorable
prospĭcĭo, ĕre, spexi, spectum, *see in*
front, discern
prōtĭnus, adv., *right onward,*
of continuity, (1) in time,
immediately; (2) in space; **protinus**
una, 416, *one unbroken line*
prōvĕho, ĕre, vexi, vectum, v. tr. *carry*
forward; in pass., *sail forth,* 72,
proceed
proximus, see propior
prūdentĭa, ae, f., *foresight*
(=providentia)
pūbes, is, f., *the youth; collective, males,*
young men
pūbesco, ĕre, ŭi, no sup. incept.,
become a youth, grow up
pŭer, ĕri, m., *boy*

pulcher, chra, chrum, adj., *fair,*
beautiful
pulso, āre, āvi, ātum, *strike, beat*
puppis, is, f., *poop, stern;* hence *ship*
purpŭrĕus, a, um, adj., *of purple hue,*
bright
Pyrrhus, i, m., king of Epirus, son of
Achilles, 296, 319

quā, adv., *by what way, where*
quădrŭpes, ĕdis, m. and f., *the*
foor-footed animal; horse, steed
(quattuor+pes)
quaero, ĕre, sīvi, sītum, *search for,*
seek, ask
quaeso, ĕre, īvi or ĭi, no sup., *beg, pray,*
beseech
quālis, e, adj., *of what sort, like as,* 679;
hideous as, 641
quam, adv., *how; than*
quamvīs, conj., *although*
quando, adv. and conj., *when, since;*
indef. **si quando,** *if ever*
quantus, a, um, adj., *how great, as*
great as; huge as
quartus, a, um, ordinal num, adj.,
fourth
quătio, ĕre, no perf., quassum, *shake;*
cause to tremble, 30
quattŭor, num, adj., indecl., *four*
-quĕ, conj., *and;* -que or et...-que,
both...and
quercus, ūs, f., *oak*
quī, quae, quŏd, relative pron., *who,*
which, what
qui, quae or qua, 406, quŏd, interrog.
adj. pron., *who, what;* used as
subst. in 608
quīcumque, quaecumque,
quodcumque, relative pron.,
whoever, whatever; any possible
quĭd, interrog. adv., *why? how?*

quĭdem, adv., *indeed, truly*

quĭes, ētis, f., *rest*

quĭesco, ěre, ēvi, ētum, incept., *become quiet, rest*

quīn, conj., *that not, but that*; in corroboration, *moreover* (archaic abl. qui + ne)

quis, quae, quid, interrog. pron., *who? what?*

quis, quă, quid, indef. pron., *anyone,* see 406

quisquam, quaequam, quicquam, indef. pron., or subst. **quicque** or **quidque,** indef. pron. *each*

quisquis, quicquid, indef. pron., *whoever, whatever*

quō, adv., *whither*

quō, for **ut eo,** purpose clause, *that, thereby,* 377

quōcumquě, adv., *wherever; anywhere*

quondam, adv., *at one time, once, of old, formerly*

quŏquě, conj., *also*

quŏt, num. adj., indecl., *how many*

quŏtĭēs, adv., *as often as*

rādix, īcis, f., *root*

rādo, ěre, i, sum, *scrape, graze*

rāmus, i, m., *bough*

rāresco, ěre, no perf. or sup. incept., *become wider, begin to widen*

rārus, a, um, adj., *having wide interstices; of a loose texture; rare, scattered; disjointed words,* 314

rătis, is, f., *bark, ship*

rěcēdo, ěre, cessi, cessum, *withdraw, recede, depart*

rěcĭpio, ěre, cēpi, ceptum, *take back; duly take, welcome* (căpio)

rěclūdo, ěre, si, sum, *unclose, open* (re + claudo)

rěcordor, āri, ātus sum, *call to memory, recall*

rěcŭbo, āre, āvi, ātum, *recline, lie*

reddo, ěre, dĭdi, dĭtum, *give back; duly give; utter;* **vox reddita,** 40, *an answering voice*

rědĭmio, īre, ĭi, ītum, *bind around; wreathe around; encircle; crown*

rědux, ūcis, adj., *that is led or brought back* (from slavery, exile); *come back, returned*

rěfěro, ferre, rettŭli, rělātum, *carry back; duly carry; lay before the Senate for advice,* 59; *report, deliver,* 170

rěfŭgio, ěre, fūgi, fŭgĭtum, *flee back; retire; recede, stand back*

regno, āre, āvi, ātum, *hold sway, reign*

regnum, i, n., *kingdom, domain, empire*

rěgo, ěre, rexi, rectum, *rule, guide*

rělěgo, ěre, lēgi, lectum, *pass over again, traverse again, retrace again*

rēlĭgĭo, ōnis, f., *religion,* i.e., *utterance of sacred oracles,* 363; *religious rite* or *observance* (root lig-, *bind*)

rělinquo, ěre, līqui, lictum, *leave behind, leave*

rēlĭquĭae, ārum, f. plur., *leavings, remnant; all that are left behind,* 87

rěmētior, īri, mensus sum, *measure back; traverse again:* perf. part. as pass., **remenso,** 143

rēmĭgĭum, ĭi, n., *rowing; body of oarsmen, the rowers* (remus + ago)

rēmus, i, m., *oar*

rěnarro, āre, āvi, ātum, *relate over again; relate*

rěor, no inf. **rătus, sum,** *think, suppose*

rěpentē, adv., *suddenly*

rěpěto, ěre, petīvi or **petĭi, petītum,** *reseek; recommence, say all over again, repeat; recall, remember* rĕpōno, ĕre, pŏsŭi, pŏsĭtum, *place back; place again; place far back;* repostus, *remote lands,* 364

rĕquĭes, ētis, f., *repose, rest*

rĕquīro, ĕre, quīsīvi, quīsītum, *to seek again, to seek to know; to ask or inquire; need, want*

rēs, rĕi, f., *thing; affair; deed, fact;* pl., *fortunes, events*

rĕsolvo, ĕre, vi, sŏlūtum, *unloose, open*

rĕsŏno, āre, āvi, no sup., *re-echo*

respĭcĭo, ĕre, spexi, spectum, *look back at; look back*

rĕsŭpīnus, a, um, adj., *lying on one's back, supine*

rĕtrō, adv., *backwards*

rĕtrorsus, adv., *backwards* (retro + versus)

rĕvertor, i, versus sum, *turn back, return*

rĕvincio, īre, nxi, nctum, *bind back, bind fast*

rĕvīso, ĕre, si, sum, *revisit*

rĕvŏco, āre, āvi, ātum, *call back, recall*

rex, rēgis, m., *king*

Rhoetēus, a, um, adj., *belonging to Rhoetēum* a promontory on the Hellespont in the Troad, 108

rītĕ, adv., *duly*

rīvus, i, m., *small river, brook, rivulet*

rōro, āre, āvi, ātum, *be dewy, drip with dew* (ros)

rŭbesco, ĕre, rŭbŭi, no sup. incept., *grow red*

rŭdens, tis, m., *rope; sheet of a sail,* 267, 682

rŭdo, ĕre, īvi or ĭi, ītum, *roar, bellow* of lions, etc.; of ship's prow, 561

rŭīna, ae, f., *a falling down, fall, ruin; convulsion, desolation,* 571 (ruo)

rumpo, ĕre, rūpi, ruptum, *break, burst; break forth into speech,* 246

rŭo, ĕre, rŭi, rŭtum, fut. part. ruĭtūrus occurs rarely; *rush; rush onwards; rush downwards,* of sun, *hasten to its setting, set* 508

rūpes, is, f., *rock*

rursŭs or rursum, adv., *again* (re + versus)

săcer, cra, crum, adj., *consecrated, hallowed; holy; accursed,* 57; sacra, *sacred things, holy mysteries, sacrifice;* morem sacrorum, 408, *ritual rule*

săcerdos, ōtis, m. and f., *priest, priestess*

săcro, āre, āvi, ātum, *consecrate*

saepĕ, adv., *often*

saevus, a, um, adj., *fierce, cruel*

sal, sălis, m., *salt; the sea*

Sallentīnus, a, um, adj., *belonging to the Sallentini,* a people in the S. of Calabria near the Iapygian promontory, 400

salsus, a, um, adj., *salt* (sal)

sălūto, āre, āvi, ātum, *wish health to; greet*

Sămē, ēs, f., *an island in the Ionian sea, called afterwards Cephallenia, now Cephalonia,* 271

sanctus, a, um, adj., *sacred, holy*

sanguis, is, m., *blood, race,* 608

sănĭes, ēi, f., *gore*

săt, see satis

săta, ōrum, n. plur., *crops* (satus is past part. of sero, *sow*)

sătĭs, indecl. adj., or adv., *sufficient, sufficiently*

Sātūrnĭus, a, um, adj., *of Saturn;* as applied to Juno=*daughter of Saturn,* 380

saxum, i, n., *rock, stone, crag*

Scaeus, a, um, adj., applied to the *left*

or western gate of Troy, 351

scĕlĕrātus, a, um, adj., *wicked, guilty*

scĕlĕro, āre, āvi, ātum, *make guilty, defile*

scĕlus, ĕris, n., *guilt, crime*

sceptrum, i, n., *royal scepter*

scĭo, īre, scīvi or **scĭi, scītum,** *know*

scŏpŭlus, i, m., *rock, crag*

scūtum, i, m., *shield*

Scȳlăcēum, i, n., a town on the coast of Bruttium, 553

Scylla, ae, f., a sea-monster inhabiting a cliff above the whirlpool Charybdis between Italy and Sicily, devoured ships, 420 etc.

sē, sui, reflex. pron., *himself, herself, itself, themselves*

sēcessus, ūs, m., *a place withdrawn; retreat* (secedo)

sēclūdo, ĕre, si, sum, *shut off, shut up, seclude*

sēco, āre, ŭi, sectum, *cut, saw*

sēcrētus, a, um, adj., *withdrawn, remote, secret, secluded* (part. of **secerno,** *separate*)

sēcundo, āre, no perf. or sup., *make fortunate* or *favorable*

sēcundus, a, um, adj., *following; of wind favorable; prosperous* (sĕquor)

sēcŭs, adv., *otherwise*

sĕd, conj., *but*

sēdes, is, f., *seat, abode, settlement* (sĕdeo)

sĕges, ĕtis, f., *crop*

segnis, e, adj., *slow, lazy*

Sĕlīnūs, untis, f., a town in Sicily near Lilybaeum, 705

sĕmĕl, adv., *once*

sēmēsus, a, um, adj., *half eaten* (semi + edo)

semper, adv., *always*

sēmustus, a, um, adj., *half burned* (semi + uro)

sententĭa, ae, f., *opinion; purpose*

sentio, īre, sensi, sensum, *feel; perceive; understand,* 360

sĕpĕlio, īre, īvi or **ĭi, sepultum,** *bury*

sĕpulchrum, i, n., *tomb*

sĕquor, i, sĕcūtus sum, *follow*

sĕrēnus, a, um, adj., *calm, clear*

servĭtĭum, ĭi, n., *slavery, bondage*

servo, āre, āvi, ātum, *keep, save, protect.* **Pyrrhin conubia servas,** 319, *are you still married to/ keeping marriage with Pyrrhus?*

sese, *strengthened form of* **se**

seu, see **sive**

sī, conj., *if*

Sĭbylla, ae, f., the name given to several prophetic women, the most famous of whom was the Sibyl of Cumae, 452

sīc, adv., *so, thus*

Sīcănĭus, a, um, adj., *belonging to the Sicāni* or ancient inhabitants of Sicily, *Sicilian,* 692

siccus, a, um, adj., *dry*

Sĭcŭlus, a, um, adj., *Sicilian,* 410

sīdĕrĕus, a, um, adj., *starry, star-lit*

sīdus, ĕris, n., *star, constellation*

signo, āre, āvi, ātum, *mark, mark out; designate; affix a seal to*

signum, i, n., *sign, token*

sĭlentium, ĭi, n., *silence*

sĭleo, ēre, ŭi, no sup., *be silent*

silva, ae, f., *forest, wood; thick growth, shrub,* 24

Sĭmŏis, entis, m., a river in the Troad, 302

sĭmŭl, adv., *at the same time;* **simul ac,** *as soon as*

sĭmŭlo, āre, āvi, ātum, *pretend; counterfeit, make like.* Pass. with dat., *mimicking,* 349

sĭnĕ, prep. with abl., *without*

singŭli, ae, a, distributive num. adj.,

one to each, separate, single; each, 348

sĭnus, ūs, m., *bend; belly of sail; bay*

Sīrĭus, ĭi, m., *Sirius, the dog star,* 141

sisto, ĕre, stĭti, stătum, *place; land,* 117; *settle, rest,* 7

sĭtus, ūs, m., *site, situation, position*

sīvĕ, seu, conj., *or if;* sive *or* seu...sive *or* seu, *whether...or if*

sŏcĭus, ĭi, m., *companion, comrade;* as adj. *allied, friendly*

sōl, sōlis, m., *sun,* plur., *suns, days,* 203

sōlāmen, ĭnis, n., *solace*

sollemnis, e, adj., *yearly; religious, solemn*

sollĭcĭtus, a, um, adj., *anxious, in distress*

sŏlum, i, n., *ground*

sōlus, a, um, adj., *alone, solitary, only*

solvo, ĕre, vi, sŏlūtum, *loose, unloose; pay vow,* 404; crinem solutae, 65 *middle sense*

somnus, i, m., *sleep, slumber*

sŏnĭtus, ūs, m., *sound*

sŏno, āre, ŭi, ĭtum, *sound;* sonans, *sounding, noisy;* sonantia silvis, 442, *with its sounding or echoing woods*

sŏpor, ōris, m., *slumber; an empty dream,* 173

sorbeo, ēre, ŭi, no sup., *suck in*

sortior, īre, ītus sum, *draw lots for, obtain by lot, arrange, assign by lot*

sortītus, ūs, m., *drawing of lots*

spargo, ĕre, si, sum, *scatter, sprinkle, strew*

spĕcŭla, ae, f., *watch-tower, look-out* (cf. aspicio)

spēlunca, ae, f., *cave*

spēs, ĕi, f., *hope*

spīna, ae, f., *thorn*

spīrābĭlis, e, adj., *breathable; which we*

breathe, 600

spīro, āre, āvi, ātum, *breathe*

spūma, ae, f., *foam*

spūmo, āre, āvi, ātum, *foam*

stagno, āre, āvi, ātum, *be stagnant or marshy,* 698

stella, ae, f., *star*

stĕrĭlis, e, adj., *barren*

sterno, ĕre, strāvi, strātum, *spread out, stretch out, lie down; to throw down, overthrow;* sternimur, 509, *middle, we cast ourselves down*

stīpes, ĭtis, m., *trunk, stock of tree*

stīpo, āre, āvi, ātum, *press together; pack*

stirps, pis, f., *stock of a tree; lineage, stock; son*

sto, stāre, stĕti, stătum, *stand, stand erect, stand ranged,* 277; *be anchored,* 403; *be raised,* of altar, 63; steterant, 110, *had been built*

strātum, i, n., *bed covering, bed*

Strŏphădes, um, f. plur., islands in the Ionian Sea, S. of Zacynthus, 210

strŭo, ĕre, struxi, structum, *heap up, build*

Stygĭus, a, um, adj., *belonging to the Styx the 'River of Hate,'* in the Underworld, 215

suadeo, ēre, suasi, suasum, *persuade, recommend*

sŭb, prep. with abl., *under, under the command of,* 157; with acc., *beneath, up to, upwards towards, towards*

subdūco, ĕre, xi, ctum, *draw away from underneath, withdraw; draw up, beach ships,* 135

sŭbeo, īre, īvi *or* ĭi, ĭtum, with dat. and with acc., *go under, pass beneath; approach*

sŭbĭgo, ĕre, ēgi, actum, *bring under,*

compel (ăgo)

sŭbĭtō, adv., *suddenly*

sŭbĭtus, a, um, adj., *sudden*

subĭcio, ĕre, iēci, iectum, *throw
beneath, throw in; interpose an
answer* (iăcio)

submissus, a, um, part. of **submitto** as
adj., *lowly, submissive, on bended knee*

submitto, ĕre, mīsi, missum, *send
down; let down, lower*

subnixus, a, um, adj., with dat., *resting
on for support;* hence *confident
in,* 402 (participle of obsolete
subnitor)

subtēgmen, ĭnis, n., *that which is
woven underneath or interwoven;*
auri sub., 483, *golden embroidery*

subter, adv. and prep. with acc., *under,
beneath*

subtexo, ĕre, ŭi, xtum, *weave
underneath; spread underneath;
veil from below* (sub + texo)

succēdo, ĕre, cessi, cessum, with
dat., *go up to, come close beneath;
submit to,* 541

sūdor, ōris, m., *sweat*

suesco, ĕre, suēvi, suētum, *make
accustomed, train; grow
accustomed*

sum, esse, fui, irreg., *be*

summus, a, um, superl. adj., *highest,
topmost:* **quo summo,** 22, *on whose
top.* See **superus.**

sŭpĕr, adv. and prep. with acc. and abl.,
above, over; surviving, 489

sŭperbus, a, um, adj., *haughty, proud*

sŭpĕro, āre, āvi, ātum, *overcome;
surmount; survive*

sŭpĕrus, a, um, adj., *that is above;*
subst. **superi, ōrum, m.,** *those
above, the gods;* superl. **suprēmus,**
last, utmost; **supremum,** adv., *for*

the last time, 68; and **summus,**
highest, see above

sŭpīnus, a, um, adj., *backwards, bent
backwards, lying on the back;* of
hands, *with open palms turned
upward,* 176

suppleo, ēre, ēvi, ētum, *fill up*

supplex, ĭcis, adj., *humble, submissive,
suppliant;* as subst., *a suppliant*

sŭpra, prep. with acc. and adv., *above*

sŭpremum, adv., see **superus**

sŭprēmus, a, um, adj., see **superus**

surgo, ĕre, surrexi, surrectum, *rise*

sūs, sŭis, m. and **f.,** *pig, sow*

suspendo, ĕre, di, sum, *hang up,
suspend*

suspensus, a, um, part. of **suspendo** as
adj., *in suspense, anxious, agitated,*
372

suspĭcio, ĕre, spexi, spectum, *look
at from underneath; look up or
upwards; suspect*

sŭus, a, um, possess. adj., *his-, her-, its,
their own; his own special,* 469; **sui,**
347, *his friends*

tābĭdus, a, um, adj., *wasting, decaying*

tābum, i, n., *decay, corruption; gore,*
29, 626

tăcĭtus, a, um, adj., *silent* (tăceo)

taeter, tra, trum, adj., *foul*

tālis, e, adj., *of such kind, such*

tămen, adv., *nevertheless,
notwithstanding, yet*

tandem, adv., *at last*

tango, ĕre, tĕtĭgi, tactum, *touch*

tantum, adj., *so much; only*

tantus, a, um, adj., *so great, such;* **tanti,**
453, *of so great, value, so costly*

Tărentum, i, n., *a town on the coast of
S. Italy,* 551

taurus, i, m., *bull*

tectum, i, n., *roof, house* (tego)
tēcum, i.e., **cum te,** *with you*
tegmen, ĭnis, n., *covering*
tego, ĕre, texi, tectum, *cover, conceal, bury*
tĕgŭmen, ĭnis, n., *covering*
tellūs, ūris, f., *the earth, land, earth*
tēlum, i, n., *weapon*
tempestas, ātis, f., *weather; bad weather, storm*
templum, i, n., *temple*
tempto, āre, āvi, ātum, *try, make trial of, essay, attempt; explore, seek with difficulty,* 146
tempus, ŏris, n., *time;* in plur., *temples of the head*
tendo, ĕre, tĕtendi, tensum and tentum, *stretch*
tĕnĕbrae, ārum, f. plur., *darkness*
tĕneo, ēre, ŭi, tum, *hold, keep; maintain; gain the sea,* 192
tĕner, ĕra, ĕrum, adj., *tender*
tĕnŭis, e, adj., *stretched out, thin; slender; light*
tĕnus, prep. with abl. postpositive, *as far as, up to*
tĕpĭdus, a, um, adj., *warm*
tĕr, num. adv., *thrice*
tĕrĕbro, āre, āvi, ātum, *bore* (tero)
tergum, i, n., *back*
terra, ae, f., *dry land, earth, land, ground* (torreo)
tertĭus, a, um, ordinal adj., *third*
testor, āri, ātus sum, *invoke; summon as a witness; adjure; testify, be token of*
Teucer or Teucrus, cri, m., ancient king of Troy, son-in-law of Dardanus; hence **Teucrī, ōrum,** *Trojans,* 53 etc.
textĭlis, e, adj., *woven* (texo)
Thapsus, i, m., *a city on the E. coast of Sicily,* 689
Thrax, Thrācis, m., *a Thracian,* 14

Thrēĭcĭus, a, um, adj., *Thracian,* 51
Thȳbris, is or īdis, acc. im, n., Greek name for river Tiber, 500
Thymbraeus, a, um, adj., epithet of Apollo, who had a temple at Thymbra in the Troad, 85
tinguo, ĕre, tinxi, tinctum, *wet, dye*
tollo, ĕre, sustŭli, sublātum, *lift, raise; bear, endure; take away, carry off; kill, destroy*
tondeo, ēre, tŏtondi, tonsum, *shear; browse on, crop*
tŏno, āre, ŭi, ĭtum, *thunder*
torqueo, ēre, torsi, tortum, *twist, turn; whirl,* 208
tŏrus, i, m., *couch*
torvus, a, um, adj., *fierce, grim, glaring*
tŏt, num. adj. indecl., *so many*
tŏtĭdem, num. adj. indecl., *just as many*
tōtus, a, um, adj., *the whole*
trabs, is, f., *beam, ship*
tractus, ūs, m., *region, expanse* (traho)
trăho, ĕre, traxi, tractum, *draw, drag, drag on*
trans, prep. with acc., *across, beyond*
transmitto, ĕre, mīsi, missum, *send across, speed across; pass onto*
transtrum, i, n., *cross-beam, transom, bench for rowers,* 289
trĕmesco, ĕre, no perf. or sup. incept., *begin to tremble*
trĕmo, ĕre, ŭi, no sup., *tremble, shake, quiver*
trĕpĭdus, a, um, adj., *trembling, fearful, alarmed*
tres, trĭa, num. adj., *three*
trīgintā, num, adj. indecl., *thirty*
trĭlix, īcis, adj., *with three leashes or threads of the web of a loom; triple-twilled,* 367 (tri + licium)
Trīnăcrĭa, ae, f., *the three-cornered land, Sicily,* 440, 582

Trīnăcrius, a, um, adj., *Sicilian,* 384 etc.

Trĭōnes, um, the constellation of the *Wain (Wagon)* (currently called Ursa Major or the Big Dipper), lit. *the plowing oxen,* 516.

trĭpūs, pŏdis, m., *three-footed seat, tripod*

tristis, e, adj., *sad; bitter;* tristia dona, *mourning gifts,* 301

Trōiă, ae, f., *Troy,* 3, 11 etc.

Trōiānus, a, um, adj., *Trojan*

Trōĭŭs, a, um, adj., *Trojan,* 306 etc.

Trōiŭgĕna, ae, m., *Trojan born,* 359 (Troia + gigno)

truncus, a, um, adj., *lopped* of its branches or limbs; trunca pinus, 659, *pine trunk*

tu, tui, *you;* plur. vos, *you*

tum, adv., *then*

tŭmĭdus, a, um, adj., *swollen, swelling*

tŭmultus, ūs, m., *swelling; tumult*

tŭmŭlus, i, m., *mound, tomb*

tunc, adv., *then*

turba, ae, f., *crowd, band, troop*

turbo, āre, āvi, ātum, *disturb, trouble*

turrītus, a, um, adj., *with towers; towered, tower-like* (turris)

tūtus, a, um, adj., *protected, safe* (tueor)

tŭus, a, um, possess. adj., *yours*

ūber, ĕris, n., (1) *udder, breast; bosom;* (2) *richness or wealth of soil.* In 95, both meanings.

ūber, ĕris, adj., *rich*

ŭbĭ, adv., *when, where*

ulciscor, i, ultus sum, *avenge*

Ŭlixes, is or i, m., son of Laertes, king of Ithaca, famed for his craftiness; his wanderings on his return from Troy form the subject of the *Odyssey,* 273 etc.

ullus, a, um, adj., *any;* also as pron.,

any one (usually in negative sentences)

ultrā, adv. and prep. with acc., *beyond, further*

ultrō, adv., *beyond what is needed or asked; voluntarily, unasked,* 155

umbra, ae, f., *shade*

umbro, āre, āvi, ātum, *shadow over, shade, veil in shadow*

ūmeo, ēre, no perf. or sup., *be wet:* umens, 589, *dewy*

ūmĭdus, a, um, adj., *wet, damp*

ūnā, adv., *together, at once*

uncus, a, um, adj., *crooked, hooked, taloned*

unda, ae, f., *wave, water*

undĕ, adv., *whence*

undĭquĕ, adv., *on all sides*

undōsus, a, um, adj., *full of waves, billowy*

ūnus, a, um, adj., *one, alone:* strengthening a superlative, 321

urbs, bis, f., *city*

urgeo, ēre, ursi, no sup., *press upon* or *down*

ŭt, adv. and conj., *as, when, how; so that, in order that*

ŭterquĕ, ŭtraque, ŭtrumque, adj., *each of two, either*

ŭtĕrus, i, m., *womb, belly*

ŭtĭnam, adv., *would that!* followed by subjunctive

văco, āre, āvi, ātum, *be empty;* with abl., *be free from; be idle, at leisure, not busy*

vādo, ĕre, no perf. or sup., *go*

vădum, i, n., *a shallow place, a shallow* or *shoal; the bottom of water;* pl., *the shallows; the waters*

văleo, ēre, ŭi, ĭtum, *be strong, healthy; have power to; be able; in leave-taking, farewell*

vallis, is, f., *valley*

vărius, a, um, adj., *varying, various*

vastus, a, um, adj., *huge, vast, mighty*

vātes, is, m. and **f.,** *prophet, prophetess; bard, seer*

-ve, enclitic conj., *or*

věho, ěre, xi, ctum, *carry*

vēlātus, a, um, adj., *covered with sails, sail-clad,* 549 (velum)

vello, ěre, vulsi, vulsum, *pluck, pull up, tear up*

vēlo, āre, āvi, ātum, *cover, envelop, veil; hide, conceal; crown, garland* with fillets, 545

vēlum, i, n., *cloth, covering; sail*

věněror, āri, ātus sum, *reverence, regard with reverence, do anything reverently; gaze with awe upon,* 84; *reverently entreat;* perf. part. as pass. *entreated,* 460

věnĭa, ae, f., *favor, pardon, pity*

věnio, īre, vēni, ventum, *come, come upon, happen to,* 138

venter, tris, m., *belly*

ventus, i, m., *wind, breeze*

Věnus, ěris, f., *Venus,* mother of Aeneas, goddess of love, 475

verběro, āre, āvi, ātum, *lash, whip*

verbum, i, n., *word*

vērō, adv., *truly; but indeed*

verro, ěre, i, versum, *sweep; sweep over; toss about*

vertex, ĭcis, m., *whirl, eddy* (of wind or flame), *vortex; top* or *crown of the head; peak, summit* (verto)

verto, ěre, ti, sum, *turn:* **is vertitur ordo,** 376

vērum, adv., *but*

vērum, i, n., *truth*

vērus, a, um, adj., *true*

vescor, i, no perf. or sup. with abl., *feed on:* **vescor aurā,** 339

vester, tra, trum, possess. adj., *your*

vestīgĭum, ĭi, n., *foot-print, trail, footstep*

vestis, is, f., *raiment, dress*

věto, āre, ŭi, ĭtum, *forbid*

větus, ěris, adj., *old*

větustas, ātis, f., *antiquity, distant date,* 415

větustus, a, um, adj., *ancient*

vĭa, ae, f., *path, course, way;* plur. *travels, wanderings,* 714

vīcīnus, a, um, adj., *neighboring*

vĭcis, no nom., **vicem, vice,** plur. **vices, f.,** *change, alteration, turn;* **vices,** 634, *our several tasks;* **volvit vices,** 376, *turns the circle of changes*

victor, ōris, m., *conqueror,* as adj., *victorious* (vinco)

victrix, īcis, f. adj., *conquering, victorious;* unusually, with neut. pl., **victricia arma,** 54

victus, ūs, m., *that on which one lives; sustenance, support, food* (vivo)

vĭdeo, ēre, vīdi, vīsum; *see,* **videor,** *seem;* **videtur** impersonally with dat., *it seems proper, right,* or *fit*

vīmen, ĭnis, n., *that which binds: twig, shoot*

vīnum, i, n., *wine*

vĭr, vĭri, m., *man, hero*

virgĭněus, a, um, adj., *of* or *belonging to a maiden* or *virgin*

virgo, ĭnis, f., *maiden*

virgultum, i, n., *thicket* (virga, twig)

vĭrĭdis, e, adj., *green*

vĭrīlis, e, adj., *manly, courageous* (vir)

virtūs, ūtis, f., *manliness, virtue* (vir)

vis, vis, f. plur. **vires, virium,** *force, power, violence,* in plur., *strength; military forces*

viscus, ěris, n. mostly plur. **viscera,** *entrails, bowels*

vīsum, i, n., *sight*

vīsus, ūs, m., *sight, portent*

vīta, ae, f., *life*

vīto, āre, āvi, ātum, *shun*

vitta, ae, f., *fillet*, ribbon used by priests and for religious decorations

vivo, ĕre, vixi, victum, *live*

vīvus, a, um, adj., *alive; natural* of rock, 688

vix, adv., *scarcely*

vŏco, āre, āvi, ātum, *call, summon, invoke, name*

vŏlĭto, āre, āvi, ātum, *keep flying, flutter* (freq. of vŏlo, *fly*)

vŏlo, āre, āvi, ātum, *fly*

vŏlo, velle, ui, no sup. *wish, be willing;* volens, 457, *graciously*

vŏlŭcer, cris, cre, adj., *swift*

vŏlŭcris, is, f., *bird*

vŏluptas, ātis, f., *pleasure, delight*

vŏlūto, āre, āvi, ātum, *roll, turn, twist; grovel*

volvo, ĕre, vi, vŏlūtum, *roll; turn over* in mind, *ponder,* 102; **fumum,** 206, *send up whorls of smoke;* **volvit vices,** 376, *turns* (the circle of) *changes*

vos, pl. of **tu,** *you*

vōtum, i, n., *vow* (voveo)

vox, vōcis, f., *voice;* pl., *words, sounds*

vulgō, adv., *commonly; everywhere, all over*

vulnus, ĕris, n., *wound*

vultus, ūs, m., *countenance*

Xanthus, i, m., a famous river in the Troad, also called Scamander, 350, 497

Zăcynthos, i, f., an island in the Ionian sea off the coast of Elis, 270

Zĕphўrus i, m., *West wind,* 120

Index

This index lists grammatical, metrical, and stylistic items mentioned in the commentary; numbers refer to lines in the Latin text and the corresponding commentary notes. Terms with an asterisk are defined in the glossary.

Ablative

Absolute: 17, 27,138,143, 156, 369, 565, 614, 666, 705, 718

Archaic: 456

attendant circumstance: 498

cause: 214, 218, 271, 327, 585, 672, 706

comparative, after: 214

description: 28, 350, 426, 492, 677

degree of difference: 116

extent, space over which: 124, 204, 268, 277, 417

impersonal agent: 570

manner: 56, 83, 314, 524, 665

material: 304

means: 38, 136, 222, 233, 279, 280, 298, 383, 400, 417, 442, 650, 665, 668

quality: 13,45, 286, 535, 538, 618, 685

place where: 111, 296

respect: 164, 591, 614, 621

separation: 72, 300, 577

source: 138

special use, after *tenus*: 427

special verb: 224, 278, 296, 355, 352, 475,339, 352, 392, 607, 622

supine: 26, 365

time: 333

Abas

shield of, 278-93, 286

Accusative

cognate: 56, 68, 343, 572, 610

double construction: 370

duration of time: 203

extent of space: 191

Greek: 122, 517, 525, 572

indirect statement: 52,121,185, 236, 374, 414, 430, 578, 580

motion towards: 154, 254, 507, 601, 614

respect: 47, 65, 81, 405, 428, 545, 595

Achaemenides

306, 405, main note 588-612

as competing narrator: 613-54 614, 633

Achates 523-4, 707-15

Actium

main note: 278-93

games: 28

battle of: 527

Adjectives

as substantive: 232, 588

epic compound: 75, 221, 359, 550, 553, 642, 660, 680, 704

for genitive: 117, 212, 441, 466, 551, 678, 706

in hyperbaton: 176